The Public Speaker/
The Public Listener

The Public Speaker/
The Public Listener

Andrew D. Wolvin

University of Maryland
College Park and University College

Roy M. Berko

Speech Communication
Association—National Office

Darlyn R. Wolvin

Prince George's Community College

Houghton Mifflin Company   Boston   Toronto

Dallas   *Geneva, Illinois*   *Palo Alto*   *Princeton, New Jersey*

Sponsoring Editor: Margaret Seawell
Senior Development Editor: Lance Wickens
Project Editor: Jean Levitt
Design/Production Coordinator: Karen Rappaport
Senior Manufacturing Coordinator: Marie Barnes
Marketing Manager: Karen Natale

Cover design by Ron Kosciak

Printed in the U.S.A.

Library of Congress Catalog Card Number: 92-72407

ISBN: 0-395-54011-9

123456789-DH-96 95 94 93 92

About the Authors

Andrew D. Wolvin is a professor and chair of the department of speech communication at the University of Maryland—College Park. He has his Ph.D. from Purdue University. In addition to his many publications, he is a noted authority on listening behavior and has been the president of the International Listening Association and the Eastern Communication Association. He is a professional speaker, and he serves as a speech coach and trainer to a number of federal agencies, private corporations, and trade associations in Washington, D.C.

Roy M. Berko is the director of education services at the national office of the Speech Communication Association. He formerly was on the faculties of Towson State University and Lorain County Community College, and served as an adjunct/visiting professor at the University of Maryland, Cleveland State University, and Pennsylvania State University. He holds a Ph.D. from Pennsylvania State University, an M.A. from the University of Michigan, and a B.A. from Kent State University. He was selected as a Teacher on Teaching by the Speech Communication Association and was the first recipient of the Outstanding Teacher Award by the Community College Section of SCA. He is a speech consultant, and his books include *Communicating: A Social and Career Focus*, *This Business of Communicating*, *Communicating With Competence*, *Basic-ly Communicating*, and the forthcoming *Interpersonal Communication Competency: A Culture-Sensitive Perspective*.

Darlyn R. Wolvin is a professor and chair of the department of speech communication and theatre at Prince George's Community College, Largo, Maryland. She did her undergraduate and graduate work at the University of Nebraska—Lincoln. Active in the field, she has published widely and has been the president of the Eastern Communication Association and has served in a number of leadership positions in the Speech Communication Association.

Contents

3   The Responsible Public Communicator   46

4   Getting Started   66

7 Sources of Supporting Materials   122

8 Structuring the Speech   138

9 Formats for the Speech 168

10 Oral and Physical Presentation 186

Preface

We think it is significant, as we complete our text, that a new book has appeared in the popular market, *Lincoln at Gettysburg,* by Gary Wills (Simon and Schuster, 1992). The book is a rhetorical and historical analysis of Abraham Lincoln's Gettysburg Address, a three-minute speech of 272 words that, Wills persuasively argues, changed the course of American history. That an entire book, intended for a large readership, is devoted to the analysis of a single speech, no matter how famous, and has become a best seller, is remarkable. It is also ample testimony to the central role of public communication not only to politics and history, but, indeed, to the conduct of human affairs in general.

What Is This Book About?

The Public Speaker/The Public Listener is intended to help students to develop their understanding of skills as public communicators. Delivering or listening to speeches plays a role in the lives of almost everyone. We are asked to present our ideas to either large audiences or smaller, informal groups, both in classes and at work. We also listen to numerous presentations, such as political or other public addresses, class lectures, sermons, or informal talks.

As a speaker, one should present a speech that is immediately understandable, well-structured, and clear in its ideas—in short, one that gains and holds an audience's attention.

As a listener, one should listen responsibly and attentively so as to be receptive to a well-informed and sufficiently documented speech, while at the same time being skeptical at the prospect of manipulative or questionable tactics on the part of the speaker.

The Student of Public Speaking

We have provided students with the resources and techniques for learning how to be effective public speakers and listeners. Moreover, we have included some historical background to help in understanding the role of public communication in everyday life and in appreciating public communicators. And finally, we examine the role of the professional public speaker.

We hope to reinforce students' commitment to effective, responsible communication. Only through public discourse can we, as both listeners and speakers, ensure the durability of thoughtful, legitimate deliberation of the significant issues and policies necessarily affecting our decisions and our way of life as global citizens.

We have taken care to write directly for our readers, using a conversational tone, provocative examples, and an easily mastered format. At the same time, we have developed our ideas with the most recent scholarly research in mind.

The Structure of the Book

The fourteen chapters of this book have been further divided into sections, which are double-numbered—providing the chapter and section number. This format enables teachers to assign either a whole chapter or simply a section of a chapter at a time.

The first chapter of the book probes the role of the public speaker, and in a parallel fashion Chapter 2 explores the role of the public listener. Then Chapter 3 synthetically examines the roles of both speaker and listener as responsible public communicators. Chapters 4 through 9 assist the reader in gaining the skills for developing a public speech; Chapter 10 elaborates on the oral and physical presentation of the speech. Chapters 11 through 13 examine specific kinds of speeches such as the informative, persuasive, and ceremonial. Finally, Chapter 14 takes a look at public communication as a profession.

The Ancillary Package

The following are available to adopters of *The Public Speaker/The Public Listener:*

◆ The **Instructor's Resource Manual with Test Items** was written by Andrew Wolvin, Roy Berko, Darlyn Wolvin, and Barbara Finegan. For each chapter, the manual contains sample syllabi, classroom activities and teaching suggestions, and test questions.

◆ **Speech outlining software** (IBM and Macintosh), a computer program especially tailored to this text, leads students through the process of outlining their own speeches. The self-directed, step-by-step program takes students through formats for each major speech design discussed in the text.

◆ **Transparencies** feature line art from the text as well as key "Listening" features.

◆ **Test generating software** is available.

In addition, a videotape illustrating student speeches is available to adopters. Users should contact Houghton Mifflin representatives for details.

Acknowledgments

No book of this scope is possible without the support and assistance of many individuals. We appreciate all that we have learned through the years from our speech communication colleagues, audiences, and students, for it is really their influence that has shaped our understanding of public speaking and public listening.

We are grateful for the institutional support from the University of Maryland—College Park and for the work of our research assistants, Ted Barkley for his bibliographic help and Colleen Ryan for her development of the profiles of notable American speakers. Special appreciation goes to Barbara Finegan for her assistance with the *Instructor's Resource Manual* that accompanies this text. We would also like to thank Margaret Seawell for launching this project and the Houghton Mifflin team that guided us through the writing and production process: Jean Levitt, Lance Wickens, and Jeffrey Greene.

We are also grateful to the following teachers for their thoughtful and constructive readings of our manuscript:

Blanton Croft, Northern Virginia Community College

Robert H. Fogg, Millersville University

Steve Kosokoff, Portland State University

Tommy L. Neuman, American River College

Mabry M. O'Donnell, Marietta College

Charles Tucker, Northern Illinois University

Enid S. Waldhart, University of Kentucky

George W. Ziegelmueller, Wayne State University

And thanks to you, our readers, for your engagement in and commitment to improving public speaking and public listening.

A.D.W.
R.M.B.
D.R.W.

The Public Speaker/
The Public Listener

1

The Public Speaker: A Perspective

Chapter Outline

Learning Outcomes

After reading this chapter you should be able to:

Define public speaking.

Understand the need for public speaking.

Understand the need for you to be an effective public speaker.

Appreciate the historical roots of public speaking.

Understand the process of public communication.

Define and understand the role of the source, the code, perceptions and attitudes, the message, the channel/the conduit, the receiver, feedback, noise, and the environment as they relate to public speaking.

When you decided to register for this course in public speaking, you may have been thinking, "I like to get up and speak to audiences, so this class should be no problem." Maybe, though, your thoughts were more in the line of "Me, get up before a class and give a speech? No way!" If that was your response, feel some comfort in realizing that for most of us there is an element of uncertainty, or in some cases out-and-out fear, when it comes to **public speaking**—the act of communication that occurs between one person and an audience.

Some people actually do enjoy speaking before groups. If that were not true we would not have politicians, teachers, media performers, and religious leaders. On the other hand, research shows that 61 percent of the people in the United States are afraid of giving speeches.[1]

☰ 1.1 You and Public Speaking

One of the purposes of this book, and the course you are taking, is to teach you the skills necessary to prepare and present an effective speech or to reinforce the skills you already have. People who are confident of their public speaking abilities have more positive attitudes about communicating to an audience than those who lack these skills.

You may also be wondering why you need to know anything about public speaking, especially if you've decided to try to avoid it. A study aptly titled "Do Real People Ever Give Speeches?" identified the various levels of public speaking that people do. The researcher concluded that people at all levels do indeed give presentations.[2] Fifty-five percent of the respondents gave at least one speech every two years to ten or more people; 71 percent of these speakers gave at least four speeches during that time. People with more education and income give speeches most frequently. Knowing this, a person who wants a high-income job is wise to get a solid education and prepare to become an effective speaker.[3]

No matter your career choice, most college graduates enter occupations that require some form of speaking before groups, whether within the organization, at conferences or conventions, or as a representative of the company. Businesses are acutely aware of this requirement. A survey of Fortune 500 companies revealed that presentation skills were identified as "somewhat important" for secretarial staff and hourly wage workers; "important" for supervisors and technical staff; and "very important" for sales staff, executives, middle managers, and human resource staff.[4] Eighty-two percent of the Fortune 500 companies responding to this survey indicated that presentation skills were important enough that they provide speech training in order to increase employee performance.

Public speaking occurs both internally, within the organization to groups of employees, and externally, to the various groups of outside users, potential customers, and interested constituents of all kinds. Because communication is so central to productivity and effectiveness, many organizations have begun to develop communication plans to help guide officers in making decisions about their public speaking. One such company with an intricate communication plan is Honeywell. Honeywell's corporate communication department has established a speakers bureau with a specific public communication objective: to identify appropriate speaking platforms, negotiate media interviews, publish speakers' remarks, and provide opportunities to reach customers and prospects.[5]

Interest in effective public communication is also reflected in the growth of speakers' agents, who book speakers for the annual sales meetings, conventions, and other large meetings companies and organizations often sponsor. A former chief executive officer of Chrysler Corporation stresses that public speaking, which "requires a lot of preparation," is "the best way to motivate a large group."[6] The speaking industry is lucrative. Popular speakers can command as much as $25,000 or more for a speech.[7]

Skill in public speaking is important not only in the business world but also in the academic arena. Students are asked to do classroom presentations of research projects, reports, experiments, and studies. Outside of class you might give a report to a student organization, make a proposal to your fraternity or sorority, represent a political candidate, or give a speech as part of a job interview.

Public communication is the lifeblood of political, legal, advertising, and promotional work—and is central to any media-related position. One need only recall how the world was riveted to the television screen for regular briefings by General Norman Schwarzkopf, commander of the American forces in the Persian Gulf during Operation Desert Storm,

Profile: Thomas W. Faranda, *professional speaker and management consultant*

Calling effective public speaking his "most visible and important skill," Thomas Faranda, president of Faranda and Associates, an international management training and development firm, acknowledges the value of developing and maintaining excellence as a speaker. When combined with effective listening and creative problem solving, public speaking serves as a powerful tool for expressing his ideas to corporations and having those ideas accepted. Fifteen years as a professional speaker on the lecture circuit have taught Faranda some important lessons. His advice? Do some serious work *before* you put yourself in a public speaking situation.

◆ Develop technical expertise in an area.

◆ Learn to interview people to gain information.

◆ Learn to listen so you really hear and understand what people are telling you.

◆ Learn to present your ideas professionally, using effective speaking techniques so your ideas are accepted.

After you are satisfied with the work you have done in these areas,

◆ Practice until you cannot stand to hear yourself talk anymore.

◆ Listen to yourself on tape. Observe your gestures and mannerisms on video.

◆ Constantly seek to improve your skills.

Learn not only by watching yourself but also by observing others:

◆ Spend money to go watch the masters of the profession . . . they are your best teachers.

◆ Learn how they touch the audience with their voice, gestures, feelings, and words.

◆ Emulate them, but do not copy them. Be an original, not a copy. People always pay more for an original than a copy.

Finally, and perhaps most important,

◆ Care about what you do so much that you will not accept anything but excellence.

to appreciate what public speaking skills can accomplish. Schwarzkopf's success, though resounding, was not unique. Public speaking has a long and historic record. Being aware of this history allows us to realize that public speaking customs and processes are based on many trials and errors, theories, imitations of great speakers, and research into effective speaking.

1.2 The Historical Roots of Public Speaking

"Give me liberty or give me death." "Ask not what your country can do for you, ask what you can do for your country." "We have nothing to fear, but fear itself." "Four score and seven years ago . . ." "Read my lips . . ." A review of lines from famous public speeches is a review of the history of people—of our conflicts, our ideals, our dreams, and our despairs.

The art of public speaking has a rich tradition in the study of **rhetoric**, or persuasive discourse.[8] *The Instruction of Ptah-hotep and the Instruction of Keg' emni,* an ancient book discovered on the banks of the Nile River in Egypt, advises a young Egyptian man how to become governor of a city and counselor to a king. In these instructions, effective **speechmaking**, the presentation of speeches, is recognized as a chief means for social control. In ancient Greece, where the popular assembly was very powerful, the prominent statesman Pericles advocated and practiced skill in speechmaking. His funeral oration, delivered as a memorial to the first Athenian soldiers who fell in the Peloponnesian War in 431 B.C., is considered one of the greatest eulogies ever delivered. Pericles trained as an orator with Zeno of Elea, noted as one of the first teachers of the art of speechmaking. Another great orator was Demosthenes, remembered for his seaside practice of speaking with pebbles in his mouth in order to perfect his delivery. Demosthenes delivered his speech "On the Crown" in Athens in 330 B.C., urging loyalty and honesty in politics. It is still considered a model of speechmaking.

During the middle years of the fifth century B.C., education was very much in the hands of a group of teachers known as the **sophists**, the first speech teachers to take money for their work. In preparing Athenians for civic life, they focused on the ability to speak effectively with **eloquence**, or with a memorable style. The Greek philosopher Plato was concerned about the Sophists' emphasis in speech education. He attacked their prevailing rhetorical practice for encouraging the deception of listeners and for stressing superficial knowledge. Responding to Plato's charges, the philosopher Aristotle wrote *The Rhetoric*, probably the most significant work in the history of public speaking. Aristotle's work, divided into three books dealing with the speaker, the audience, and the speech, insisted on worthwhile content and provided a thorough explanation of audience control. Aristotle's *The Rhetoric* today forms the foundation for our understanding of the process of persuasive speech.

In the classical Roman era, Cicero emerged as a prominent rhetorician and orator. He was a rare individual who combined his oratorical skill with a scholarly written work, *The Orator*, which stressed a liberal education as the foundation for developing speaking abilities. In addition to his memorable speeches, Cicero is noted for clarifying the classical **canons of rhetoric**, the categories for understanding what is involved in the speechmaking process. The five Ciceronian canons, still relevant to the present day, included *invention,* gathering the materials for the speech; *disposition,* organizing the materials into the speech form; *elocution,* practicing clear pronunciation of language; *memory,* developing a command of the materials; and *action,* delivering the speech.

Another significant figure in Roman speech history is Quintilian, whose *Institutes of Oratory* (dated about 95 A.D.) is an exhaustive manual for teachers, offering a plan for the education of the perfect orator. Stressing the need for teachers to adapt to the individual abilities of their students, Quintilian insisted on high ethical standards. Indeed, he defined the perfect orator as "the good man trained in speaking."

From Quintilian's time to about 1500 A.D., the church was the center of most public communication. Most of the population of the Western world was not able to read or write, so people depended on the clergy to enlighten them and to pass on religious teachings and traditions through the spoken word. St. Augustine's *On Christian Doctrine* was an especially dominant effort to return rhetoric to the teachings of the Greeks and Romans.

As the English language developed, British rhetoric in the 1500s and beyond emerged from the classical Ciceronian tradition. Bishop Richard Whateley's *Rhetoric,* 1828, was an important text based on Aristotle, Cicero, and Quintilian's ideas. Some other specialized approaches to the study of speechmaking emerged. One approach, characterized by Henry Peacham's *Garden of Eloquence* (1577), stressed the use of figurative, ornamental language. Another emphasis, typified by John Walker's *Elements of Elocution* (1781), focused on the mechanics of speech delivery.

British eloquence flourished during the eighteenth century—the golden age of oratory in the English Parliament. The American Revolution occasioned speeches about the British position and the colonial position, notably by William Pitt, the Earl of Chatham, who argued that the British had no right to tax the colonies, and by Edmund Burke, who urged conciliation with the American revolutionaries. Speakers in Parliament would often present discourses lasting two or three hours, reflecting phenomenal command of the issues and of the English language.

These British rhetorical traditions underpinned educational practices in early American schools. Public speaking was included as part of the curriculum when Harvard was founded in 1636. Though some schools based their oratorical training on the Ciceronian canons, which combined speech content and delivery, other teachers (of elocution) focused solely on the speaker's delivery. Early colonial speakers of note included Patrick Henry, whose famous "Give me liberty or give me death" speech was delivered before the Virginia Convention of Delegates in 1775, and Jonathan Edwards, a New England preacher whose sermon "Sinners in the Hands of an Angry God" painted a vivid portrait of sin, hell, and punishment.

One of the greatest periods of American oratory occurred during the 1800s at the time of the Civil War. Daniel Webster, a senator from

Massachusetts, presented a masterful reply to Senator Robert Hayne of South Carolina on issues that were beginning to divide the North and the South in 1830. John Calhoun of South Carolina was an eloquent champion of the South, and Henry Clay of Kentucky emerged as the "Great Compromiser" in the historic debates over Southern secession. Charles Sumner, another senator from Massachusetts, became a militant spokesman for the abolition of slavery. His senate speech "The Crime Against Kansas," which he delivered in 1856, provoked the nephew of an opposing senator to physically attack him on the senate floor. Abraham Lincoln, "The Great Emancipator," accomplished a great deal through his oratorical skills as president. His commemorative "Gettysburg Address" remains one of the most eloquent speeches of all time.

Other American speakers took their place in the history of influential public communication. One of the most famous female orators was Susan B. Anthony, noted for her antislavery and temperance stands. Her eloquent speech "On Woman's Right to Suffrage" played a vital role in gaining American women the right to vote. William Jennings Bryan's famous speech "The Cross of Gold," delivered at the Democratic National Convention in Chicago in 1896, favored free coinage of silver at the ratio of 16 to 1. Attorney Clarence Darrow presented eloquent courtroom speeches, notably his plea against capital punishment in the Leopold and Loeb case in 1924. Russell Conwell, a Baptist minister, made a career as a speaker with his motivational speech "Acres of Diamonds." The speech was so popular that he was able to found Temple University from the profits. Humorist Will Rogers was highly popular on the speaking circuit.

World War II brought about another era of compelling oratory. Adolf Hitler's oratorical control over the German masses contributed greatly to his rise to power. President Franklin D. Roosevelt utilized the radio to speak reassuringly to people alarmed about domestic economic pressures and the dangers of the war in Europe. Britain's prime minister, Winston Churchill, will always be noted in history as an eloquent speaker. His oft-repeated messages of hope and inspiration included such famous phrases as "blood, sweat and tears" and "their finest hour." His warning about the "Iron Curtain," in a speech in 1946, significantly influenced subsequent military and foreign policy in the Western world.

Public communication as practiced today in the Western world has been shaped by the powers of many contemporary speakers. President John F. Kennedy was one of the first to understand the significance of television as a communication medium and to recognize how to use it to his advantage. Religious leaders such as Reverend Billy Graham also have learned to adapt their oratorical style to the medium of television. The Reverend Martin Luther King, Jr., eloquently reached out to many

On Listening Listeners must recognize that they can have a profound effect on the speaker and, consequently, the outcome of the public communication. Analyzing some of the research on these effects, listening researcher Ethel Glenn concluded that the behavior of listeners can be a significant factor in the anxiety level of speakers. As a result, listeners should provide supportive, encouraging, reassuring, positive feedback to public speakers.

See Ethel Glenn, "Speech Apprehension and the Perception of Audience Listening Behavior," paper presented at the International Listening Association convention, Indianapolis, Ind., March 1990.

Americans as a leader in the fight for civil rights. President Ronald Reagan successfully used his background as a radio sports announcer and Hollywood actor to earn the nickname "The Great Communicator."

The history of public communication truly is the history of ideas and their expression by competent speakers living in the midst of important human events. As nations confront crises, domestic or foreign, spokespersons emerge to respond to those events. By studying their responses, scholars of public communication can help us come to an understanding of the components in this complex process.

☰ 1.3   The Components of Public Communication

The process of public communication, like all communication, is highly complex and involves the interrelationship of a number of basic components. These are the source, the code, perceptions and attitudes, the message, the channel/the conduit, the receiver, feedback, noise, and the environment. A model of this process is represented in Figure 1.1.

The Source and the Code

The process of public communication originates with a **source**, the speaker, who consciously or unconsciously is stimulated to communicate by some event, object, or idea. The speaker's need to send a message results in the search for a **code**—the appropriate verbal and/or nonverbal language with which to symbolize the message.

Figure 1.1
*A Model of Public
Communication*

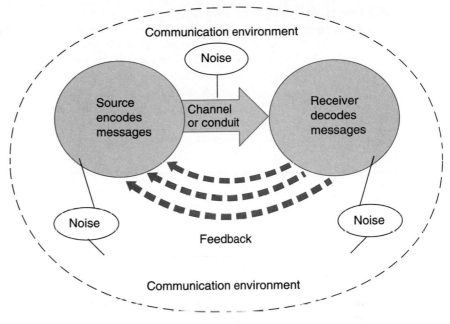

Perceptions and Attitudes

As the source of communication, speakers are influenced by a number of factors. **Perceptions**—the way a person views the world—affect a speaker's choice of topic and style of composing the message. Likewise, speakers are influenced by their own as well as the listener's **attitudes**—predispositions to respond—which usually are positive or negative expectations. These personal perceptions and attitudes affect the choices we make as communicators. A speaker's mental and physical state also may have a bearing on decisions about communicating. For a speaker who does not feel well or is preoccupied, it will be much more difficult to focus on communicating the message.

The Message

The encoded **message**, the speech itself, is composed of verbal and/or nonverbal symbols and supplementary aids, such as visual aids, selected by the speaker to convey his or her ideas. The language is **symbolic** in that the words represent the ideas, objects, and events that the communicator is expressing. The word *chair*, for instance, is an arbitrary selection of sounds that represents a particular type of furniture. The semanticist who studies the symbolic nature of language stresses that just as maps are not the actual terrain but rather representations of that terrain, so are words representations, not the actual objects or ideas.

The Channel or Conduit

The encoded message is carried through a **channel** or channels—speaking, hearing, seeing, smelling, tasting, and touching. As speakers and listeners, we rely primarily on the channels of sight and sound, but sometimes a speaker may have members of the audience also smell, touch, or taste objects in order to convey meaning.

An encoded message may be conveyed to listeners via a **conduit**, a mechanical or electronic means of carrying a message, such as radio, television, overhead projector, tape recorder, videocassette playback unit, or laser disk. Selecting and using the appropriate conduit is a matter for careful decision making for speakers. This is because different messages may very well require different modes of transmission. For example, the advent of television changed the nature of political communication. Presidential candidates once traveled throughout the country giving speeches from the rear of campaign trains. Because they had personal contact with individual audiences at each train stop, they could tailor-make their messages. Today, through the use of television, they can reach a larger number of people without traveling, but they need to code their messages differently. Thirty second spots do not lend themselves to long, eloquent speeches adjusted to individual audiences.

The Receiver

Regardless of the channel used, the message must be decoded before communication is accomplished. The **receiver**, the listener, receives the verbal and nonverbal signals and translates them. The decoded message will not be identical to the one encoded by the speaker, for each listener's symbol system is based on a unique set of perceptions. Just as speakers are influenced by their own perceptions, attitudes, and physical and psychological states, so, too, are listeners affected by these factors at any given moment in the communication process. How the listener interprets a message will depend, to a great extent, on how these factors interact to shape his or her decoding of the message.

Feedback

Once the listener assigns meaning to the message received, he or she is in a position to respond. This response, called **feedback**, can be a verbal or nonverbal reaction (or both) to the message, the speaker, the channel, or even the rest of the audience itself. The speaker should carefully observe feedback because it can indicate whether the listener understands (e.g., nodding), misunderstands (e.g., "I don't understand"), encourages the speaker to continue (e.g., attentive expression, leaning forward), or disagrees (e.g., "No way!"). The act of responding, by which the listener sends feedback to the speaker, actually shifts the receiver's role to that of a source.

On Listening

One of the most grating expressions we hear frequently is the admonition "Just listen." The expression grates because listening is one of the most complex of all human behaviors—and, indeed, one of the most difficult. It's not possible to "just" listen, for listening inevitably calls up an incredible reserve of information-processing skills in every individual.

In American society, we have come to regard listening as a very passive act, something we can do with little or no effort or involvement. As a result, there is a tendency to assume that the speaker must do all the work, bearing sole responsibility for the successful outcome of the communication. This passive view of listening is most unfortunate, for listeners must assume at least 50 percent (and we'd prefer to stipulate 51 percent) of the responsibility for communication. It is critical for our society to improve its communication efforts, both among ourselves as U.S. citizens and throughout the world as citizens of the international community.

Listening is an active process that requires a great deal of time, energy, and concentration to do well. It is not possible to sit back and, like sponges, passively let the verbal and nonverbal messages flow into us. To receive, attend to, interpret, and respond to messages meaningfully, listeners must be thoroughly engaged both physically and mentally. Good listening takes a great deal of work.

Consequently, "Just listen" is a phrase that should be replaced with a more meaningful directive. Perhaps "Listen actively" and "Listen responsibly" and "Listen with care" better describe what good listening is all about.

Noise   The content of a message is influenced not only by the source's coding and the receiver's decoding but also by noise. **Noise** is any internal or external interference in the communication process.[9] It can be caused by environmental factors, physiological impairment, problems with semantics or syntax, organizational confusion, or social or psychological factors. Control of noise is an important consideration for both speaker and listener in any public communication situation.

Environmental noise is outside interference that prevents the listener from receiving the message. This type of noise can occur during a lecture when the students around you are talking so loudly that you cannot hear the instructor, when people are shuffling through their notebooks

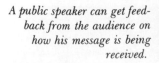

A public speaker can get feedback from the audience on how his message is being received.

looking for a clean page on which to take notes, or when some aspect of the room, such as the air conditioning or the lighting, distracts you from the speaker. In each of these cases, some form of environmental noise is blocking clear reception of the message.

A **physiological impairment**, unless compensated for, can also block the effective sending or receiving of a message. For example, to receive an oral message, a person who is hearing impaired must use a mechanical device, such as a hearing aid, or read the speaker's lips. To send a message to a hearing audience, such a person might use sign language that an able translator would then deliver orally to the listeners. Similarly, an individual with a speech impediment may be difficult for some people to understand. Physiological impairments can cause frustrating communication experiences, for both speakers and listeners.

Problems may also arise with semantics—the meaning of words. **Semantic problems** often result when speakers use language that is common only to one specific group of people, from a particular region or country, for instance, or from a particular field, profession, or organization. Listeners can experience semantic problems when speakers use words without defining them. College professors, physicists, computer technicians, and other experts sometimes forget that those who don't have as much knowledge of their field may not be familiar with its vocabulary.

One semantic problem that is particularly widespread is the use of initials to refer to organizations, equipment, or activities instead of their full names. For example, federal agencies often are referred to with initials, such as SEC (Securities and Exchange Commission) and NOAA (National Oceanic and Atmospheric Administration). Government officials become so accustomed to this usage that they forget that most Americans don't recognize the "alphabet soup." In order to avoid semantic problems, public speakers must be aware that although they know the meaning of a term or a phrase, the listener must have a similar background to understand it as well.

Each language has a syntax—a customary way of putting words together into sentences—and if a speaker uses an unfamiliar syntax the receiver may be confused. Various types of **syntactical problems,** or flawed grammatical usage, can interfere with communication. For example, listeners may become confused if a public speaker changes tenses in the middle of a story being used to make a point ("She is walking down the street and then she said to him . . ."). Or they may be confused by the use of double negatives ("He doesn't have no intention of doing that") or by other incorrect grammar.

Internationals who are learning English often put words in the wrong order. The usual sequence of a grammatically correct English sentence is subject-verb-object: "I give him the book." But other languages—Spanish, for example—do not follow this pattern. In Spanish the same sentence would be "Le doy el libro," or literally "To him I give the book." Thus it is clear that someone who is learning a new language must master not only the vocabulary but an entirely different system of syntax as well. Until the speaker becomes more fluent, the language may be quite difficult both to encode and to decode. Public speakers whose native language is not English may have trouble communicating their ideas fully. Conversely, to communicate most clearly with an international audience, English speakers might be wise to ask an interpreter to carry the burden of clarification. This holds true not only for syntactic noise, but for semantic noise as well.

A common problem for listeners is being unable to follow the structure of a speech. When the source fails to realize that certain ideas are best grasped by presenting them in a structured order, **organizational confusion** may be the result. If, for example, a sociology instructor presents ideas in a random fashion, starting by talking about India, then jumping to China, then Greece, and back to India, after a while his students may become confused as to which country his comments pertain. If the speaker presents material in a specific pattern, the listener can process the ideas and readily grasp the meaning. If the message is not so organized, the receiver must try to sort out the information.

Social noise, a strong factor in communication, is the set of preconceived, unyielding group attitudes that prevents the receiver from dealing objectively with a message. A prime example of social noise is the attitude that any action by a representative of one's own group is always right, whereas the same action by a member of another group is wrong. Thus an individual who has always voted for one political party may well ignore the negative aspects of that party while easily accepting the negative aspects of an opposing party. Such social noise prevents listeners from receiving and interpreting a message effectively.

Social noise can also arise from the topic chosen for a speech. Certain controversial subjects might cause members of the audience to become negative listeners. Religiously conservative audiences, for instance, may not be able to listen with an open mind to a speech about homosexuality, and a predominantly homosexual audience might be incensed by a speech that proposes mandatory AIDS testing. This does not mean that controversial subjects are taboo. What it does mean is that a person who picks such a topic must be aware of the possibility of negative reactions, or must confront the issue in a way that will at least get the audience to give it a hearing. This adjustment takes careful audience analysis and knowledge of speaking techniques that compensate for negative reactions. Some speakers use the negative feedback to their advantage, as Barbara Bush did in her commencement address at Wellesley College in June of 1990. Mrs. Bush was aware that many members of the audience felt she was not an appropriate speaker because she was not a professional woman in her own right but had received her position in society only through her husband's political achievements. Rather than avoiding the issue, she confronted it directly. She spoke about her choice to concentrate on her family, thus diffusing the hostility.

Finally, **psychological noise** confronts both speakers and listeners. We sometimes find ourselves in situations where stress, frustration, or irritation causes us to send or receive messages ineffectively. Think about what happens when you are so angry that you "can't think straight." Or remember the time when you got such stage fright that you were unable to speak, or when you couldn't concentrate on listening to a speech because of some problem at home. In all these cases, psychological noise is getting in the way of effective communication.

The Environment

Communication does not occur in a vacuum; it always exists in some context, some **environment**. Where we are and who is with us affect the message we receive. Such factors as the size of the room, the color of the walls, the arrangement of the chairs, the lighting, the ventilation, and the size of the audience can all affect communication. Environmental control—of the lighting, the sound, the room temperature—can especially determine whether a speech is effectively presented and received.

The communication setting also results from the **occasion**, or the

The environment can affect how a speaker presents his message as well as the impact that the speech has on listeners.

context itself. Just what is the purpose for the speech event? The speaker and listener must understand the nature of the occasion, what it is that brings them together and, to a great extent, shapes the very purpose and the outcome of the speech.

Environment combines with the other components of communication—the source, the code, perceptions and attitudes, the message, the channel, the conduit, the receiver, feedback, and noise—to form a very complex process. Some public speakers assume that all they have to do is present material and the audience will automatically listen, but effective speakers realize that a speech often is dynamic and transactive. Live communication is **dynamic** in the sense that it is continuous, ongoing. As the speaker presents the message to the audience, the feedback from listeners can be instantaneous. Suddenly, both speaker and listener are encoding and decoding messages at the same time. Just as the speaker is encoding and sending the speech, he or she is receiving and decoding feedback from the listeners; likewise, as the listeners receive the speaker's message, they encode and send their feedback. This simultaneous sending and receiving of messages represents the **communication transaction**. The transactional feature of communication is important to recognize, for it is descriptive of what truly occurs when speakers and listeners communicate.

Public communication is dynamic also in the sense that it is ever changing. In this age of information, what both speakers and listeners know is in continuous flux. We are constantly learning new information and adjusting our beliefs and attitudes. **Public speaking competency**, the ability to create appropriate and effective messages, is based on an understanding of the symbolic, dynamic, and transactional nature of communication. Successful communicators make a considerable effort to become skilled senders and receivers of messages. As you embark on your study of public speaking, remember that communicators throughout history have recognized that public speaking competency can be developed through careful attention to the details of speaking and listening. It is worth the effort to acquire the skills of an effective speaker— they can improve your academic work and aid you in social and job-related encounters.

Summary

This chapter investigated the historical roots and the basic components of public speaking. The major concepts discussed were

- ◆ Public speaking is the act of communication that takes place between one person and an audience.
- ◆ Skill in public speaking is important.
- ◆ No matter your career choice, most college graduates enter occupations that require some form of speaking before groups.
- ◆ The study of public speaking has a rich tradition in the study of rhetoric, or persuasive discourse.
- ◆ The history of public communication is the history of ideas and their expression by competent speakers living in the midst of important human events.
- ◆ The basic components of the public communication process are the source, the code, perceptions and attitudes, the message, the channel/the conduit, the receiver, feedback, noise, and the environment.

Key Terms

public speaking	source
rhetoric	code
speechmaking	perceptions
Sophists	attitudes
eloquence	message
canons of rhetoric	symbolic

feedback   organizational
noise   confusion
environmental noise   social noise
physiological impairment   psychological noise
semantic problems   environment
syntactical problems   occasion
channel   dynamic
conduit   communication transaction
receiver   public speaking competency

Learn by Doing

1. Research a historical era of public speaking or the history of public speaking in a non-Western society (e.g., China, Japan) and prepare a report on the rhetoric of that country.

2. Research a specific type of rhetoric, such as the rhetoric of the women's movement, the rhetoric of the gay rights movement, or the rhetoric of sermons. Prepare a report on your findings.

3. Identify which type of noise is present in each of these public speaking situations:

    a. The people sitting behind you are talking so loudly that it is difficult for you to hear the speaker.

    b. The speaker uses numerous curses. You have been taught that intelligent people don't use profane language. You become angrier and angrier with the speaker and finally stop actively listening.

    c. In a lecture your theater instructor uses terms such as "fly space," "wings," and "scrim," which you have never heard before. You cannot comprehend the major points of what she is saying.

    d. The speaker is supposed to be informing the audience about international trade restrictions. His native language is Japanese and he has difficulty forming grammatical sentences in English. You are having trouble interpreting his ideas.

    e. The speaker is explaining how to operate a new computer system. She describes the first operation, then the second, and then the third. She then says, "Oh, I forgot to tell you, between the first and second operation you should not turn off the machine." She begins to describe the fourth operation but then says, "Oh, also, before you start, be sure to use a new computer disk." She then jumps back to the fourth operation. By now, you are lost.

Notes

1. Tony Rodriguez, "The Bruskin Report, updated," Unpublished paper, Cerritos College, California, 1983.

2. Kathleen Edgerton Kendall, "Do Real People Ever Give Speeches?" *Central States Speech Journal,* 25 (Fall 1974), pp. 233–235.

3. Ibid.

4. Lloyd E. Corder, "A Survey Report of Presentation Skills Training in *Fortune 500* Industrial Companies," Unpublished report, Pittsburgh: University of Pittsburgh, 1989.

5. *Honeywell 1988 Corporate Communication Plan* (Minneapolis: Honeywell Corporation, 1988), p. 43.

6. Lee Iacocca with William Novak, *Iacocca* (New York: Bantam Books, 1984), p. 55.

7. Sharon Warren Walsh, "The Lucrative Business of Speaking," *The Washington Post* (March 14, 1988), pp. 1, 34.

8. For a more detailed overview of the history of rhetorical theory, see Andrew Thomas Weaver, Gladys Louise Borchers, and Donald Kliese Smith, *The Teaching of Speech* (Englewood Cliffs, N.J.: Prentice-Hall, 1952), Chapter 2. See also Karl R. Wallace, ed., *History of Speech Education in America* (New York: Appleton-Century-Crofts, 1954). The history of public speaking is described in Lewis Copeland and Lawrence Lamm, eds., *The World's Great Speeches* (New York: Dover Publications, 1942).

9. Factors that cause communication difficulties are sometimes called interference. In this text they will be referred to as noise.

The Public Listener: A Perspective

2

Chapter Outline

Learning Outcomes

After reading this chapter you should be able to:

Explain the difference between hearing and listening.

Explain the listening process.

Clarify what influences listening.

List and describe the levels of listening.

Recognize how to listen to speeches.

Understand the techniques for improving listening in the public speaking setting.

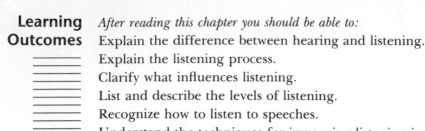

he process through which the listener receives, perceives, attends to, assigns meaning to, and responds to messages is complex. The listener must be actively involved throughout and work to overcome any barriers that may arise during the listening experience.

2.1 The Importance of Public Listening

The importance of listening has been well documented. In fact, listening may take up as much as 45 percent of our communication time.[1] Some studies show that listening is more critical to success in school than is either reading or academic aptitude.[2]

As one observer points out, educated people

have an obligation to strive to become responsible listeners. Responsible means responsiveness; instead of being passive we treat listening as part of ongoing communication with the other person. We make decisions about how to listen based on the nature of our relationship with the other person. In making those decisions however, we need take special care to listen to and appreciate points of view other than our own.[3]

In the process of public communication, this responsibility for listening is particularly significant. Communication will be successful only insofar as the listener remains an active participant throughout the speech.

2.2 The Listening Process

Many people assume that hearing and listening are the same. However, the two are not synonymous. **Hearing** is a biological activity that involves reception of a message through sensory channels; as such, it may be

Profile: Bill Moyers, *journalist and "public listener"*

Any discussion of public speaking would be incomplete without a look at the role of listening in communication. Public speakers, particularly good ones, can wield considerable power in society. Effective public listeners—those who are educated about public speaking and dedicated to listening—are equally important in determining the outcomes of significant events. Journalist Bill Moyers exemplifies the very best qualities of a "public listener."

At age fifteen, Moyers dove into journalism as a cub reporter for the *Marshall News Messenger,* in Marshall, Texas. He graduated from the University of Texas and has worked in broadcasting for over twenty years, devoting most of his energy to uncovering and scrutinizing the social, political, and international issues facing the United States. A *Television Quarterly* survey of critics recently named Moyers among the top ten journalists who have had the most significant influence on TV news.

Moyers has produced over 125 programming hours, including *Special Report: After the War, God and Politics, Facing Hate with Elie Wiesel,* and *The Arab World.* His best-selling book, *Listening to America,* and his current PBS television series of the same name point to his understanding of the importance of listening in public communication. To watch him as he leads discussions is to witness active, effective public listening. Fully engaged in the communication event, he often leans toward his guests with interest. He sits back, chin in hand, and concentrates as he sorts out difficult issues and arguments. Most of all, his face tells speakers that he is committed to listening to what they have to say. Moyers's furrowed brow and tilted head seem to welcome the spoken word and encourage his guests.

Bill Moyers does not sit back and "just listen." He "sits up and listens." As a result, his insightful questions and attentive manner focus his viewers' eyes and ears on America's social, political, and international problems and triumphs.

affected by all of our senses. But hearing—the active processing of all auditory stimuli—is only one part of listening. **Listening** also involves reception, perception, attention, the assignment of meaning, and response by the listener to the message that is presented.

The process of listening is illustrated in Figure 2.1. Since all the components of this process occur almost simultaneously, they are shown as overlapping. Throughout, each step in listening is affected by listening influencers.

Reception   The initial step in the listening process is the **reception** of the stimulus or message. This includes both the auditory message and the visual, nonverbal message. The healthy human ear has the capacity to distinguish approximately 340,000 different tones. Obviously, proper care of the ears is important because auditory acuity enhances one's ability to listen efficiently. The National Institutes of Health estimates that approximately 13 million Americans (almost one out of every twenty peo-

Figure 2.1

The Listening Process

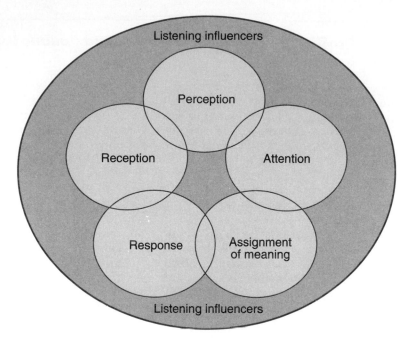

ple) have some type of hearing impairment.[4] In order to keep these statistics from rising, people who work near loud machinery are now required to wear ear protectors. But the workplace is not the only source of potential danger. For example, individuals who expose themselves to loud rock music, especially by listening through earphones, also should be aware that they can damage their hearing mechanism. Indeed, the use of earphones is considered to be the source of much of the ear damage suffered by Americans.[5]

In addition to using our ears, we also listen through our eyes. Barring physical defects, human eyes have the phenomenal capacity of 5 million discriminations per second. Closely watching a speaker's facial expression, posture, and movement and noting his or her physical appearance provides us with important cues that may not be obvious merely by listening to the verbal part of the message. It has been estimated that 93 percent of the total meaning of a message can emerge from nonverbal and visual cues.[6] Thus, sensitivity to these visual cues becomes a very important part of effective listening behavior.

Perception   As the stimulus or message is received, the listener's perceptions come into play. **Perception** is a screening process that filters the message according to the listener's background, experiences, roles, mental and physical state, beliefs, attitudes, and values—in short, everything that makes up the listener's orientation to the world. Listeners are constantly influenced by their perceptual filter. Studies on listening perception suggest that "the louder, the more relevant, the more novel the stimuli, the more likely they are to be perceived by the listener."[7] Good listeners, therefore, should recognize the influences of their own perceptions on what they hear and deal with these influences appropriately. For example, the listener who understands that, to many Americans, someone who speaks with a British accent sounds more authoritative may want to work harder to understand the content of the person's public speech before drawing any conclusions about it.

Attention   Once the stimulus—the word and/or its visual cues—is received and sent through the perceptual filter, it finally reaches the listener's attention. **Attention** represents the focus on a specific stimulus that is selected from all the stimuli we receive at any given moment. At this point, all other stimuli recede in our consciousness so that we can concentrate on a specific word or visual symbol. Consider, for example, what happens when you are listening to a speech. Perhaps the person sitting next to you is wearing too much perfume, and perhaps the argument you had with a friend just before you arrived is still bothering you. In addition, the sound system is humming and you are worried because you left your car in a no-parking zone. Obviously, your attention is being pulled in several directions. But if the speech is well presented, with compelling information, you will focus on what is happening on the stage, and all the other factors will be relegated to the back of your consciousness.

Attention to a stimulus occurs in an individual's short-term memory. The capacity of the short-term memory—our **attention span**—is about sixty seconds.[8] The ability of the listener to focus attention is therefore limited indeed. In fact, professional speakers have observed that their typical listeners cannot handle a speech that continues much beyond a fifteen-minute time frame. The reasons for this have not yet been traced, although some believe "it's entirely possible that our capacity for sustained attention and deliberate thought is being altered by television viewing."[9] Most of us who have been raised on television have come to expect a seven- to ten-minute viewing format, followed by a commercial break.

Undoubtedly, one of the most difficult tasks we have as listeners is to achieve the ability to concentrate. Motivation plays a great part in acquiring this skill. For example, efforts to anticipate the next point or sequence of points in a speech can sometimes assist us in receiving a message (although it should be recognized that if you anticipate a message and the speaker takes a different approach, you can be thrown off the track). In the same way, constructing internal summaries throughout the speech and concentrating on isolating the main points should also help.

Paraphrasing—making a summary of the ideas you have just received—will provide you with a concise restatement of the speaker's message. It will also allow you to determine whether you understand the material or not. After all, if you cannot repeat or write down a summary of what was said, then you probably didn't receive the whole message or didn't understand it. Keep this in mind when you're in class listening to the instructor or any other speaker and taking notes. Instead of writing down direct quotes, try to mentally paraphrase the material. If you can't do it, that ought to be a clue that you should ask for clarification or make a note to look up that particular material later on.

Human beings can think three to four times faster than the normal conversation rate of 125 to 150 words per minute.[10] And because we can receive messages much more quickly than the other person can talk, we tend to tune in and out throughout a message. The mind can absorb only so much material. In addition, the brain operates much like a computer. It turns off, recycles itself, and turns back on in order to avoid information overload.[11] It's no wonder, then, that our attention fluctuates even when we're actively involved as listeners. Think back to the last class lecture or sermon you attended. Do you recall a slight gap in your listening at times? Were you conscious of the moment when your mind tuned out? This is a natural part of the listening process, but you must remember to make a conscious effort to tune back in so that you can concentrate on the message. When you turn off, the major danger is that you will begin to daydream rather than quickly turn back to the message. But by taking notes and forcing yourself to paraphrase you will avoid this pitfall.

Concentration on the message is an important key to effective listening. Developing the skills of concentration requires physical and mental effort. The listener must be thoroughly engaged in the communication and be able to focus his or her energies on the speech as it is presented. Listening to a speech while concentrating can be exhausting, but the reward of gaining the speaker's message is often well worth the effort.

The Assignment of Meaning

Once we have paid attention to the material a speaker has presented, the next step in the listening process is to categorize the message in order to assign meanings to the verbal and nonverbal stimuli. We are only now beginning to understand something about this cognitive structuring. Some researchers suggest that once we receive a stimulus, we process it mentally and put the stimulus into some predetermined category.[12] This process, the **assignment of meaning**, develops as we acquire our language system, which provides us with the mental categories for interpreting the messages we receive. For instance, our mental categories for the word *cheese* might include "food," "dairy product," "taste," and "nourishment"—all of which help us to relate the word *cheese* to the context in which it is used.

The categorical assignment of meaning that provides listeners with the interpretation of the message is affected by the human cognitive process. This categorical context creates what psychologists have identified as **schema**—scripts for processing information. The cognitive process involves interpretation from all the schema that an individual develops throughout life, and it is these schema that provide the mental links for understanding and creating meaning from the stimuli that we receive.[13]

Today's research suggests that the two hemispheres of our brain handle information differently and have different functions. The left hemisphere deals with verbal and numerical information in a linear form, providing the analytical function, while the right hemisphere specializes in processing shapes and images, performing a more spatial, intuitive function.[14] As researchers come to understand the implications of this division of function in more detail, we communicators probably will better understand why we respond as we do in assigning meanings to the messages we receive. This understanding could also allow us to become better listeners, because we may find it possible to teach individuals to better use whatever part of the brain deals with particular materials presented in a speech.

A strategy useful to listeners in assigning meaning to messages is to differentiate **factual statements** (those based on observable phenomena or common acceptance) from opinions (inferences or judgments made by the speaker).[15] Speakers who have a strong, assertive style are likely to sound very authoritative and factual, but the message may be based more on their own opinions than on fact. The listener should be alert to such phrases as "In my opinion," "It seems to me," "I think," and "It would appear" as indicators that the content of the message is primarily based on the speaker's opinions. Likewise, it is helpful for the listener to be alert to the verbal obscurity of messages. Unclear terms and phrases, euphemisms, and evasive language make interpretation difficult.

The assignment of meaning is a complex step in the listening process. Effective listeners are sensitive to how and why they are interpreting a message and use such self-monitoring to understand the influence of messages on their listening behavior.

Response   Once you, as a listener, have assigned meaning to a message, you continue your processing of the information with an internal or an external

A public speaker should be aware that some listeners may respond negatively.

response (an intellectual or emotional reaction) to the message. In general, on a cognitive level, this response may be seen as a type of information storage; you recognize you have gained some idea by saying something like "Oh, I understand," either out loud or to yourself. In some cases this acquisition is below our level of awareness. In fact, some psychologists hypothesize that every stimulus we received is stored somewhere in our brain, whether we recognize it or not.

How can you remember information you've heard? The authors of a study skills program for students recommend using the following techniques: (1) choose to remember, (2) visualize the material to remember, (3) associate the material with something familiar to assist in recalling it, and (4) practice with the material so that recalling it becomes easy.[16] For example, when you are introduced to a new idea during a speech, you must first decide that you want to remember that idea and get ready to remember it. You might then picture the idea in a particular context. Then try to tie the idea to something you are familiar with, such as finding a rhyme for a key word in the concept. Finally, repeat the idea several times or write it down. If you carry through with these techniques, the odds of your remembering the information increase greatly.

One response that cannot only assist the listener in storing information into long-term memory but also provide meaningful feedback to the speaker is to ask questions. Asking questions provides listeners with the opportunity to ensure that the message they have received and interpreted is consistent with the original intent of the speaker. Questions offer the speaker a chance to clarify any points that seem confusing and demonstrate that listeners are indeed involved in the communication transaction.

To be effective, however, questions must necessarily be relevant to the message the speaker has presented. Questions that are off the topic or beyond the scope of the speaker's message can disrupt the communication flow. Questions intended to increase the listener's understanding must be direct and to the point. Too frequently, listeners use the opportunity to ask questions that take stands on issues and present their own messages rather than to probe for understanding of the speaker's intentions. This, of course, does little to help listeners comprehend the speaker's points. Question-and-answer sessions following speeches should concentrate on such requests as: asking for clarification of the ideas presented or seeking more information, inquiring into the validity of sources the speaker refers to, or soliciting the speaker's in-depth views about ideas alluded to in the speech. Attention to feedback skills such as these is a critical part of being an effective listener. Good feedback is appropriate to the speaker, the message, and the situation, and it should be clearly presented so that the speaker understands your feedback message.

Listening Influencers

In a public setting a listener may be influenced not only by the speaker but also by the other members of the audience, as illustrated in Figure 2.2. Research in listening has demonstrated that certain key influencers can facilitate or deter the process at almost any point.[17]

The speaker, of course, is a major listening influencer. The speaker's credibility (which is the listener's perception of the speaker's trustworthiness, competence, and dynamism) can lead the listener to accept or to reject a message. If you feel you can't trust the speaker, you're not likely to trust his or her message. On the other hand, some listeners are so in awe of a particular speaker's outstanding credentials or reputation that they lose all objectivity in analyzing the message the speaker presents. The speaker's physical presentation, such as clothing and posture, can also have an instantaneous effect on whether or not you attend to the message.

Another major influencer is the message itself. A critical factor in

Figure 2.2
Public Listening

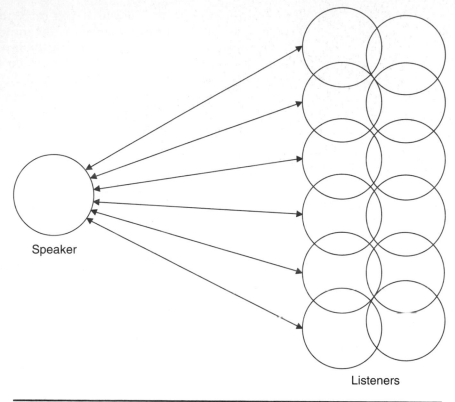

Speaker

Listeners

understanding oral messages is how well the message is structured. If the presentation is not clearly organized—if the arguments are not well ordered—it will be difficult for the listener to concentrate and stay tuned. Likewise, the tone and the treatment of the message can influence listening. If you don't agree with the point of view, or if the speaker is too strident or too ambivalent in the arguments presented, your listening comprehension will be affected. For example, speakers who make emotional appeals so strong that the audience is overwhelmed by the desperation of the predicament can turn listeners away from the message.

The communication channel also influences listening ability. Some people probably are more auditory and some are more visual in orientation, so channel preference can be a factor. The speaker who couples the message with some clear visual aids may assist listeners in comprehending the material.

Noise, any sort of interference in the communication channel, certainly diminishes the effectiveness of the listener. Static on the radio or distortions on the television screen can interrupt good listening. Noise in the environment also affects listeners. If the lighting is so poor that you can't see the speaker easily, or if the room temperature is too cold or too hot, you may have greater difficulty attending to the speaker's message.

Listeners are influenced not only by a vast array of external factors but also by internal variables, such as their physical state (general health, gender, age), experiences (background, life history, training, culture), attitudes (predispositions) and expectations, and memory. These internal factors are always with you and can enhance or detract from listening. A listener who feels ill, for example, will have difficulty focusing on the message. Some research illustrates that men and women listen differently, as do people of different ages.[18] Life experiences likewise can be quite influential. People from different cultures have different ways of attending to each other in terms of eye contact, physical distance between speakers and listeners, and amount of patience afforded the speaker. Though there is little research on the effects of modeling on listening behavior, it appears safe to assume that we are influenced by how those around us listen. Teachers, parents, and other people with whom we come in contact on a regular basis, who are good listeners, can provide models for children to emulate as they build their listening skills.

The positive or negative attitude that one carries into a listening situation, coupled with the expectation one has for the listening experience, is important. If you go to a speech convinced beforehand that it will be a waste of time, you probably will carry that negative attitude into the session and be unable to listen comprehensively. A person's attitude toward listening is a type of self-concept. Most of us have received very little praise or external reward for good listening, but we probably have heard lots of negative messages: "Sit down and listen" or "Keep quiet and listen" or "Why don't you ever listen to me?" These negative messages create a negative attitude about our own listening abilities. Most listeners who have received such negative messages probably have poor images of themselves as listeners. They expect to listen poorly, so they do.

Memory plays a significant role in listening. The listener must be willing and able to hold the message in short-term memory long enough to assign meaning to it. Sufficient auditory and visual memory is required to maintain this focus. As pointed out earlier, taking notes can serve as a useful aid to memory. It is also necessary for the listener to have the time—and to take the time—to listen with discrimination and comprehension in order to respond to the message.

On Listening

A coalition of organizations in higher education has issued a statement deploring the heckling incidents involving controversial public figures invited to speak on various campuses. The list of notables who have been heckled by members of campus audiences is growing; it includes Jeane Kirkpatrick, U.S. Ambassador to the United Nations; the social activist Eldridge Cleaver; and Sheik Ahmed Zaki Yamani, the Saudi Arabian oil minister.

The possibility that the demonstrations have political overtones has alarmed some people, but whether or not that is the case, the heckling should be of concern to all educators as a problem of basic communication.

One of the objectives of American education should be the development of effective communication skills and attitudes in students. Ours is a communication society, and speaking and listening play a prominent role in our careers and in maintaining our social relationships.

Studies have revealed that a major part of the time that people spend in communication each day is spent listening. Yet we're doing very little in our colleges to train students to listen.

That our students lack the requisite skills to be effective listeners came to light in a study conducted by New York's Center for Public Resources. In addition to decrying the decline in basic mathematics and science skills in the work force, the corporate executives and labor-union officials who were questioned in the study complained of a decline in their employees' speaking and listening skills. At the same time, the educators who were questioned observed that they were satisfied with their students' preparation in communication skills. Clearly, there is a gap between the employers' and educators' perceptions about how students are being prepared for the realities of the workplace. The heckling issue reflects that gap.

The students who are not willing to give controversial speakers a fair hearing are short-circuiting the listening process in communication. The first step in listening is to receive and comprehend a message *before* forming judgments about its merits or its source.

Carl Rogers, the well-known psychotherapist, argues that the greatest barrier to human communication is the tendency to form snap judgments about a person or what he or she is saying and then "tune out." That tendency must be recognized and overcome—we must hear people out before deciding whether to accept or reject their message.

The listener shares equally with the speaker the responsibility to uphold the right to freedom of speech. Just as speakers who take that freedom seriously must strive to preserve it by not abusing it, so, too, should their hearers preserve it by listening.

> The coalition of higher-education organizations summed up the issue in a "Call to Action":
>
> "Unless there is freedom to speak and to teach, even for those with whom we differ on fundamentals," it said, "and unless there is freedom for all to listen and to learn, there can be no true college or university no matter how fine the buildings or modern the equipment."
>
> From "Heckling on Campus: Freedom of Speech Depends on Teaching Students to Listen," by Andrew D. Wolvin from *The Chronicle of Higher Education*, July 20, 1983, p. 20.

☰ 2.3 The Levels of Listening

We have seen that listeners may be influenced by a wide range of factors that can enhance or detract from the listening process. Reading specialists suggest that a person who establishes a clear goal before beginning to read some material will read more effectively.[19] The same principle applies to listeners.

We listen on a number of levels. Listeners probably function differently depending on their particular level of listening or on their objectives for listening. These levels represent the basis on which to build listening skills.[20]

Discrimination Level

At the **discrimination level**, we listen to distinguish auditory and visual stimuli. Distinguishing the message stimuli is at the base of all listening we do, and experience and practice are our best strategies for improving discrimination. At first, we tend not to discern subtle shades of meaning and vocal nuances until we become accustomed to the communication style of a particular speaker. It takes some time to develop these skills. The more experience we have in listening to a speaker, the easier it generally becomes to discriminate the message. For example, during the first few class lectures, you may find yourself confused by your professor's way of speaking. Soon, however, you will probably find that there is a system to the way he or she organizes the lecture and stresses ideas, such as writing key terms on the chalkboard. Getting acquainted with a style of speaking helps you to listen more effectively.

Discrimination of both auditory and visual cues can enable listeners to be more sensitive perceivers of a message. Through discrimination we can come to understand differences in verbal sounds (dialects, pronunciation) and nonverbal behavior (gestures, facial expressions). We can then determine, for example, if a person is being sarcastic, evasive, or enthusiastic, realizing that the same set of words can be taken in a variety of ways. If we don't listen with discrimination to how something is said, we may miss the meaning of the message.

Comprehension Level

The objective of the **comprehension level** of listening is to recognize and retain information. Comprehensive listening is what you do most in college classes. Listening comprehension is a critical factor in the success or failure of college students. "Among the students who fail," one researcher commented, "deficient listening skills were a stronger factor than reading skills or academic aptitude."[21]

Some techniques enhance listening comprehension. One strategy is to concentrate on getting the main points of a message rather than all of the supporting details. As you listen to a speaker discuss an idea, focus on the main point being made rather than on the elaboration and the details. When taking notes, it is wise to sort out the main points and the supporting details.

At the next class you attend, try this method for taking notes: Draw a vertical line down the middle of your paper from top to bottom, and put the main points in the left-hand column and the supporting ideas in the right-hand column. By abbreviating commonly used words, you save time in writing, which allows for more listening time. Many note takers like to provide examples to help clarify material. You will have to

At the comprehension level of listening, the objective is to recognize and retain information.

determine for yourself how much detail you will need in your notes. (See Figure 2.3.)

You may also need to develop a number of memory techniques in order to recall the main points at a later time. You can forget as much as 50 percent of any given information after the first day unless you take notes and review them.[22] Because it is so easy to forget information, good academic listeners have found that they retain ideas best if they review the information immediately after it is presented and then go over it daily rather than waiting to do a cram review session on the night before an examination.

Therapeutic Level

The **therapeutic level** of listening is important for those in such fields as psychology, social work, speech therapy, and counseling. Therapeutic listening requires you to act as a sounding board so that a speaker can talk through a problem and, ideally, reach his or her own solution. This type of listening utilizes many of the techniques of a counseling interview.

Therapeutic listening is not restricted to professional counselors, however; it also applies to public speaking. At times listeners may assume the role of sounding board for public speakers. Speakers often tell stories, and these personal anecdotes may reveal something about the speakers' emotions. Knowing this could be useful to a listener trying to understand the point a speaker is developing or to identify the speaker's perspective. Identification is an imperative of public speaking: "You persuade a person only insofar as you can talk his language by speech, gesture, tonality, order, image, attitude, idea, *identifying* your ways with his."[23]

Therapeutic listening requires a willingness to suspend judgment and to listen with empathy—to understand where the speaker is coming from. A speaker who talks about his wartime service, for instance, might be telling "war stories" essentially to "purge" himself of the experience or to rationalize some of his behaviors while in uniform and thus needs a supportive, understanding audience.

Critical Level

At the **critical level** of listening, we comprehend and evaluate the message that has been received. A critical listener assesses the arguments and the appeals in a message and then decides whether to accept or to reject them. Ideally, this analysis should occur only after you have recognized, understood, and reflected on the entire message that the speaker has presented.

As in critical thinking, an understanding of both the tools of persua-

Figure 2.3

Note-taking Format

Lstng

Lstng Process

Hearing – biological process
Lstng – active processing of info heard
Reception – get message
Perception – screen info
Attention
    focus on ideas
    anticipate next point
    paraphrase – restate in own words
    get ready to lstn rapidly
Assignment of meaning – categorize symbols
Response – info storage
    choose to remember
    visualize what is to be remembered
    associate info
    practice material
Lstng Influencers
    speaker
    message
    channel
    noise
    internal variables
    attitude
    memory
    time

Levels of Lstng

Discrimination
Comprehension

---

sion and the process of logic and reasoning will enable critical listeners to analyze the merits of the messages they receive. Analysis includes such factors as:

1. *The personal appeal of the speaker.* The speaker's personal appeal, or credibility, stems from the level of expertise, trustworthiness, and dynamism that is projected. The critical listener needs to recognize the extent to which the speaker's credibility influences the message, and be able to consider the validity of what is said apart from how the speaker sounds or looks.

2. *The speaker's arguments and evidence.* Does the speaker present a logical

argument that is supported with data that have substance and relevance to the point? Is the information acceptable to you from the evidence presented? Does the conclusion the speaker reaches seem reasonable based on the information presented?

3. *The speaker's motivational appeals.* How does the speaker attempt to get listeners involved in the message? What appeals does the speaker utilize to elicit your response to the persuasive message? Are these "tricks" intended to make you a believer or are they relevant ideas?

4. *Assumptions on the part of the speaker.* Beware of when a speaker assumes that something is a fact when it has not been established as such. If you hear a phrase such as "It is readily apparent that" or "Everyone knows," be alert to the possibility that the speaker is making up evidence.

5. *What is not said.* In some cases, a speaker may imply an idea that is never actually stated, so that the listener is forced to read between the lines to supply the message. "You know what our objectives are" and "You know what I mean" are two phrases of implication that should alert the listener to think about the information presented very carefully.

6. *Use of passive language.* Sentences stated in the passive voice eliminate the subject and thus can be too vague. "It has been proved" and "It was previously demonstrated" are all-too-common examples of this kind of language. Again, be wary of these nonfactual attempts to lead you to "factual" acceptance.

The critical listener analyzes information to assess the merits or demerits of a particular message. Campaign speeches, radio and television news reporting and commentary, and persuasive briefings are all examples of public speaking that require critical content analysis.

Appreciation Level

At the **appreciation level**, we listen for enjoyment or for the sensory stimulation a message gives us. Listeners can appreciate a speaker's style, vocal tone, humor, approach to the audience, or any of the other elements in public communication, even the setting itself. A public speaker presenting an evening of poetry or describing a visit to a beautiful vacation spot may inspire appreciative listening. Appreciation is a highly individual matter—there are no rules on how to go about it. Some people believe that the more knowledge you have about a particular subject, the more you can appreciate it. Others feel that the more you know, the more critical you become, thus losing your ability to appreciate any speech on the subject but the very best. Public listening is appreciative when you have a pleasurable experience as a participant in the communication process.

2.4   Listening to Speeches

As a listener in a speaker's audience, you are not the only one receiving the message and not the only one for whom the message is intended. As a result, your listening experience can be influenced by the speaker's efforts to target the audience as a group and by the responses of the various listeners within that group. Though in most public communication settings you will not have the opportunity to give direct verbal feedback throughout the speech, you will be sending nonverbal cues to the speaker through your attentive posture and facial expression. And you may be given the opportunity to ask questions or otherwise respond following the presentation.

Besides giving indirect feedback to the speaker, the public listener may be asked to make critical judgments about the speech and the speaker following the presentation. In public speaking classes, for instance, students will often be asked to comment on what they feel is effective and what might be improved in a speaker's presentation. Likewise, after presidential debates and speeches by diplomats and other politicians, listeners sometimes offer their views on the speaker's effectiveness. Some useful guidelines for evaluating speeches include:

1. Did the speaker have a worthwhile purpose?
2. Has the speaker made an attempt to be objective and fair to himself or herself, to the audience, and to the subject?
3. Did the speaker know the subject?
4. Had the speaker analyzed the audience?
5. Was the speech structurally sound?
6. Did the speaker utilize effective language?
7. Did the speaker make use of factors of attention and interest in both the content and the delivery of the speech?
8. Did the speaker's supporting materials meet the tests of evidence?
9. How effectively did the speaker make use of the visual aspects of delivery?
10. How effectively did the speaker use his or her voice?
11. Was the speaker a credible spokesperson on the subject?
12. What was the total impression left by the speech?

2.5   Improving Listening

You can do a great deal to improve your ability to listen. Improving listening skills starts with understanding what is involved in the process so that you can monitor your own listening behavior, recognizing what

On Listening

Have ZOOL 211 students no manners at all? During the seminar presented by Dr. Walter Neupert on "Translocation of Proteins into Mitochondria" on April 8, many of them completely embarrassed and infuriated those of us who came to hear him speak.

A distinguished lecturer should not be "walked out" on by a third of his audience, especially from the front rows, nor should this mass exiting be punctuated by repeated door-slamming! They not only destroyed the concentration of the remaining audience, but disrupted the speaker's train of thought as well.

This type of behavior not only looks bad for their class, but also paints a gloomy picture of campus students. Similar actions at other seminars will no doubt put this university on the "black list" of many potential speakers. Seminars such as Dr. Neupert's provide a great source of information on subjects of current interest, given by prominent people in the field, and are a tremendous asset to others working in similar areas. Loss of these types of seminars would not only limit one's education, but hurt the campus as well.

If we are fortunate enough to have another distinguished lecturer speak and you decide to go, please do not talk during the seminar. If you know you must leave during the talk, sit near the rear so your exiting will not disturb others, and close the door quietly.

STEWART ALCORN
plus nine others
graduate students/faculty
microbiology

See Stewart Alcorn, "What happened to our manners?" Letters to the Editor, *Diamondback*, University of Maryland, April 13, 1992, p. 4.

you are and are not doing at any given point. Taking the next step toward being a better listener may require you to break old habits and put new strategies in their place—and then to practice these new skills until they feel comfortable to you.

Techniques

The following suggestions will help listeners develop greater skill as participants in communication.

1. *Recognize that both the sender and the receiver share the responsibility for effective communication.* As a receiver, you should ask questions and

provide feedback if you cannot understand the speaker's point. If possible, restate the major ideas so that the speaker can check to be sure you have accurately grasped the meaning.

2. *Suspend judgments.* One of the greatest barriers to human communication is our tendency to form instant judgments about almost everything we encounter. As listeners, we are prone to making premature assessments of speakers even before comprehending their message. Statements such as "I don't like his voice," "This is a boring lecture," or "I disagree with her point" all set up barriers to effective listening. The good listener works to set aside these judgments and to listen for the message.

3. *Be a patient listener.* Avoid interrupting or tuning out while the speaker is communicating the message. We often find ourselves beginning to respond before we have completely understood what's being said. Think about how difficult it is to assemble a new product until you have thoroughly comprehended the instructions. Or remember the times when you filled out a form only to realize later on that you had written your name when the directions said to print and that you had put your first name down when the last name should have come first. Patience in listening will help you avoid having to go back over messages you missed the first time around or didn't understand because you didn't let the whole message come through.

4. *Carefully note your emotional responses to words.* Some words can bring about instant reactions. **Inciting words** are words that trigger strong feelings within us, either positive or negative. How do you react to the words *child beater, rapist,* and *income tax?* Words like these often send us off on tangents, cause daydreaming, or break our concentration. You should be aware that we can be led astray through our emotional responses. There is no easy way to prevent yourself from reacting to inciting words. However, by monitoring your body you might catch yourself physically pulling in or daydreaming, or you might feel yourself flushing as you become upset.

5. *Be aware that your posture affects your listening.* When you listen to an exciting lecture, how do you sit? Usually you lean slightly forward, feet on the floor, and look directly at the presenter. On the other hand, if you slump down and stare out the window, it's very unlikely that you're actively participating in the communication act. What happens to you when you curl up in a comfortable chair, turn on soft music, and try to read? Most likely, instead of reading you fall asleep or do a lot of daydreaming.

Have you ever left a classroom feeling totally exhausted? It may well be that you were concentrating so hard that you became physically tired. After all, good listening is hard work. An effective listener learns when it is necessary to listen in a totally active way and when it is possible to relax. Consider this analogy: When you're driving a car with an automatic transmission, the car shifts gears when it needs more or less power. Unfortunately, people don't have automatic transmissions. We have to shift gears for ourselves. When you need to concentrate, you shift into your version of first gear (feet on the floor, posture erect, looking directly at the speaker in order to pick up any necessary nonverbal clues). Once you feel that you understand the point that's being made (a test for this would be the ability to paraphrase what has been said), then a shift of posture to a more comfortable position may be in order. When a new subject arises—or when you hear transitional words or phrases such as "therefore" or "in summary"—then you shift back into your active listening position.

6. *Make a conscious effort to listen.* If it is important for you to listen carefully to a message, then you must tune in to that message. As discussed earlier, hearing and listening are not synonymous. Listening requires a concerted effort on your part to receive, perceive, attend to, assign meaning to, and respond to the message. This does not happen automatically. If you are going to take notes, take out the paper and a writing instrument. If you know you are easily distracted, move away from the window or from friends who might prevent you from concentrating.

7. *Control distractions.* All of us are surrounded by noise. Sometimes the sound of other audience members talking, or even the hum of an air conditioner, can interfere with efficient listening. If the message is important to you, you should try to adjust the interference or control it. If possible, move to a different seat or ask someone to please be quiet. There is little point to being a participant in communication if you can't hear or see the speaker.

8. *Concentrate.* Focus your attention energy on the message. An effective speaker will provide listeners with verbal and nonverbal cues to assist concentration. You should recognize **transitions** (words indicating a change of idea or topic, such as "therefore," "another idea is," "finally"); **forecasts of ideas** (statements that indicate a series of ideas will follow, such as "there are three ideas," "the next point is"); and **internal summaries** (restatements of ideas that have just been explained, such as "and so we have seen that"). All these are vehicles for furthering your grasp of the major points that the speaker is presenting. The vocal dynamics, or **paralanguage**—the rate, volume, and pitch of speech and the length of pauses—used by the speaker can also help you understand the points being developed. By stressing words, pausing before an idea, or increasing the volume of a phrase, the speaker is telling you that something is important, unusual, or significant.

The speaker's physical movements can carry meaning that might reinforce or even contradict the verbal message. Be aware of a speaker's use of forceful gesture or enumeration of ideas with the pointing finger. We often have to listen with our eyes as well as our ears in order to pick up all the cues that will help us understand the real message. It is important to look beyond the words themselves for the full intent of the message.

A Willingness to Listen

Once the listener develops a clear understanding of the complexities of the listening process, recognizes how she or he is functioning within that process, and builds some new skills to perform more effectively in listening, it still requires considerable commitment to be an effective listener. The good public receiver is one who is willing to listen.

Unfortunately, listening has been the most underrated of the communication modes. Many people have come to perceive listening as a passive act, assuming that the speaker can and should bear almost the total responsibility for the outcome of the communication. This, of course, is not true. The key to effective listening is caring to be a good listener—learning the skills to be effective, practicing these skills, and putting them into effect.

Summary

Listening is an important part of the communication process. This chapter developed the following points about effective listening:

- A great deal of our communication time is devoted to listening.
- Hearing is a biological process that involves the reception of a message through sensory channels; it may be affected by all of our senses.
- Listening is the active processing of the information we receive.
- Listening involves reception, perception, attention, the assignment of meaning, and response by the listener to the message that has been presented.
- Auditory acuity enhances an individual's ability to listen efficiently.
- Listeners use the visual system as well as the hearing mechanism.
- Attention represents the focus on a specific stimulus selected from all the stimuli we receive at any given moment.
- Making a summary of the ideas presented, or paraphrasing, can be a helpful technique for sharpening concentration.
- Both the interest level and the difficulty of the message affect our listening concentration.

◆ Studies of compressed speech indicate that we can comprehend at a much faster rate than people normally speak.

◆ Putting a stimulus into some predetermined category enables a listener to assign meaning to a message.

◆ Schema are scripts for processing information.

◆ The two hemispheres of the human brain process information differently.

◆ Once we have assigned meaning to a message, we continue the listening process with an internal or an external response (feedback) to that message.

◆ Memory capacity can be increased by choosing to remember, visualizing what is to be remembered, associating the information with something familiar, and practicing with the material.

◆ Listening influencers include the speaker, the message, the channel, noise, internal variables, attitude, memory, and time.

◆ The effective listener receives, perceives, attends to, assigns meaning to, and responds to messages while being influenced by a wide range of factors that enhance or detract from the process at any given time.

◆ There are five levels at which we listen: the discrimination level, the comprehension level, the therapeutic level, the critical level, and the appreciation level.

◆ Inciting words can interrupt good listening.

◆ Listening to speeches requires an understanding of your own response to the public communication and your adaptation of that response to the communication purpose.

Key Terms

hearing
listening
reception
perception
attention
attention span
paraphrasing
assignment of meaning
schema
factual statements
response

discrimination level
comprehension level
therapeutic level
critical level
appreciation level
inciting words
transitions
forecasts of ideas
internal summaries
paralanguage

Learn by Doing

1. Contrast hearing and listening. Draw an analogy between listening and reading.

2. Analyzing your own listening, name one listening behavior that you have that does not match the characteristics of a good listener as described in this chapter. Consider how you could change this behavior so that you can be more effective as a listener.

3. Now that you are aware of some of the principles of effective listening, put them into practice. At the next speech or class lecture you attend, sit up, concentrate on what the speaker is saying, and focus all of your attention energy on comprehending the material. Work out strategies to provide internal summaries and paraphrases to assist you in concentrating and comprehending. After the session is over, analyze your listening behavior and determine what else you can do to improve your listening comprehension.

4. Make a list of terms that stimulate a strong emotional response in you. Go back and review those terms. Why do you think they are inciting for you? If time is available your instructor will divide the class into groups of four to six students. Discuss your terms and what implications they have for your habits of communication.

5. Attend a speech presentation and listen on an appreciative or therapeutic level to the speaker's style and use of stories. What does the speaker do to enhance your appreciative or therapeutic response to the presentation?

Notes

1. Paul Tory Rankin, "Listening Ability: Its Importance, Measurement, and Development," *Chicago School Journal,* 12 (January 1930), 177–179. Other studies support Rankin's findings: Donald E. Bird, "Teaching Listening Comprehension," *Journal of Communication,* 3 (November 1953), 127–130; Lila R. Breiter, "Research in Listening and Its Importance to Literature," M.A. thesis, Brooklyn College, 1957; and Elyse K. Werner, "A Study of Communication Time," M.A. thesis, University of Maryland, 1975.

2. Margaret Conaway, "Listening: Learning Tool and Retention Agent," in A. S. Algier and K. W. Algier, eds., *Improving Reading and Study Skills* (San Francisco: Jossey-Bass, 1982), pp. 51–63. For a comprehensive review of information on listening, see the 1990 issue of the *Journal of the International Listening Association.*

3. William F. Eadie, "Hearing What We Ought to Hear," *Journal of the International Listening Association,* 4 (1990), 4.

4. "Hearing Loss: Ways to Avoid, New Ways to Treat," *U.S. News & World Report,* October 18, 1982, pp. 85–86.

5. Ibid.

6. Albert Mehrabian, *Silent Messages* (Belmont, Calif.: Wadsworth, 1971), p. 41.

7. Larry L. Barker, *Listening Behavior* (Englewood Cliffs, N.J.: Prentice-Hall, 1971), p. 31.

8. D. A. Norman, "Memory While Shadowing," *Quarterly Journal of Experimental Psychology*, 21 (February 1969), 85–93.

9. Dorothy Singer and Jerome Singer, "Is Human Imagination Going Down the Tube?" *Chronicle of Higher Education*, April 29, 1979, p. 56.

10. Ralph G. Nichols and Leonard A. Stevens, *Are You Listening?* (New York: McGraw-Hill, 1957), p. 107.

11. Norbert Wiener, *Cybernetics* (Cambridge, Mass.: M.I.T. Press, 1961), and *The Human Use of Human Beings* (Garden City, N.Y.: Doubleday, 1964).

12. See Carl H. Weaver, *Human Listening* (Indianapolis: Bobbs-Merrill, 1972), pp. 42–59.

13. Jack C. Richard, "Listening Comprehension: Approach, Design, Procedure," *Tesol Quarterly*, 17 (June 1983), 219–240.

14. See Sally P. Springer and George Deutsch, *Left Brain, Right Brain* (San Francisco: W. H. Freeman, 1981).

15. William V. Haney, *Communication Patterns and Incidents* (Homewood, Ill.: Richard D. Irwin, 1960).

16. *Harvard Milton College Study Skills Program Level HI* (Reston, Va.: National Association of Secondary School Principals, 1983).

17. Andrew D. Wolvin and Carolyn Gwynn Coakley, *Listening*, 4th ed. (Dubuque, Iowa: William C. Brown, 1992). Chapter 3 includes an analysis of the major variables that affect the listening process.

18. Ibid.

19. Ivan Quandt, *Self-Concept and Reading* (Newark, Del.: International Reading Association, n.d.), p. 31.

20. See Wolvin and Coakley, *Listening*, Part 2, for a detailed description of this listening taxonomy.

21. Conaway, p. 57.

22. H. F. Spitzer, "Studies in Retention," *Journal of Experimental Psychology*, 30 (1939), 641–656.

23. Kenneth Burke, *A Rhetoric of Motives* (New York: World Publishing Company, 1962), p. 579.

THE EARTH
SHOULD LAST FOREVER...
OUR GARBAGE
SHOULDN'T
USE
BOTTLES

The Responsible Public Communicator

3

Chapter Outline

**Learning
Outcomes**

After reading this chapter you should be able to:

Define freedom of expression and explain how it relates to the public forum.

Explain how people reach conclusions through critical thinking, theological reasoning, and philosophical thought.

Explain the role of evidence in critical thinking.

Define ethics and explain the role of ethics in our society.

Contrast differing ethical views.

Explain the role of ethics in public speaking and listening.

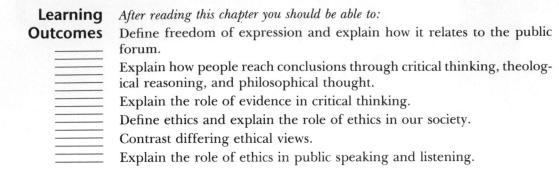

*D*uring the Vietnam conflict of the sixties and seventies, many college campuses in the United States were the focus of prolonged civic unrest. When in 1970 four students were shot and killed by the National Guard during its efforts to quell a peace demonstration at Kent State University, Americans were divided over the extent to which people should be allowed freedom of expression. The same question arose in 1991 during Operation Desert Storm, when peace activists decided to take a stand and protest the United Nation's war actions against Iraq's invasion of Kuwait. Whether the issue is animal rights, the environment, abortion, homosexual rights, or religious and racial intolerance, colleges and universities are usually hotbeds of debate concerning freedom of expression.

3.1 Freedom of Expression

The legal guarantee of **freedom of expression**—the right to present one's views in a public forum—extends not only to protest speeches but also to speeches by hatemongers. It protects members of the audience who harass invited speakers, and it protects speakers who use language that listeners might find offensive. Scholars, students, the national press, and the courts continue to face the question of what is really meant by freedom of expression, often in the highly charged, emotional context of recent events.

Many universities, often considered to be the last bastions of open speech, are developing policies on freedom of expression. These are important to public speakers, as they often set the guidelines for what can and cannot be said in university settings, including individual classrooms. One university's policy, fairly representative of those of many public institutions, states, "This policy statement . . . recognizes the particular importance that the university, as an institution of learning, places on the free exchange of ideas."[1] It goes on to indicate the university's commitment to open, vigorous debate and speech. It places each member of the campus community on notice of his or her obligation to promote free expression and prohibits interference with such expression. It further encourages the members of the campus community to "consider the hurt which may result from the use of [discriminatory] slurs or epithets."[2] The policy sets forth guidelines for the protection of free speech in areas of campus designated as "public forums." It also acknowledges the right to dissent.[3]

Policies of this nature are important to public speakers. The fact that the First Amendment to the U.S. Constitution protects speech seems clear; however, speech is such a broad concept that the Constitution's implications are subject to an array of interpretations. The Supreme Court has determined that some speech has no value under the First Amendment. Categories of speech excluded from protection include defamation, invasion of privacy, fraudulent misrepresentation, obscenity, advocacy of imminent lawless behavior, and fighting words.[4]

First Amendment advocates contend that it is impossible to know specifically what the original intent was of any of the items in the Constitution or the Bill of Rights.[5] They believe that concepts change with time and that a document has to be interpreted according to the times. Since the framers of the Constitution were white male Protestant landowners, and they represented similar people, what they wrote is not necessarily applicable today, given the dramatic changes our nation has undergone in terms of expanded voting rights and representation. What was "politically correct" in the late 1700s may not pertain to today. The disenfranchised, such as urban African-Americans and Mexican-Americans, have seized new powers. They want to be heard and to demonstrate their power, as was evidenced during the Los Angeles riots in 1992.[6] These conditions were not present and didn't have to be considered by our nation's forefathers.

As a public communicator you will constantly be making judgments concerning what you communicate, to whom you communicate, and how you listen to speakers. You will make decisions about who has the right to speak, about what, and under what conditions. You will, as both a speaker and a listener, be continually challenged to think, to reason to conclusions, and to act on those conclusions. Rhetoric itself is neither moral nor immoral. Public speaking itself is neither good nor bad. What we can make judgments about, however, is what people do with their communication skills as speakers and as listeners.

≡ 3.2 Reaching Conclusions

Because of different backgrounds and experiences, people process information differently; therefore, we reach conclusions and solve problems in a wide variety of ways. To be an effective public speaker, you must understand how you tend to reach conclusions and present your ideas. In addition, you might want to consider whether the way in which you develop your ideas, as well as the process you use to listen to others' ideas, needs some evaluation. You should recognize that other people may be using a different means of developing their message to you and of listening to your message. This section explores the different ways people reason and reach conclusions.

Critical Thinking

Some people reach conclusions through the process of **critical thinking**, which is reasonable, reflective thinking that is focused on deciding what to believe and do.[7] Proponents of critical thinking propose that it is essential for competent problem solving, clear understanding, and efficient processing of information, and as a tool to evaluate information received.

Critical thinking can be likened to the legal process in which the presentation of evidence substantiates claims and allegations. **Evidence** in critical thinking is all the means by which any alleged matter of facts is established or disproved. It includes testimony, records, documents, and objects that assist in building a logical case. The purpose of this information is not to decorate, but to prove. Just because there is a lot of information (quotes, for example) doesn't in and of itself prove that the information is either valid or leads to a particular conclusion. The relevant issue is whether the information helps develop the specific contention, and is valid and presented in a reliable way.

There are some common elements of critical thinking that communicators should incorporate into the sending and receiving of messages. Some may sound theoretical, but together they form a practical basis for applying the principles of critical thinking:[8]

1. Seek a clear statement of the thesis or questions.
2. Seek reasons.
3. Try to be well informed on the topic or issue.
4. Use and mention credible sources.
5. Take into account the total situation.
6. Try to remain relevant to the main point.
7. Keep in mind the original or basic concern, issue, or topic.

Public communication specialist James R. Andrews suggests that the public listener must adopt strategies for listening actively. "Since a piece of communication is designed to get a response from you," says Andrews, "you ought to ask yourself what it is doing to and for you as you listen." He recommends that the public listener listen "defensively," understanding his or her own response to the communication and actively adapting that response to the communicator's objective. The "defensive" public listener must be able to concentrate all of his or her time, energy, and attention on the message itself.

Andrews offers seven suggestions for being a more effective public listener:

1. Think about your own identity.
2. Listen with a purpose.
3. Understand the setting.
4. Try to understand to whom the speaker is talking.
5. Examine your assessment of and knowledge about the speaker.
6. Consider the speaker's purpose.
7. Listen defensively.

See James R. Andrews, *Essentials of Public Communication* (New York: Wiley, 1979), p. 34.

8. Look for alternatives.
9. Be open minded.
10. Take a position (and change a position) when the evidence and reasons are sufficient to do so.
11. Seek as much precision as the subject permits.
12. Deal in an orderly manner with the parts of a complex whole.
13. Be sensitive to the feelings, knowledge, and degree of sophistication of others.
14. Be aware of other speakers' attempts to manipulate you with the use of doublespeak, false facts, partial information, biased stands, and emotional appeals disguised as logical ideas.

Applying critical thinking skills to information you receive helps you *diagnose* the information (identify how reasonable it is in terms of personal experience, expert opinion, and factuality) and *evaluate* the information (determine how appropriate it is to the goal you want to attain or concept you want to understand). Critical thinking also enables you to *implement* a plan or idea because it gives you a clear sense of how and why the plan or idea was derived. Critical thinking, however, is only one way in which individuals reach conclusions.

Theological Reasoning

Some individuals claim that one should reach conclusions by acknowledging "the belief in the existence of a supreme personal being as the necessary foundation of the entire scheme of thought."[9] Public speakers and listeners who use **theological reasoning** determine whether an action is right or wrong by relying on a rule, a law, or the outcome of a moral debate that presupposes the existence of a prime mover, such as God, a natural force, or some other supernatural instigator.[10]

Most of the world's established religions have a tradition of revelation that usually is incorporated into sacred scriptures such as the Old and New Testaments, the Torah, and the Koran. Believers of these revelations turn to them as the basis for a theological defense of a particular argument. For example, a speech based on a theologically reasoned stand against the use of birth-control devices might characterize the procreative nature of the sexual act as God-given. Following this reasoning, any form of contraception would be wrong because it inhibits procreation.

Philosophical Thought

There are those who have reservations about using a formal system of reason as the principal guide to life. This group of thinkers makes use of **philosophical thought**. "Those who express such reservations," explains one source, "would point to the positive value of certain levels of human existence that lie beyond the province of conceptual analysis and the practical uses of intelligence altogether, and yet that should also be given their due weight in an adequate philosophy of life."[11] As public speakers and listeners, they would, of course, reach conclusions in yet another way.

Some philosophers present alternative ways of thinking about life that are similar to those espoused by some Eastern religions, most notably Hinduism and Buddhism, that are found in countries such as India, China, and Japan. These traditions have always stressed certain insights or "modes of awareness" not normally found in the dominant religious traditions of the West—including, for example, transcendentalism, metaphysical speculation, intuition, and the transmigration of souls. The enlightenment sought by such Eastern sages as the Buddha or Lao-tse was the redemption of the individual, a redemption that was not believed attainable through solely intellectual and logical means. Over the last few decades, more people in the West have become interested in systems of thought originating in the East. Nevertheless, listening to a speaker who reaches conclusions primarily by nonintellectual means can be a frustrating experience for someone who is used to critical thinking or theological reasoning.

Conflicts Between Systems for Reaching Conclusions

Which reasoning system or systems do you use? How do you react to the type of reasoning used by others? It is significant to note that each individual's reasoning process is probably not so neatly categorized as the previous discussion might imply. We often approach different problems in different ways. This makes it difficult sometimes for you not only to know exactly how you came to a conclusion but also to follow someone else's line of reasoning.

If we fail to recognize that not all people use the same type of reasoning, conflicts and misunderstandings can result. Let's say that, following a speech you've attended, you become involved in a disagreement concerning the validity of what the speaker has said. Did you stop to consider that you and the speaker might have different but equally defensible ideas about what constitutes valid evidence? Efforts to change the opinion of a devout religious believer by use of scientific proof may be futile, for example. Similarly, quotations from religious scholars and the Bible will probably not convince someone who thinks scientifically.

It's important to recognize that different individuals may select different solutions to a problem because they use different reasoning processes. Consider, for example, two speeches actually given by individuals who confronted the same problem: how to handle the birth of a child to parents with incompatible blood types. One speaker explained that because he had Rh-positive blood and his wife had Rh-negative blood, they were aware of the possibility that their child might die or have a birth defect. They were told by their doctor that the baby might have to fight off the blood incompatibility and undergo transfusions. The speaker went on to state that on the advice of their physician, they had arranged for the birth to take place in a hospital noted for its excellent pediatric care, even though it was a considerable distance from their home.

The other speaker was a woman who also was aware that she and her husband had incompatible blood types. These parents-to-be were practicing Christian Scientists. She explained that because their religion taught them to consider a human being as a God-created spiritual entity and not a material being, they believed that their baby would be made not of material elements like blood, brain, and bones but rather of spiritual qualities like intelligence, love, kindness, and health. Their solution to the problem, she explained, was to contact their Christian Science teacher, who helped them do prayerful work for their unborn child.[12]

The speeches clearly showed the audience that each of these couples used a different reasoning process to arrive at a solution. Each couple was satisfied with the solution they had chosen, and neither would have chosen the other's solution. It is wise to recognize that a major breakthrough in communication takes place when we accept the concept that it is possible to respect others' beliefs even if we do not share these beliefs. This does not mean, however, that a listener should blindly accept a speaker's contentions; the speaker must earn the listener's respect by developing ideas clearly and consistently.

3.3 Ethics

As you communicate with others in your daily and professional lives, you are influenced both as a sender and a receiver by your ethics. In fact, your ethical system is the underlying core of everything you say and everything you do. Your **ethics** are the values that have been instilled in you, which you have knowingly or unknowingly accepted, and how you act according to those values. Your ethics tell you right from wrong. Your **ethical value system** forms the basis for your decision making and for your personal understanding of why you will or will not behave in a certain way. You must also realize that other people have their own systems of ethics.

Ethics and Society   Ethics are action oriented. A personal ethics system that enables you to make considered decisions and to explain and defend your actions calls for consistency among your beliefs, your words, and your actions. Unfortunately, what some people believe and what they do are not necessarily parallel. Recently there has arisen a strong emphasis on ethics in communication, in professional responsibilities, and in decision making. The reasons for this new emphasis are complex; perhaps it has come about because "large sections of the nation's ethical roofing have been sagging badly, from the White House to churches, schools, industries, medical centers, law firms and stock brokerages."[13]

There are many examples of questionable ethical conduct among those in American public life. Political candidates are often subject to ethical questioning, such as in 1992 when Democratic presidential candidate Bill Clinton was accused of marital infidelity, and when Republican Pat Buchanan was discovered hypocritically exhorting the nation to "Buy American" while owning a German-built Mercedes-Benz. Perhaps the most deeply felt ethical crisis in recent history occurred in 1974, when President Richard Nixon was forced to resign from office because he was suspected of covering up a break-in into the Democratic Party's Watergate offices. Well-known religious leaders, such as the Reverend Jim Bakker, have likewise been removed from their positions because of financial and sexual misadventures.

The upshot is that "Watergate-style revelations and reports of corporate bribery and white-collar crime have contributed to a sense of uneasiness within the country about the state of professional and private virtue in American life."[14] If we combine this sense of uneasiness with recent technological advances—in reproduction and organ-replacement techniques, in computer use, in machinery for prolonging life, in space exploration—additional moral dilemmas arise. An individual's system of ethics must be firmly enough established to serve as a guide to consistent behavior, yet flexible enough to adapt to a rapidly changing reality. This is a tall order indeed.

Ethics and You

Your ethical system underlies the way you resolve conflicts that arise in your personal life and in your work. Your communication ethics are based on such matters as your selection of words, your style of presentation, and the manner in which you defend and develop your ideas. To be an effective communicator, it is helpful for you to understand your own ethical system. Such an understanding has several benefits: making sense of your life; fulfilling personal, professional, and social responsibilities; making informed political judgments; and guarding against social or political excesses that promote bigotry and repression.

Making sense of your life. To have consistent and coherent beliefs and actions you need to understand that your ethics are the basis for what you do and what you refrain from doing, what you communicate about and what you refrain from communicating about. Have you ever asked yourself precisely why you believe or don't believe in the death penalty? How would you react if a friend of yours told you he had AIDS? Why would you react that way?

Fulfilling personal, professional, and social responsibilities. Life is a pattern of setting goals and then carrying them out. In order to do this you must understand how these goals affect your daily life, your work environment, and your interaction with others. Why have you chosen your college major? Why do you want to do that type of work? If you have chosen a career that involves helping other people, such as psychology or counseling, do you really want the responsibility for assisting others to make life decisions? How would you react if your intervention did not prevent a person from committing suicide or a violent crime? It is difficult to say precisely what constitutes a "moral life," but consistent principles that govern one's words and deeds and are applied uniformly in all areas of human responsibility—personal, professional, and social—would seem to be a significant part of such a life.

Making informed political judgments. As a member of a democratic society, you have an obligation to realize your role as a voter and a citizen. How do you select the candidate you decide to vote for in an election? How much of that decision is yours, based on an understanding of your ethical system, and how much is influenced by well-contrived advertisements emphasizing such extraneous factors as the candidate's physical appearance? Do you select a candidate according to factors that have little to do with the duties of the office, such as whether the candidate has the same religion as you? Carefully analyzing your ethical system will help you to better understand why you make the political decisions you do and help preserve your integrity and autonomy as a member of a democratic society.

Guarding against social or political excesses that promote bigotry and repression. Other people's ethics will not always be similar to yours. Hatred of those who are different and the desire for power over others are prevalent trends in human history. In order to guard against unknowingly participating in acts based on these ethics, you must be aware of your own value system. What are your prejudices? Would you be willing to put your career or even your life on the line to support civil rights for all? Why or why not?

A Code of Ethics

Because there seems to be no universal code of ethics that is true for all people at all times and in all places, we sometimes become confused about what is right and what is wrong. We are forced to think about what price we are willing to pay for decency, compassion, and sensitivity in our dealings with others. We must ask ourselves whether words such as *honesty* and *integrity* form the basis for the way we want to live. There seem to be five driving forces behind the way individuals apply ethics.[15]

Stimulating the moral imagination. Each moral choice we make has repercussions for ourselves as well as for others. This is true regardless of our occupation or role in society. Questions such as the following lead to moral decisions: How would I decide whether extraordinary means should be used to keep someone alive? What effect does the grading system my instructor uses have on my entrance into graduate school? Why shouldn't I adjust my tax return in my benefit if I need the money more than the government does? If I behave according to the adage "Spare the rod and spoil the child," what effect will this have on my children's lives? As a businessperson, do I believe that pollution control should take a back seat to profits?

Profile: Campus Speech Codes

"Speech that wounds or insults or demeans by reason of race, gender, religion, or sexual preference has no place on a university campus. In fact, such expression seems least tolerable in an academic setting, where the values of rational discourse and the quest for truth are paramount. Universities also have a special need to establish an environment hospitable to persons who have felt unwelcome there for far too long, and whose very ability to learn may depend on civility and respect.

"Yet it is also in this setting—and for the most central educational reasons—that, in the words of the recent American Association of University Professors statement, 'no viewpoint or message may be deemed so hateful or disturbing that it may not be expressed.' And, as the statement adds, 'by proscribing any ideas, a university sets an example that profoundly disserves its academic mission.' Thus penalties or policies that might be found acceptable in the industrial workplace simply do not belong in the classroom or the laboratory, or even the dormitory or the locker room.

"What, then, are the options? Strong condemnation of racist and sexist epithets and slurs is surely appropriate, indeed essential. But many institutions rightly feel that they need to do more than simply make strong statements or even promote educational programs designed to increase sensitivity and enhance the campus climate. Such steps are well and good, they say, but may be—or may be seen as—less than an unpleasant or hurtful situation requires or the campus community expects.

"Several more tangible options do exist. We have never fully exhausted the potential of rules aimed at conduct and not at speech. Most of the inflammatory incidents of recent years have, in fact, involved some punishable conduct—whether it be defacing property, disrupting scheduled university events, or physically intimidating or harassing a fellow student.

"To take an example that is not hypothetical: You do not need a speech code to deal forcefully with a drunken student who awakens his dormitory mates at 3 in the morning—whether his words are racist or profane or simply nonsense or lyric poetry, for that matter. Such disruption of the essential life and tranquility of the academic community can and should be punished without reference to the content of the words, or the thought—hateful or benign—that may have impelled the disrupter."

From "A Time to Re-evaluate Campus Speech Codes," by Robert M. O'Neil from *The Chronicle of Higher Education,* July 8, 1992, p. A40.

Recognizing ethical issues. Ethical issues are by their very nature overriding—that is, once we recognize an issue as an ethical matter, we attach more significance to it than we did previously. When we are aware that we are making an ethical decision, we may attempt to identify hidden assumptions and to determine whether there is a reasonable ground for making a judgment or for reaching a conclusion. We might ask ourselves: Do I have enough evidence to reach a decision? Is the person giving me advice or counsel a credible source? Is this a decision I should be making?

Developing analytical skills. Words such as *justice, dignity, privacy,* and *virtue* are not always used with clarity and consistency. People have a need to examine and make distinctions among concepts that center on ethical principles and moral rules. We must be aware of the need to challenge and think hard about ethical concepts so that we apply them consistently. We need to understand the logical and practical consequences of these applications and the extent to which such consequences are worth considering.

Eliciting a sense of moral responsibility. Part of the process of adopting an ethical system is that our ethical values will be reflected in our personal conduct. When we attempt to act consistently with our values, some basic questions about reaching conclusions arise: Do I have the freedom to make moral choices? If so, how should I go about making decisions? What is the connection between thinking about my ethics and my personal conduct? What would I do, for example, if faced with deciding for myself whether to get an abortion? How would I advise someone I am involved with in a relationship who is facing that question? Why would I make that decision? Do I have the right to make that decision? How would I feel about this decision if I were a doctor or nurse? Questions about moral responsibility cannot be set aside easily, since they concern matters that affect us daily.

Tolerating—and resisting—disagreement and ambiguity. Even if ethical certainty is impossible, ethical reasoning about choice can be precise. In other words, even though there may not always be "right" answers, we can reason clearly about the issues. If we know how we reached a conclusion we can explain how the decision was made, thus bringing some consistency and coherence to our decision-making process.

Anita Hill exercised her moral responsibility in speaking out against sexual harassment during the Clarence Thomas Supreme Court appointment hearings.

Differing Ethical Views

To understand your own ethical system and that of others, you should ask yourself some basic questions regarding the choices you make and the choices others make that affect you: Do I understand that it is possible to tolerate differences of choice and to refrain from labeling opposite choices as immoral?

As you think over ethical ideas and then communicate with others, you will encounter **dilemmas of principles**—situations in which you are torn between conflicting moral obligations that cannot be fulfilled at the same time. You probably will be faced with situations in which what you want to do may not be what you believe you should do. You probably will encounter situations in which you must choose between deception and telling the truth. Is the "little white lie" that protects you from punishment at home or at work really a harmless action? Is the answer to "Will I get caught?" your bottom line in deciding whether or not to tell the truth?

In your decision-making process you will probably come face-to-face with **utilitarianism**, a moral theory that bases the "rightness" of an action on whether it achieves its intended results. A utilitarian outlook may put you in situations that are in direct conflict with your moral beliefs. For example, let's say that workers in a chemical processing plant become aware that the materials they are producing cause birth defects and cancer and have additional long-term fatal effects for the general population. The ethical question they must answer might be: Should I continue to work for an organization that is producing a product that might result in human disease and death? Does my need for financial security override my need not to negatively affect other people's lives?

Utilitarianism is not always a bad system to use in decision making, however. Depending on the size of the group to be served (society rather than the individual, for example), the time frame (long term as opposed to immediate benefit), and other relevant factors, utilitarianism can produce very humane policies.

Although utilitarians believe that ethics has to do with achieving some desired goal or result, followers of the eighteenth-century philosopher Immanuel Kant believe that morality is the act of fulfilling duties and obligations. In other words, according to Kant, our obligations to ourselves should never be given moral priority over our obligations to others merely for the sake of achieving personal goals. For Kant, being moral means having a concern for others simply because they are persons, not because they contribute to some goal or because they are part of a particular group—as utilitarianism would allow. A worker in the chemical processing plant who is a follower of Kant would have a clear-cut decision: The destruction of others is indefensible, no matter what the personal gain. Such a worker would, therefore, have to quit his or her job or take some action to stop the dangerous product from being produced. This stand puts concern for others ahead of personal gain.

Defining the idea of "being moral" as "having a tendency to be concerned about happiness in general" has a long history in Western cultures. This viewpoint is epitomized by the golden rule: "Do unto others as you would have them do unto you." In contrast, certain Eastern philosophies (Buddhism and Confucianism, for example) understand morality less as doing unto others and more as *not* doing unto others. The essence of this morality, sometimes referred to as the silver rule, is thus "What you do not want done to yourself, do not do unto others." According to these philosophies, the purpose of morality is the achievement of personal peace, contentment, and tranquility—not a concern for others.[16]

Though it may seem idealistic, each person must become increasingly aware of the nature of morality and engage in self-examination. Only through such self-examination, understanding, and awareness can you bring consistency and coherence to your ethical decisions and actions.

The Ethics of the Public Speaker

Over the decades, speech communication instructors have stressed that competent public speakers should, by necessity, be ethical speakers— that a speaker should give the listener assistance in making wise decisions, and should consider moral principles when planning what to say. Speech instructors would also stress that although propagandists (such as Hitler) are certainly persuasive and compelling speakers, they bring about much human destruction because of their skewed ethical values.

It is a generally accepted principle that the spoken word can have a significant effect on a listener. We are aware that the use of language develops, enlarges, and enhances human personalities. Furthermore, we would all acknowledge that a speaker who uses language that degrades or injures human personality by exaggeration, pseudotruths, twisting words, and name calling is clearly acting unethically.[17]

Ethical public speakers are generally defined as those who conform to the moral standards the society establishes for its communicators. Though this definition seems plausible, it contains a major flaw: The words ring hollow because it is practically impossible to gain universal acceptance for a certain set of moral standards. Nevertheless, research in the field of speech has isolated specific traits of what could be generally considered an ethical speaker. According to this research, an ethical public communicator:

Speaks with sincerity.

Does not knowingly expose an audience to falsehoods or half-truths that cause significant harm.

Does not premeditatedly alter the truth.

Presents the truth as he or she understands it.

Raises the listeners' level of expertise by supplying the necessary facts, definitions, descriptions, and substantiating information.

Employs a message that is free from mental as well as physical coercion, by not compelling someone to take an action against his or her will.

Does not invent or fabricate statistics or other information intended to serve as a basis for proof of a contention or belief.

Gives credit to the source of information and does not pretend that the information is original when it is not.

The basic concept of ethical speaking might be stated as follows: "You must understand that you are a moral agent and when you communicate with others and make decisions that affect you and others, you have a moral responsibility because there are human consequences based on your actions.[18]

The Ethical Responsibilities of a Public Listener

Just as the speaker has a personal responsibility for ethical, honest communication, so, too, does the listener. You learned in the previous chapter that listening is far from a passive act; it requires a full commitment from the listener to be at least an equal partner in the communication. "To be an effective communicator, a listener should assume at least 51 percent of the burden of the communication. Such a responsibility requires that the listener be committed to active, involved, dynamic listening and engage constantly in the communication."[19]

This view of listening is part of **participative communication**, a concept consistent with the participative democracy on which our government is founded: "[Participative communication] suggests a more balanced approach to the power relationship in communication, an ideal of both speaker and listener, message-maker and message-receiver, sharing together the responsibility of creating meaning."[20] Consequently, the listener must first bear the responsibility for deciding to listen to the speaker. Just as speakers have the freedom to speak, so listeners have the freedom to listen.

If you do decide to engage in a public speech as a listener, then you have a responsibility to participate fully. This includes being willing to provide the speaker with a fair hearing and to receive and comprehend the message before making a decision to agree or disagree with it. This can be difficult, for most of us have a very natural human inclination to form instant judgments and to tune in or tune out a speaker based on that fleeting first impression. This tendency to quick evaluation is considered by some to be the greatest barrier to human communication.[21] As an ethical communicator, it is important to recognize this tendency and to try to get past your initial impression in order to truly listen to the speaker.

It is your responsibility to yourself to listen constructively and objectively.[22] To listen constructively, you should determine the speaker's purpose, evaluate the message, and relate the message to your own frame of reference. Listening objectively requires that you identify your own predispositions on the topic, avoid jumping to conclusions, avoid emotional reactions, and avoid becoming too influenced by the responses of other audience members. "Responsible listening," observes a public communication specialist, "requires concentration, critical examination of ideas and arguments, careful thought, and judicious decision making."[23]

An ancient Greek philosopher characterized the responsible listener. His words are as relevant today as when they were written, especially if you consider the amount of public information you are exposed to each day through the media:

> There are others who think that the speaker has a function to perform, and the hearer none. They think it only right that the speaker shall come with his discourse carefully thought out and prepared, while they, without consideration or thought of their obligations, rush in and take their seats exactly as though they had come to dinner, to have a good time while others toil. And yet even a well-bred guest at dinner has a function to perform, much more a hearer; for he is a participant in the discourse and a fellow-worker with the speaker.[24]

Summary

This chapter investigated reasoning to conclusion, ethics and freedom of expression. The major ideas presented include:

◆ Freedom of expression is the right to present one's views in a public forum.

◆ The First Amendment to the U.S. Constitution protects speech.

◆ As a public communicator you will constantly be making judgments concerning what you communicate, to whom you communicate, and how you listen to speakers.

◆ People process information and reach conclusions in a wide variety of ways, such as through critical thinking, theological reasoning, and philosophical thought.

◆ Critical thinking is reasonable, reflective thinking that is focused on deciding what to believe and do.

◆ Theological reasoning is based on the concept that there is a prime mover that causes things to happen in a prescribed manner.

◆ Philosophical thought recognizes that some areas of human existence "lie beyond the province of conceptual analysis and the practical uses of intelligence" and involves alternative, nonintellectual ways of reaching conclusions.

◆ It is possible to respect others' beliefs without actually believing as they do.

◆ Ethics are the values that have been instilled in you, which you have knowingly or unknowingly accepted, and how you act according to those values.

◆ It is helpful for you as a communicator to understand your own ethical system in order to be a responsible public speaker and listener.

◆ You experience a dilemma of principle when you are torn between conflicting moral obligations that cannot be fulfilled at the same time.

◆ Ethical communicators are those who conform to the moral standards the society establishes for its communicators.

◆ Public speaking itself is neither good nor bad. It is what you do with your public communication skills that can be ethically judged.

◆ In listening to a speech, it is your responsibility to yourself to listen constructively and objectively.

Key Terms

freedom of expression	ethics
critical thinking	ethical value system
evidence	dilemmas of principles
theological reasoning	utilitarianism
philosophical thought	ethical public speakers
	participative communication

Learn by Doing

1. As a homework assignment, determine what you would do in each of these situations. Write a brief answer for each. At the next class session, you will be divided into groups of four to six students to discuss your answers. After this session write a short paper examining what you learned about your ethical values.

   a. You are taking a public speaking course. The instructor requires three quoted references in the speech that you are to present in about five minutes, but you didn't have time to do the necessary research. Would you (1) make up three references, (2) not give the speech and get a failing grade, (3) give the speech without the references and hope for the best, or (4) take some other action? If you would take another action, what would it be?

   b. The business you work for is illegally storing chemical waste.

You have just given a speech to the local chamber of commerce on the topic of your company's role in building community values. You are asked, during a question-and-answer session, about the rumor of the stored chemical waste. If the practice was discovered, the legal fine against the business would bankrupt it. Do you tell the truth?

c. You are a politician who is giving a speech one day before the election. It is a very close race. Whatever you say will probably not get into the newspaper because it is past the news deadline. Your opponent indicates that she has knowledge of your election committee having committed fund-raising manipulation, as well as indiscretions among your staff. What would you say?

d. A friend has asked you to introduce his speech at your school's honors day assembly. You know he plagiarized much of the material he is going to present. You have been announced as the introducer. What do you do?

2. How free is your speech? The student government association on your campus has announced its speaker series for the semester. There will be five guests: a member of the Ku Klux Klan, a known anti–African-American racist, a neo-Nazi who has given anti-Semitic speeches, a minister who believes all gays and lesbians should be banned from public academic institutions, and an atheist who condemns all members of organized religious groups. The speakers' fees will be paid out of the student activity fund to which all students are required to contribute. Do you feel that these speakers should be allowed to make their presentations on your campus? Be prepared to defend your answers.

3. Recall the experience of listening to a speech in which the speaker used a reasoning system different from yours. What were your feelings? Did you verbally react in some way? How did you feel about the speaker? Did you listen intently to the speech or stop listening because you disagreed?

4. Each class member should bring in a letter to the editor from a local paper or your school newspaper in which the writer takes a stand. The class will be divided into groups. Group members are to read the letters, assuming that they are speeches that were given by the writers. Discuss the method or methods the writers of these letters used to develop their conclusions.

Notes

1. Susan L. Bayly, *Freedom of Expression: Policy and the Law* (College Park, Md.: Office of Legal Affairs, 1991), p. 2.

2. Ibid.

3. Ibid.

4. Ibid, p. 3.

5. "Imprisonment of Ideas: What Is the First Amendment," a speech presented by Melvin Dershowitz, Eisenhower Symposium, Johns Hopkins University, October 20, 1991.

6. Ibid.

7. Lorenz Boehm, *Critical Thinking/Critical Literacy: Teaching—As If It Matters* (Des Plaines, Ill.: Critical Literacy Project, Oakton Community College, 1990).

8. Based in part on Robert Ennis, "A Taxonomy of Critical Thinking Dispositions and Abilities," in J. Baron and R. Sternberg, eds., *Teaching for Thinking* (New York: D. H. Freeman, 1987).

9. William P. Alston, *Religious Belief and Philosophical Thought* (New York: Harcourt Brace Jovanovich, 1963), p. 15.

10. For more information on theological reasoning, see Father R. W. Mulligan, S.J., "St. Thomas Aquinas," *Encyclopedia International* (New York: Grolier, 1966), pp. 500–501.

11. Milton K. Munitz, *The Ways of Philosophy* (New York: Macmillan, 1979), p. 323.

12. A true story with the Christian Science explanation given by Mary Mona Fisher, the mother, in a class presentation at Lorain County Community College, Elyria, Ohio, where she served as an adjunct instructor of communication. This critical thinking presentation was by Roy Berko, professor of communications, to the same class.

13. Ezra Bowen, "Ethics—Looking to Its Roots," *Time*, May 25, 1987, p. 26.

14. "Applied Ethics: A Strategy for Fostering Professional Responsibility," *Carnegie Quarterly*, 28 (Spring/Summer 1980), 2.

15. Ibid., pp. 3–4.

16. Based on the concepts and writings of Charles Buckalew, Associate Professor of Philosophy, Lorain County Community College, Elyria, Ohio.

17. Synthesized from an unpublished paper entitled "Ethics and Effectiveness," which refers generally to J. W. Gibson et al., "The Basic Course in Speech at U.S. Colleges and Universities," *Communication Education*, 29 (1980), 1–9.

18. Thomas Nelsen, *Ethics in Speech Communication* (Indianapolis: Bobbs-Merrill, 1966), p. 139.

19. Andrew D. Wolvin and Carolyn Gwynn Coakley, *Listening* (Dubuque, Iowa: William C. Brown, 1988), p. 108.

20. Michael Osborn and Suzanne Osborn, *Alliance for a Better Public Voice* (Dayton, Ohio: National Issues Forums, 1991), p. 14.

21. Carol R. Rogers and F. J. Roethlisberger, "Barriers and Gateways to Communication," *Harvard Business Review*, 30 (July 1952), 46–52.

22. Robert N. Bostrom, *Communicating in Public* (Santa Rosa, Calif.: Burgess Publishing, 1988), pp. 46–47.

23. Thomas L. Tedford, *Public Speaking in a Free Society* (New York: McGraw-Hill, 1991), p. 62.

24. Plutarch, *Plutarch's Moralia*, trans. Frank Cole Babbitt (Cambridge, Mass.: Harvard University Press, 1927), p. 245.

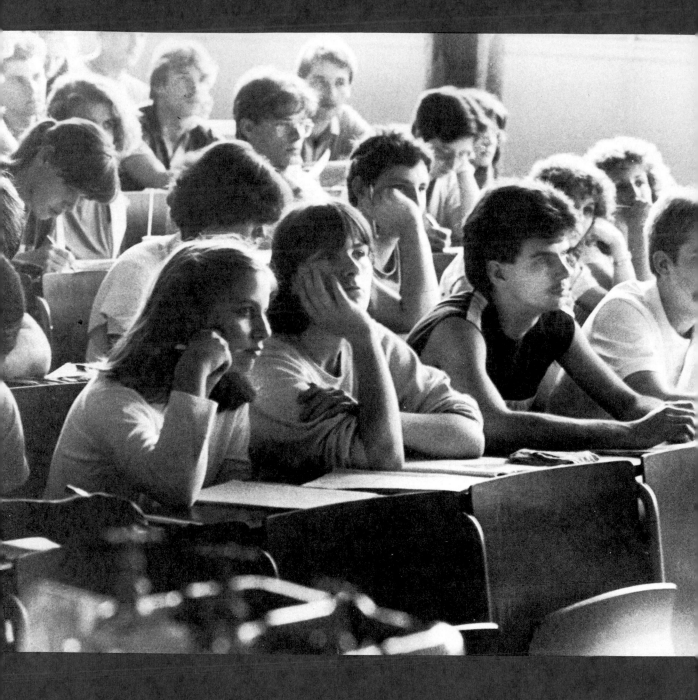

Getting Started

4

Chapter Outline

Learning Outcomes

After reading this chapter, you should be able to:

List and explain the components and process of communicative analysis.

Define and explain prior speech analysis.

Prepare a personal speaker inventory.

Conduct an audience analysis by investigating the prospective listeners' demographics, psychographics, and rhetorographics.

Understand why and how to conduct process speech analysis.

Understand why and how to conduct postspeech analysis.

The first questions usually asked by someone who is going to present a speech are "How do I get started?" and "Then what do I do?" When preparing a speech, many people first decide on a topic and formulate a purpose statement. Next, they do any necessary research to collect material that develops the purpose statement. After this preliminary work, they construct an introduction that will get the audience's attention and give listeners the necessary background material so they will be ready to hear the details of the subject. After providing these details, many speakers move on to the statement of the central idea, which tells the audience what the speech is all about. The main part of the presentation then fulfills the purpose of the speech. The conclusion summarizes the major points and wraps up the presentation. Though not all speakers follow this exact order, such a structure will assure the presenter of a well-constructed speech. In order to prepare an effective speech, it is helpful for you to understand how to analyze yourself, the audience, the setting, and your purpose for speaking.

4.1 Components of Analysis

Any act of communication has three components: the participants, the setting, and the purpose of the communication.

The **participants** are the persons engaged in the communication event—the speaker and the members of the audience.

The **setting** consists of the place, time, and emotional climate of the speech.

The **purpose** is what the communicator is trying to accomplish (e.g., answer a question, change a point of view, influence others to take an action).

In public speaking, these three parameters affect the topic selected, the language used, the types of supporting materials (such as examples and illustrations) chosen, and the supplementary aids needed to reinforce and clarify ideas.

To prepare effective speeches, you need to be able to analyze these components and use what you learn. Determining the purpose for your speech (see Chapter 5) depends on your thorough analysis of the participants and the setting. This investigation is done in three stages: prior analysis, process analysis, and postspeech analysis. Though the majority of the work takes place during **prior analysis**, which you do before you give the speech, watching the audience for feedback, or **process analysis**, and paying attention to the reactions after the speech, or **postspeech analysis**, are also vital.

4.2 Prior Analysis

In some instances, you are given a topic and told who is going to be in attendance and how long you are to speak. At other times, you may be left on your own to figure out what you are going to do with the time you have before the audience. You must also eventually decide on the appropriate presentation style, the language, and the supporting materials to be used. Taking personal and audience inventories can help you make those decisions.

Personal Inventory

If you are given total freedom to choose a topic, spend some time examining yourself. What are you interested in speaking about? What do you know about that would be of interest to the audience to whom you will speak? What subject would you feel most comfortable with and most knowledgeable about? Do you think you could develop an interesting and successful presentation on this subject that will hold the audience's attention?

In searching for a topic, consider your **personal speaking inventory**— your life experiences and interests. Consider such areas as your hobbies and special skills, your work, places you have traveled, things you know how to do (sports, machinery you can operate, cooking skills), jobs you have held, your experiences (accidents, special events), funny things that have happened to you, books you have read, movies you have seen, interesting people you know, people you admire, your college major, class topics that you found interesting, social and political views you hold, or your religious or ethnic background. We all have an inventory of possible ideas to share. Do not assume that because you are not the world's greatest authority on something or that because you have had limited experiences in certain areas, you have nothing to talk about. If necessary, you can supplement your knowledge with research and interviews.

To discover your personal speaking inventory, complete activity 1 in the Learn by Doing section at the end of this chapter. If you are giving the speech for a class assignment, you may want to see which of the areas in your speaking inventory fit the requirements.

Audience Inventory

Individual listeners who make up a speaker's audience play a critical role in the communication process and should always be the center of focus for the speaker. They come to a speech event with a variety of individual objectives, but in general they tend to focus on themselves and their needs and wants. In order to gain and hold their attention, you must often center on satisfying a very basic self-centered human question: "What's in it for me?"[1] One listener may have come to gain information he or she feels is important, another to critically analyze the speaker's arguments, and still another out of vague curiosity, with no specific set expectations. In all cases, they will tend to actively listen only if they feel that their needs are being met. Since physical limitations allow a person to focus for not more than about 60 seconds at best on a single stimulus, even when interested, concentrating on a speaker's message requires considerable energy as well as the desire to want to listen.[2]

Besides having individual needs, as people assemble to become an audience they begin to exhibit group dynamics. They develop into a group with its own specific characteristics, which the speaker must address in some way. **Polarization** takes place as the individual members become an audience and begin to center their attention on the speaker and the message.[3] In order to get the audience to polarize, the speaker must find a way to grab and hold their attention.

How do you find out what will gain the audience's attention? How can you match that with what you learned in your personal speaking inventory and choose an effective topic? The act of collecting the necessary information is called **audience analysis**. It is based on analysis of the listeners' **demographics** (characteristics such as age, gender, and interests), **psychographics** (attitudes, such as positive or negative predispositions toward the speaker, the speech, and the occasion), and **rhetorographics** (the setting, including the situational and environmental aspects of the speech event).

Demographic analysis allows you to profile the features that distinguish your intended group of listeners. This will assist you in choosing a topic, appropriate language, and the types of aids that will help the audience grasp the meaning of the speech and motivate them to listen. You are looking for the common bonds among audience members— their uniqueness and differences.

Psychographic analysis enables you to determine whether the listeners are accepting of or hostile to your point of view, and perhaps to find out why they hold this attitude. This knowledge can assist you in developing the psychological strategies necessary to help alter their attitude. It may also lead you to decide on the overall method of organization to use for the speech.

Rhetorographic analysis has to do with such factors as where the speech will be given, the time allowed, and the characteristics of the place that might require you to use special equipment or restrict your topic choice. Seating arrangements, acoustics, style of lectern, and light are important rhetorographic findings.

Knowing generally what you are looking for is the first step in prior analysis. The process continues by knowing specifically how to probe for and find the demographics, psychographics, and rhetorographics.

Demographics If you are preparing a speech for a class or work situation, look around at the people in the room. Try to figure out who they are. If you are going to speak to a group of strangers, ask the person who engaged you for some information about the group: "Why are these people gathered together?" "What types of presentations have they liked in the past?" "Are there special considerations I will need to make about the topic I pick, the approach I take, or the language I will be using?"

Some of your questions and observations can center on audience factors: age, gender, religion, cultural and ethnic uniqueness, intellectual level, and occupation. By finding out this demographic information, you can decide which topic from your personal inventory may fit this particular group. In addition, it should help guide you in developing the speech and eventually in selecting the language and supporting materials to use.

Age. The general age of the audience can have an effect on the topic and the approach you will take. A person near the age of retirement may be interested in hearing a speech about the present structure and payoff of the Social Security system, but an 18-year old college student will probably be more interested in the financial implications of this system for young people. This does not mean that if you are knowledgeable in and wish to talk about Social Security you should avoid the topic. It simply means that you may have to adjust your approach if this is your topic choice.

Gender. Sometimes speakers should take the gender of an audience into consideration. A group of pregnant women who are deciding whether to breast-feed will have particular listener interests that a male audience might not have. Similarly, a group of single fathers will have their own particular interests and concerns. This does not mean that

Knowing the demographics of your audience is essential to prepare an effective speech.

the topic of breast feeding or single fatherhood cannot be presented to audiences of the opposite gender, but a speaker who addresses a mixed audience on such a topic may need to make some adjustments.

Be aware that making statements based on stereotypes about gender can bring problems. For example, former president Ronald Reagan found himself in trouble when he addressed a female group by saying, " 'If it wasn't for women, us men would still be walking around in skin suits carrying clubs!' "[4] This statement was intended to acknowledge the contributions of women to American society but came just after the resignation of a member of his staff who had accused him of not offering equal opportunities for women in his administration. Because of the way in which the statement was worded, it was taken as demeaning and as encouraging the stereotyped view that a woman's primary role is to nurture others.

Religion.   The way a speaker handles a topic can establish or destroy a bond with specific religious groups represented in the audience. It seems unwise, for example, to propose before a Catholic audience that Catholicism has been responsible for the decline of many civilizations, such as the Mayans and the Incas. Politicians especially can get into difficulty by making comments that alienate the audience. Jesse Jackson, a candidate for the presidential nomination in 1988, discovered this during a primary campaign when he referred to Jewish people as "Hymies" and New York as "Hymietown."[5] That slip of the tongue cost him many votes. Treating your audience with as much respect as you can will help you avoid this type of grave mistake.

Cultural and Ethnic Uniqueness.   Effective speakers study the cultural and ethnic background of their audience and are open to new ideas, values, and ways of looking at the world. Considering what makes your audience unique and what topics its members might enjoy hearing about is time well spent. For example, a film producer planning a presentation for the members of an African-American cultural center might speak on "The Changing Role of African-Americans in Motion Pictures." A speaker asked to address a cooking club might want to find out about the ethnic backgrounds of its members and give a talk on the origins of foods from those areas of the world. This sort of audience analysis is necessary if you want to gain your listeners' attention and accomplish your public speaking goal.

Culture is the sum total of a group's social behavior, beliefs, and traditions. One of the most pervasive elements of a culture is its language system. Both the verbal and the nonverbal language symbols, developed by and agreed upon over time by the group of people within the culture, serve to unify individuals and to provide a common basis for communication. People from the same ethnic background usually have a shared language and national origin. **Cultural values**, what people of a specific culture hold to be of importance and worth, are the basis for understanding and preparing speeches for diverse audiences.

Cultural misunderstandings can cause difficulties for public speakers. For example, in 1992 many Japanese people were offended by accusations made by a group of American business leaders about trade restrictions on U.S. products. Concurrently, Americans were offended by comments made by a Japanese diplomat, who suggested that the U.S. economy was declining because American workers were lazy. Though speakers on both sides later indicated that they were misunderstood due to translation problems and different values and customs, the strong negative response of both Japanese and American publics to those speeches well illustrates the result of poor audience analysis.

Taking into consideration the cultural and ethnic uniqueness of the audience is increasingly important in both academic and business settings. College classrooms are rapidly growing more ethnically and racially diverse. As a student of public speaking, you should bear in mind the unique backgrounds of your classmates when choosing your topic, approach, supporting materials, and language.

More and more, speakers in business, industry, and the social sciences are being called upon to communicate with diverse audiences. American organizations are experiencing great changes in their work force. For example, white males no longer constitute the majority in American business; women and minorities make up at least 52 percent of the workers in organizations.[6] By the year 2000, approximately 46 percent of the U.S. work force will be female. In addition, African-Americans, Hispanics, and other minorities will comprise 29 percent of new additions to the U.S. work force, and will make up more than 15 percent of the work force in the year 2000.[7] The number of Asian, Eastern European, Central American, and South American immigrants has increased as those areas of the globe continue to experience political and economic upheaval. The new workers bring with them their own cultural values and customs and are often confused by American ways. Such demographic changes demand public speakers who understand how to analyze and adapt to different audiences. Gender is an especially significant factor in audience analysis. Since males and females often have culturally different ways of communicating and acting, the inclusion of more females in the work force has required some male speakers to confront their use of verbal sexism, sexually harassing language, and sexually inappropriate topics.

Intellectual Level.　An analysis of the audience's intellectual level, educational background, and training in a particular area can help you select a topic. Remember that people may feel threatened if what you are talking about is beyond their understanding. Some people may be put off, for example, by a communication expert who begins a speech by saying, "There appears to be a definite anthropological basis, as developed through the works of Hall, for the proxemic behavior of all people." Instead, for an audience that does not include specialists in the field, the speaker might be better off discussing an elementary aspect of nonverbal communication. At the same time, it is important not to make audience members feel as though you are talking down to them. Most people are intelligent enough to understand technical terms if they are clearly defined.

Occupation.　It is an excellent idea to form a bond with an audience by using occupational interests and experiences as the basis for your communication. This is a comparatively common practice we all engage in daily: Students discuss their school activities with each other, factory workers discuss production problems, doctors and nurses discuss hospital procedures. Problems arise when speakers fail to realize that their occupational concerns may be of little or no interest to the audience, or are of interest to only a select group, and may not be appropriate to a public speech.

Psychographics　As mentioned earlier, psychographics allows you to discover how the audience feels about the topic you want to discuss. Such audience factors

Profile: Sharon Pratt Kelly, *mayor of Washington, D.C.*

For the mayor of the nation's capital, public speaking situations are part of the daily routine. As with most political figures, Mayor Sharon Pratt Kelly's statements, activities, and innumerable public messages are carefully recorded and reported. Therefore, she must strive for flawless presentation in every situation.

Audience analysis and careful preparation help Mayor Kelly deal wisely and effectively with the great variety of contexts in which she is called upon to appear. She must be at ease whether she is speaking before a council meeting, at a parade, or with a group of concerned citizens. Her presentations encompass both good news and difficult topics and may be viewed by schoolchildren, reporters, or the entire nation. She must be prepared to speak in almost any environment to almost any audience.

Says Mayor Kelly, "I would encourage those aspiring to become effective speakers to prepare their speeches thoroughly. In preparation for speaking in front of any group, regardless of its size, one should know the demographics of the audience. Researching the group or area to be addressed will enable the speaker to comment on those issues which are of concern to the audience."

She realizes that her style of delivery contributes to the effectiveness of the presentation as well as to her public image. She recommends that a speaker "take time before his or her scheduled speech to relax and release all tension from the body. Tension, the public speaker's worst enemy, causes nervousness, loss of thought, and shaky speech."

However, for the mayor of Washington, D.C., staunch belief in the message is what contributes most to the speaker's potency. According to Sharon Pratt Kelly, "Perhaps the most important elements a speaker should exhibit are confidence and conviction."

as political affiliation, conservative or liberal disposition, social and economic levels, and listening/learning style can help you make decisions about the topic, language, and supporting materials.

Political Affiliation. The speaker rose from his seat, crossed to a position behind the lectern, looked at his audience, and said, "The changing role of politics in America indicates that the Democratic Party is out of touch with the mainstream and should be considered a dead institution." He then went on to develop the reasons for his stand, ending his presentation with the statement, "There will be no Democratic Party beyond the next five years." When he was finished, there was a stony silence in the room. After a few moments, the members of the audience rose from their seats and began to talk, ignoring him and his topic completely. The setting? A Democratic women's club meeting in a small midwestern town. The speaker obviously did not consider the audience's political beliefs and the fact that they had raised a great deal of money for the party of their choice.

Another speaker, realizing that she would be a Democrat speaking to a predominantly Republican group, started her presentation by explaining those views she held that were most like those of her audience. She wisely built a bridge to show that she was not completely out of touch with the audience. Her effort to build goodwill helped reduce the antagonism she might have created by focusing only on topics of disagreement.

Conservative or Liberal Disposition.   When you speak on such controversial issues as abortion, the death penalty, homosexuality, biological engineering, law enforcement, individual rights, feminism, protection of the environment, universal health care, and prayer in school, you are taking on topics in which the listeners may well have an emotional investment according to their conservative or liberal dispositions. In attempting to persuade an audience to believe the way you do or to take some action such as vote for a candidate, give money, or sign a petition, you are well advised to know the disposition of your listeners. If the majority are on your side from the outset, your task will be very different than if they are opposed to your views or solutions. Chapter 12 presents some of the methods speakers use to work toward change of opinion. Knowing the predispositions of your listeners is a valuable tool to aid you in this process.

Social and Economic Levels.   In selecting a topic, you might want to determine the social and economic levels of the audience members so that your approach fits their needs, interests, and attitudes. Different socioeconomic groups hold radically different beliefs, biases, and prejudices. For example, in addressing a gathering of wealthy patrons of the arts, it may be appropriate to comment on the strong financial support for a recent symphony performance. The same comment made to a group of less affluent people may elicit hostility. Keep in mind that different groups will enter the public speaking environment with preconceived ideas about certain topics.

Listening/Learning Style.   People listen and learn in different ways. Think back to some of the classes you had in which you learned the material rather easily. Now recall those classes in which you had difficulty tuning into the material. The reason for your difficulty may be tied to your left- or right-brain dominance and your listening/learning style. Public speakers who want to help the audience understand and act on the message presented must adapt to people's various listening/ learning styles. Ignoring this important psychographic consideration can limit the possibility of a speech's success.

The human brain is divided into right and left hemispheres. In most cases a person has a dominance that allows for learning and listening in

On Listening

"Those who perceive audiences as shapeless masses subject merely to the ability of speakers of any ethical stripe to influence must put this concept aside. We are dealing with those partners who *most* influence the outcomes of any speech communications; we are dealing with listeners. Listening . . . is an active and influential process. Listening, when it takes place, is *directed* at speakers and speaking. . . . Our language permits us to conceive of listeners listening but never of audiences *audiencing*. . . . The speaker who can improve his understanding of the fascinating interplay between listeners and speakers—the complexities of motivation, perception, and behavior that comprise the communication process—will become a more effective communicator in the day-to-day role of listener-speaker."

From Paul D. Holtzman, *The Psychology of Speakers' Audiences* (Glenview, Ill.: Scott, Foresman, 1970), pp. 1–2.

a patterned way. For example, "the left hemisphere of the brain is most responsible for rational, logical, sequential, linear, and abstract thinking."[8] Among other things, the left side of the brain is the "word" side. As you listen, as you speak, you are pulling the words out of the left side of the brain. The right hemisphere of the brain is responsible for intuitive, spatial, visual, and concrete matters: "It is from the right side of the brain that we are able to visualize."[9] The right side interprets the printed word, creating characters, places, and things in our mind's eye.

It is important to analyze your brain dominance so you understand the way in which you function as a speaker and a listener. If you have a very strong **left-brain dominance** you will probably desire to listen to a lecture rather than be an active participant, require handouts and other written material to review the presentation, and favor serious and logical ideas. As a speaker you will tend to be specific, use few examples, use few metaphors and analogies, and present logic-based arguments.

A listener with strong **right-brain dominance** tends to desire examples rather than technical explanations, needs word pictures to remember ideas, likes to explore ideas individually rather than be lectured to, prefers metaphors and analogies to facts, likes humor, and wants to know how information can be specifically useful or applied. As a speaker, the person with right-brain dominance tends to present materials in a creative rather than a structured format, relies on intuitive thinking, will present visual images, will give visually oriented instructions rather than word-oriented instructions, will explore possibilities without always coming to a conclusion, enjoys interaction rather than straight lecturing, and favors humor.

Complete activity 5 in the Learn by Doing section at the end of this chapter to determine your brain dominance. It may be impractical to give your audience such a survey, but the occupational and educational backgrounds of the audience members may indicate their general brain dominance. For example, persons with left-brain dominance tend to enter scientific, mathematical, legal, engineering, research, and computing fields; while persons with right-brain dominance may be found to favor writing, the arts, the social sciences, advertising, and media. Understanding that audience members do not all listen and learn in the same way allows you to plan your speech so that all segments of the audience can gain information. You should be structured (left-brained) but give an overall view of the ideas (right-brained); use allusions, metaphors, analogies, and examples (right-brained) while presenting concrete information (left-brained); have visual aids that both illustrate (right-brained) and list facts and statistics (left-brained); draw relational concepts (right-brained) while verifying information (left-brained).[9]

Another factor that affects listening/learning style is how people use the information they receive. Some people receive information and act on it quickly; others must let the ideas sit for a while and think about them before reaching any conclusions. In preparing your speech, give both types of listeners a chance to use their style. If you want a decision by the conclusion of the speech, give the information early and let the "thinkers" ponder it as you expand on the ideas. If the decision does not have to be made immediately, conclude by reinforcing the need to eventually make a decision, thus giving the thinkers a chance to do their pondering with a guideline for action. **Feeling-doers**, those who act on information impulsively, respond well to emotional appeals. **Watcher-thinkers**, those who need to ponder decisions, respond best to facts and logical appeals. Again, keeping in mind that you normally have both types in the audience, use both approaches as you plan your speech.

Rhetorographics   Important rhetorographic factors, which together comprise the setting, are the place, time limit, time of day, and emotional climate for the speech.

Place.   The effect of place on the tone and topic of a speech is sometimes fairly obvious. For example, a detailed dissection lecture is more suitable for a biology class than a banquet hall. A speaker who wants to convey the beauty of the Hawaiian Islands by means of a slide show will not be able to communicate fully unless the lights can be dimmed and a screen set up.

The angle you take on a topic also varies with the setting. Suppose, for example, the subject is "Changing Sex Roles in American Society." In a sociology class, a speaker may consider the history of male and female roles in the United States, the differences in sex roles in various cultures, and the factors that have brought about changing attitudes toward male and female roles. In contrast, a speaker at a meeting of liberal female legislators, realizing the audience has already accepted the idea that society discriminates against women, may focus on a particular aspect of this issue by discussing a strategy for obtaining new legislation to ensure equal opportunities for women.

Such factors as the size of a room, the temperature, the lighting, the arrangement of the furniture, and the physical comfort or discomfort of the audience all affect your communication. For example, we tend to speak in proportion to the size of a room; a large, crowded room leads to larger gestures and louder speech, and close, intimate conditions lend themselves to quiet speech. Physical proximity cuts down the broadness of gestures. A brightly lit room fosters louder sounds than a dimly lit one, and a furniture arrangement that encourages people to sit in clusters produces more intimate transactions than one that allows audience members to spread out.

Time. Both the time limit and the time of day affect a speaker's performance. Time limits are set for various reasons. For example, the room may have to be vacated by a particular hour, or audience members may have other commitments. The time limit may also be dictated by radio or television coverage. The speaker may impose certain restrictions. For example, the length of a speech may be planned on the basis of past observations of how long a particular group was capable of paying attention. Or a speaker may set a time limit because audience members can dedicate only a particular segment of their meeting to the presentation. Whatever the reason for the time limit, a speaker has an obligation to stay within the prescribed boundaries. This requires careful narrowing of a topic and careful structuring of the presentation.

Speakers should also be aware that the time of day can affect an audience. Early morning and late evening hours often are difficult times to hold people's attention. An audience may have difficulty paying attention to presentations immediately after lunches and dinners because of the drowsiness that typically follows a meal. In these cases, special care should be taken to select unusual, dramatic, or humorous material to hold the audience's attention.

Emotional Climate. The setting for public communication may also be affected by its emotional climate—the overriding psychological state of the participants. A community recently devastated by a tornado, for example, certainly would have a special emotional climate. Thus a speaker called on to present a speech in such a setting would have to adapt the message to the tragedy and deal with the fears, bitterness, and trauma experienced by the audience. Similarly, a speaker invited to address a civic organization in a town that had just been named "outstanding community of the year" would want to adjust the message to reflect the pride and satisfaction felt by the participants. Special occasions like this often create an emotional climate and provide a framework for selection of both materials and language.

☰ 4.3 Process Analysis

From the information obtained in the prior analysis you should be able to reach a reasonable conclusion about a topic that will fit you and the audience, and make judgments about the language and supporting materials to help you develop the speech. But your audience analysis should not stop there. It is important for you to analyze the listeners' responses during the speech—to perform process analysis—so you can make adaptations as you present the message.

The audience can convey verbal and nonverbal cues of attentiveness, boredom, agreement, and hostility through posture and facial expression. Some speakers and theater performers are sensitive to what they term a **cough meter.** If you have lost your audience, you will hear the results as the people clear their throats, cough, and become restless. Effective process analysis requires that you interpret these cues accurately and then adapt to them. Be careful not to assume, for instance, that a hostile response from one or two people represents the response of most of your listeners. The more experience you have in reading and adapting to feedback, the more accurate your process analysis will be.

There are various ways to adapt to the feedback you receive. For example, if you feel the audience does not understand a point, add an illustration, clarify your terms, or restate the idea. If you sense that the audience is not attentive, change the volume of your voice, use a pause, move forward, ask a direct question, or insert an interesting or humorous anecdote.

☰ 4.4 Postspeech Analysis

Postspeech analysis enables you to determine how the speech affected the audience. This information can be useful in preparing and presenting future speeches. One very direct way to conduct the postspeech analysis is to have a question-and-answer session—the questions your audience asks may reveal just how clear your presentation really was.

The tone of the questions may also reflect the general mood of the listeners, telling you how positively or negatively they have received you and your message. Informal conversations with members of the audience after the speech will also reveal a good deal.

Other postspeech techniques include opinion ballots, tests, questionnaires, and follow-up interviews. Some researchers even use electronic devices to measure such physical characteristics as pupil dilation, heart rate, and perspiration on the listeners' palms. These electronic techniques are usually appropriate only in laboratory settings and are of little practical value to public speakers.

One technique for postspeech analysis available to classroom speakers is the audience reaction sheet. Many instructors devise a form for student listeners to use in providing positive and constructive responses to their classmates' speeches. In some instances the instructor also fills out an evaluation sheet for the speaker. In other cases, instructors and students give constructive criticism verbally. Still another technique is to videotape or audiotape the speech and then critique it. All of these procedures allow speakers to get feedback from the audience.

Summary

This chapter examined important elements in the planning of a public communication. The major ideas presented were:

◆ Three factors should be considered when planning a public communication: the participants, the setting, and the purpose of the communication.

◆ Prior analysis of the audience takes place before the speech is given.

◆ Process analysis is the act of responding to the feedback a speaker receives during a speech.

◆ After the presentation, postspeech analysis helps to determine the effectiveness of the speaker's efforts and allows for adjustments in future speeches.

◆ A personal speaking inventory can aid a public speaker in selecting a topic.

◆ Listeners act not only as individuals but as members of a group that responds dynamically to the speech setting.

◆ The audience inventory encompasses demographics, psychographics, and rhetorographics.

◆ Demographic factors include the age, gender, religion, cultural and ethnic uniqueness, intellectual level, and occupation of the audience.

◆ Psychographic factors include political affiliation, conservative or liberal disposition, social and economic levels, and listening/learning style.

◆ Rhetorographic factors include the place, time limit, time of day, and emotional climate for the speech.

◆ People listen and learn in different ways.

Key Terms

participants   psychographics
setting   rhetorographics
purpose   culture
prior analysis   cultural values
process analysis   left-brain dominance
postspeech analysis   right-brain dominance
personal speaking inventory   feeling-doers
polarization   watcher-thinkers
audience analysis   cough meter
demographics

Learn by Doing

1. One of the keys to giving an effective oral presentation is to choose a subject you are interested in and about which you have some knowledge. To learn about your interests, complete the following.

   My Speaking Inventory
   a. Hobbies and special interests _____
   b. Places traveled _____
   c. Things I know how to do (sports I can play, skills I have) ____
   d. Jobs I have had _____
   e. Experiences (accidents, special events) _____
   f. Funny things that have happened to me _____
   g. Books I have read and liked _____
   h. Movies and plays I have seen and liked _____
   i. Interesting people I have known _____
   j. People I admire _____
   k. Religious and ethnic customs of my family _____
   l. Talents I have (musical, artistic, athletic) _____

2. A student volunteer is blindfolded, handed ten pennies, and told that a wastebasket (preferably a metal one) is placed somewhere in the room. It is the student's task to throw the pennies, one at a time, into the wastebasket. The student is spun around several times to become disoriented. The class is not to make any sounds while the

experiment is going on. After the student tosses all the pennies, he or she is given the opportunity to repeat the activity, but this time everyone in the class is to give directions simultaneously. Then the experiment is run a third time, but now the student is to select one person who will give directions. After the three attempts, the class will discuss the value of audience feedback, what happens when there is too much or not enough feedback, and how feedback can be used during public communication. This is an excellent way to gain an appreciation of process analysis during a speech.

3. What questions would you ask the guidance counselor at a local high school if she asked you to come speak to the senior class about life as a college student?

4. Imagine a specific situation in which you would alter a speech because of the differing attitudes of two audiences. What is your topic? Who are the audiences to which you are going to speak? What adjustments would you make for the second audience that you did not make for the first audience?

5. Answer all of these questions quickly and do not stop to analyze them. When there is no clear preference, choose the one that most closely represents your attitudes or behavior.

Left/Right Brain Dominance[10]
1. Do you usually have a place for everything, a system for doing things, and an ability to organize information and materials?
   a. _____ Yes
   b. _____ No
2. In thinking about the activities of your day, which is most typical of your "style"?
   a. _____ I make a list of all the things I need to do, people to see.
   b. _____ I just let it happen.
3. Concerning hunches,
   a. _____ I would not rely on hunches to help me make important decisions.
   b. _____ I frequently have strong ones and follow them.
4. I think of daydreaming as
   a. _____ a waste of time.
   b. _____ a viable tool for planning my future.
5. In a problem-solving situation, do you
   a. _____ think about and write down all alternatives, arrange them according to priorities, and then pick the best?
   b. _____ wait to see if the situation will right itself?

6. In school did you prefer
   a. _____ geometry?
   b. _____ algebra?
7. Sit in a relaxed position and clasp your hands comfortably in your lap. Which thumb is on top?
   a. _____ Right
   b. _____ Left
8. When you want to remember directions, a name, or a news item, do you
   a. _____ visualize the information?
   b. _____ write notes?
9. In sports or performing in public, do you often perform better than your training and natural abilities warrant?
   a. _____ Yes
   b. _____ No
10. Do you learn athletics and dancing better by
   a. _____ imitating, getting the feel of the music or game?
   b. _____ learning the sequence and repeating the steps mentally?

Scoring and Interpretation

Give yourself one point for each question you answered "b" on numbers 1–5 and "a" on 6–10. This total is your score. To assess your degree of left- or right-brain preference, locate your final score on this continuum:

Left_____**Right**

     1   2   3   4   5   6   7   8   9   10

The lower the score, the more left-brained tendency you have. People with scores of 1 and 2 are considered to be highly left-brained. The higher the score, the more right-brained tendency you have. People with scores of 9 and 10 are considered to be highly right-brained. Please bear in mind that neither hemisphere preference is superior to the other. If you are extremely left or right dominant, it is possible to develop some traits associated with the other hemisphere, or you may already have them.

Notes
—————
=====

1. Concepts developed and presented by Jean Berns, MJSolutions, "Small Group Presentation Effectiveness," Lincoln Assurance Company, Ft. Wayne, Indiana, April 14, 1992.
2. Ralph G. Nichols, "Factors in Listening Comprehension," *Speech Monographs,* XV, 2 (1948), pp. 154–163.
3. One of the first to describe this phenomenon was F. H. Allport, *Social Psychology* (Boston: Houghton Mifflin, 1924).

4. *Time,* September 12, 1983, p. 53.

5. Bill Peterson, "Jackson's Strong Showing Brings Respect to His Candidacy," *Washington Post,* April 4, 1984, p. A8.

6. *America's Workforce Is Changing Dramatically* (San Francisco: Copeland Griggs Productions, 1989).

7. William B. Johnston and Arnold E. Packer, *Workforce 2000* (Indianapolis: Hudson Institute, 1987), pp. 85, 89.

8. Based on the information of Dr. Paul Torrance and Dr. Bernice McCarthy, 1979. See also Michael Gazzaniga, "The Social Brain," *Psychology Today* (November 1985), pp. 29–38; "How the Brain Works," *Newsweek,* February 7, 1983, pp. 40–47; Laurence Miller, "The Emotional Brain," *Psychology Today* (February 1988), pp. 34–42; Jerre Levy, "Right Brain, Left Brain: Fact and Fiction," *Psychology Today* (May 1985), pp. 38–43; Christine Wicker, "Right Brain vs. Left Brain," the *Elyria (Ohio) Chronicle-Telegram,* reprinted from the *Dallas Morning News,* April 21, 1985, p. C1.

9. Ibid.

10. Adapted from material developed by Dr. Paul Torrance and Dr. Bernice McCarthy, 1979. Complete instrument can be obtained from Excel, Inc., P.O. Box 6, Fox River Grove, Illinois, 60021.

The Speech Purpose

5

Chapter Outline

After reading this chapter you should be able to:

Explain the importance of having a purpose for a speech.

Write a purpose statement by stating the goal and topic for a speech
and specifying the method to be used in developing the speech.

peakers should know specifically what they want to communicate. Thus, before they even start to develop their presentations, many public speakers write a **purpose statement** in
which they define their subject and develop the criteria by
which they will evaluate material that may be included in the
speech.

5.1 The Purpose Statement

Writing a purpose statement assures that you will have a clear idea of
what you are trying to accomplish, determines the way in which the
speech will be developed, and aids you in selecting the materials to
include in the speech.

Taking the time to develop the purpose statement will save you time
later on, as it will actually make it easier for you to prepare your speech.
It will help you avoid the tendency of many novice speakers to rush a
speech together and then have to redo it because the ideas are disorga-
nized and the materials are not coherent. Clearly knowing where you
are going also focuses your research, since you are aware of exactly what
kinds of materials you are seeking. In addition, the development of a
purpose statement allows you to use the information you've collected
from the prior analysis to center on the participants and the setting
of the speech.

Speakers who have difficulty writing a purpose statement that states
exactly what the expected outcome of the speech will be often do not
have a clear idea of what they are trying to say. They usually make a
broad statement such as "I'm going to talk *about* income taxes." Unfortunately, this statement is so vague that it allows the speaker to wander
in both preparation and presentation. The word *about* is unclear and
nondirective. In this case, the speaker should be asking *what specifically
about* income tax the speech will address: Tax history? Tax regulations?
Tax penalties? Though developing a clear purpose statement may take

On Listening

The first step for an effective listener is to determine the purpose for listening to a particular communication. Research in reading behavior suggests that readers who know their objective before beginning to read are more likely to gain something from the reading experience. The same principle probably applies to listening behavior.

Once you identify your purpose—to listen for discrimination, to comprehend, to offer therapeutic support, to critically analyze, or to appreciate—you will need to apply your listening skills in order to accomplish it. Of course, you may find that you are listening for more than one purpose (to discriminate the speaker's auditory and visual cues, for instance). Likewise, it is important to balance your perceived listening objectives with the speaker's own objectives. If you determine that the speaker's purpose is to present information, for example, then it makes sense to decide that you are going to listen to comprehend that message. Other speakers may offer different kinds of listening challenges. A minister who has developed an excellent speaking style may lead you beyond critical listening to an appreciation of how the sermon is constructed and presented.

Just as the speaker must have a clear-cut communication objective, so too must the listener come to the communication with a carefully considered goal. The communication outcome then results from how well the speaker's and the listener's objectives mesh.

time, it will save you the frustration of not being able to stick to a narrow, specific topic.

The purpose statement typically consists of three parts: the goal of the speech, the statement of the topic, and the method or process to be used to develop the speech.

5.2 The Speech Goal

The **goal** of a speech is expressed in terms of the expected outcome: **to inform** (imparting new information or reinforcing information and understandings that the listener already has) or **to persuade** (getting the listener to take some action, accept a belief, or change a point of view). By knowing your expected outcome you can develop a plan to accomplish the goal. For example, if your purpose statement is "To inform the audience of the psychological effects of child abuse by examining

Coaches often give speeches before a game to persuade team members to play their best.

research studies," the goal is to inform. This means that you will be giving information. You will include only material that illustrates the psychological effects of child abuse. Let's say, however, that your purpose statement is "To persuade the audience to appeal to governmental officials for changes in child protection and child custody laws by showing how current laws are inadequate to prevent child abuse. In this case you would need not only to illustrate the effects of child abuse but also to suggest ways in which audience members could influence lawmakers.

☰ 5.3 The Speech Topic

State your **topic**, the subject of your speech, as specifically as possible. If you are not specific, you may find yourself mentally wandering around, unable to settle on your material. There is a difference between talking about "my trip to New Zealand" and "the art of natural wool weaving as done by New Zealand artists." There is a difference between talking about "education" and discussing "why I believe that assessment tests should be given for placement of all college freshmen into communication classes." If you are not specific in your topic choice, your listeners may never grasp your point.

Make sure you keep your audience analysis in mind when selecting the focus of the topic. A topic that fits you quite well may not fit the audience. The way you approach a subject will determine whether an audience becomes interested. Examine the topic from the audience's standpoint. If you were listening to someone else speak on this topic, what approach would interest you? For example, if you are knowledgeable about word processing, simply telling the audience what you do as a word processor may not be very fascinating. However, if you are speaking to college students, describing how they can use a word processor to improve their grades would be a better approach. Alternatively, if the audience consists of other word-processing personnel, you might share with them "five tricks I've learned that have made it easier for me to save time while operating a word-processing program."

Remember, you are only one of the participants in communication. You must also take the audience into consideration. People tend to listen to topics that they perceive have some effect on them. If given the opportunity to speak about a topic you've chosen, rather than one that has been assigned to you, select one that gives you a fighting chance to grab and hold the audience's attention. Consider the time you are allotted, the best way to structure the presentation, and the needs of your audience.

Time Allotted   You have only a certain amount of time. Make sure you can adequately cover your topic in the time allowed. Do not deceive yourself in thinking that the audience will listen merely because you are speaking. Recall the times you have mentally picked up your books and left class the instant the class period was supposed to be over, no matter how much the instructor believed there was time for "just one more idea." Audiences react the same way to a long-winded speaker.

Time limits sometimes are set for you, and sometimes you determine them on your own. In most speech classes, for example, instructors set time limits out of necessity and for educational reasons. Usually there are a certain number of class members who have to give speeches, and specific limits ensure that all will get a chance to speak. If you go over time, someone else will get less time. In addition, most instructors are aware that some speakers need to be taught to discipline themselves not to ramble, and that some speakers must be pushed to fully develop a presentation. Setting maximum and minimum time limits addresses both of these educational goals.

In the world outside the classroom speakers almost always face time

Profile: Tony Snow, *presidential speechwriter*

Often, the eloquent words we hear uttered by our great orators have flowed first from the pens of speechwriters. Speechwriters are wordsmiths who craft language to communicate clearly and artists who give color and life to spoken messages.

No special set of background experiences or education is a definitive one for people preparing careers in speechwriting. For example, Tony Snow began as a high school debater, majored in philosophy in college, and had a long career in print journalism before becoming White House Director of Speechwriting for the Bush Administration. Though the path to a speechwriting career may be varied, Snow offers some suggestions for people interested in entering this field.

1. *Study speechwriting.* As with many disciplines, we can learn the craft from those who have gone before us. Scrutinize their techniques and successes. Explore their styles. Learn from their mistakes.

2. *Learn some other discipline well.* In other words, have some other body of knowledge upon which you can draw. For example, study history, philosophy, science, or even mathematics. Furthermore, never underestimate the value of trivia. If you come out from behind your desk and participate in life, your speeches will reflect the depth of your experience.

3. *Learn how to write well.* Even the people who have the most profound ideas are rendered ineffective without the ability to communicate those ideas. In particular, know the basics, such as using the active voice and creating smooth transitions between points.

In public discourse, speechwriters often play an influential role; however, with that role comes responsibility. First and foremost, according to Snow, a speechwriter ought not to use a speaker as his or her own "mouthpiece." In Snow's eyes, a speech is composed specifically to communicate the sensibilities, ideas, emotions, arguments, or policies of the speaker. Once that speech is completed and given to a speaker, it becomes that speaker's property. Snow says, "Those writers who rely on speakers' utterances for their own reputations and places in history will be disappointed. The words will go down in history as the speaker's and that is as it should be."

One special feature of speechwriting and speaking in the information age is the need to build "sound bites" into the text. Because sound bites generally summarize arguments, Snow asserts that a good sound bite cannot exist without being preceded by a clear, strong argument. Therefore, if a writer composes an argument well, a sound bite can easily be plucked from it.

Speechwriters strive to write engaging, effective speeches. However, their written words can be either glorified or ruined by the speaker who vocalizes them. For Snow, there exists one particular quality of a good speaker which cannot be written into a speech's text. "A good speaker," he points out, "gives the audience the impression that this person is sharing a part of his or her soul with them, not merely condescending to spend a few minutes standing before them."

Based on telephone interview with Tony Snow, March 26, 1992.

limits. If you are given 10 minutes to speak about your company's new products to a group of potential purchasers, they expect you to speak for approximately 10 minutes. They have taken time out of their workday to listen to you for that period. Going 20 minutes or so can almost guarantee negative perceptions. Likewise, religious leaders, politicians, and other prominent people who speak to groups will fail to fulfill their speaking purpose if they ramble on and on. Think of a speech's time limit much in the same way as advertisers think of a television commercial. If they have 30 seconds to get their message across they must be clear, effective, and stick to the time parameters. If they go too long, the end of the commercial will be cut off the air. If they go too short, they will have dead air left over that they could have used to include more appeals for the product. Plan your speech so that it fits into the time span.

Structure of the Speech   Decide how best to approach the presentation. If the topic requires an in-depth study of one factor, then use a **vertical development** to look at a single issue in great detail. If, however, the topic requires a general survey of several ideas, use a **horizontal development**. Either approach can be successful, depending on the subject and your purpose. Say, for example, you want to speak on the subject of how a play is produced. You may narrow the topic so that you cover only the specifics of how a play is cast and go into detail about each phase of choosing the actors and actresses (vertical development). In contrast, you can use the same amount of time to discuss the overall process of staging a play. In this case, you would tell just a little about casting, blocking stage movements, and conducting rehearsals (horizontal development). In the vertically developed speech the audience becomes very knowledgeable about one phase of staging a play, whereas in the horizontally developed speech the audience has a general idea of the entire process. If you choose a horizontal approach, be careful not to spread the ideas so thin that there is little idea development.

Figure 5.1 presents outlines for two speeches about phobias. The vertically developed speech discusses one subject: agoraphobia. Listeners gain an in-depth understanding of a narrow topic. The horizontally developed speech is an overview of several phobias. Listeners will gain a broad understanding of what a phobia is and general information about four phobias.

Audience Needs   Analyze your audience and satisfy its needs. You are wise to ask yourself what phase of your topic the audience will be interested in hearing about and how to get the idea or ideas across. Narrow your topic from broad

Figure 5.1

Vertical and Horizontal Approaches to Speeches

A Speech with a Vertical Development

Purpose statement: To inform the audience about the disease of agoraphobia by defining it, identifying its causes, listing the physical symptoms of an attack, explaining the agoraphobic personality, describing its consequences, and explaining treatment for the illness.

Topics covered in speech:
A. Definition of *agoraphobia*
B. The causes of agoraphobia
C. The physical symptoms of an agoraphobia attack
D. The agoraphobic personality
E. The consequences of agoraphobia
F. The treatment for agoraphobia

A Speech with a Horizontal Development

Purpose statement: To inform the audience about phobic diseases by listing, defining, and giving examples of agoraphobia, speechophobia, xenophobia, and claustrophobia.

Topics covered in speech:
A. Definition of *phobia*
B. Representative types of phobias
    1. Agoraphobia
       a. Definition
       b. Examples of
    2. Speechophobia
       a. Definition
       b. Examples of
    3. Xenophobia
       a. Definition
       b. Examples of
    4. Claustrophobia
       a. Definition
       b. Examples of

---

to specific by deciding how to best approach your listeners. How much background will they need? If the topic is complex, devote time to providing definitions and explanatory material.

The more complex your subject, and the less experience or knowledge your audience has, the more specific you have to be. For example, in lecturing about nonverbal communication to a freshman speech class, an instructor who realizes that most students are unfamiliar with the vocabulary and the history of this field of study will lay the foundations and be alert to defining terms as she speaks. Your audience analysis should help you determine the necessary background material. Also, repeating your major concepts in various ways will help ensure that the audience understands. Break the topic into segments and approach each segment from several perspectives, so that if listeners do not grasp the material one way, they will another way.

Keeping the needs of your audience in mind will prevent you from trying to cover too much. For instance, a media major has decided to share with a class of nonmajors his knowledge about how a television show is produced, assuming that as media consumers they should be curious about how their favorite TV shows get from script to screen. After analyzing the audience, the speaker realizes that the vocabulary of TV production is complex. A typical vocabulary list for a beginning class in TV production contains about 250 terms, and an understanding of many of these terms is necessary to grasp even the most elementary phases of TV production. Obviously, the speaker cannot impart all these terms and cover all the phases of TV production. If he narrows the subject to the role of the director, and then narrows it further to the steps a director takes for getting the shots on the TV screen, the task becomes manageable. By explaining the role of the director, which necessitates defining what a "storyboard," "script," and "calls" are, the speaker has laid the necessary foundation. Then he can go into an explanation of the steps a director takes in getting the shots on the TV screen. The speaker might even use visual displays and accompany the explanation with a videotape of a show in production.

5.4 The Method of Developing the Speech

When you write out a purpose statement, use key words to indicate the **method**, or process, you are going to employ in developing your goal. In an informative speech, for example, key words can include:

"By analyzing"
"By demonstrating"
"By explaining"
"By summarizing"
"By comparing"
"By contrasting"
"By describing"
"By discussing"
"By listing"
"By showing"

Here are some examples of informative purpose statements using these key words:

◆ To inform the audience why competency testing is being used as a determination for high school graduation by discussing the three major reasons for its use.

◆ To inform the audience how to make a cut-glass sun hanger by listing the supplies needed and the step-by-step construction procedure.

◆ To inform the audience that vitamin C protects against the common cold by examining four scientific studies that provide evidence for this viewpoint.

◆ To inform the audience why I believe that the Beatles had an important effect on modern music by showing the changes in music before and after the Beatles's era.

◆ To inform the audience why I believe that the theory of color therapy is valid by examining the research and findings by color therapy investigators.

In a persuasive speech, you can use these key words in your purpose statements:

"To accept that"

"To attend"

"To join"

"To participate in"

"To support"

"To agree with"

"To contribute to"

"To lend"

"To serve"

"To volunteer to"

"To aid in"

"To defend"

"To offer to"

"To share"

"To vote for"

Examples of persuasive purpose statements follow:

◆ To persuade the audience to accept the belief that Columbus discovered America by investigating four different viewpoints concerning the discovery and showing why the Columbus version is the most plausible.

- To persuade the audience that video games have no adverse physical and psychological effects on children by presenting the research that proves this conclusion.
- To persuade the audience to fill out and sign living wills by listing five reasons for them to do so.
- To persuade the audience to accept the concept that getting help from a mental health professional can be a positive act by examining the five most common reasons people seek help and the statistics showing the success rate of treatment for those problems.

By writing a purpose statement that includes these three factors—goal, topic, and method—you can avoid some of the major pitfalls of neophyte speakers. The purpose statement helps you finish your speech in the time limit, accomplish your speaking goal, and communicate effectively with the audience.

Summary

This chapter investigated the importance of having a purpose for a speech. The concepts developed were:

- In developing a message, speakers should know specifically what they want to communicate.
- A purpose statement defines the subject of a speech and develops the criteria by which material will be evaluated for inclusion in the speech.
- Though developing a clear purpose statement may take time, in the long run it usually saves time by making the speaker select a narrow, specific topic and stick to it.
- The purpose statement typically consists of three parts: the goal of the speech, the statement of the topic, and the method or process to be used to develop the speech.
- The goal of a speech is expressed in terms of the expected outcome.
- The topic is the subject of a speech and should be stated as specifically as possible.
- Make sure the topic can be adequately covered in the time allowed.
- In vertical speech development the speaker presents a single issue in great detail.
- In horizontal speech development the speaker presents a survey of general ideas.
- Narrow your topic from broad to specific by deciding how best to approach your listeners.
- The method is the process employed in developing the speech's goal.

Key Terms   purpose statement   topic
——————   goal   vertical development
══════   to inform   horizontal development
                 to persuade   method

Learn by Doing   *1.*   Your class will be divided into pairs. Each pair is to locate a copy of
——————   a speech that has been presented—for example, one reproduced in
══════   *Vital Speeches.* Each of you is to separately read the speech and write
                     the purpose statement that the speaker intended. Compare your
                     purpose statements. If they do not agree, discuss your different
                     perceptions of the speech purpose.

                2.   Select a general topic (Operation Desert Storm, cubist painting, the
                     U.S. presidency, date rape, and so on). Prepare purpose statements
                     for a speech of 30 minutes, 15 minutes, and 5 minutes. Go back and
                     analyze each of the purpose statements you wrote. How do they
                     differ? Why did you make the changes you did?

                3.   Using the speaking inventory you completed at the end of Chapter
                     4, write five purpose statements that would be appropriate for an
                     informative speech of 5 minutes, on a topic of interest to your class.
                     Your instructor will divide the class into groups and you will evaluate
                     each other's purpose statements. You may then be assigned to give
                     a speech using that purpose statement.

                4.   Select three controversial issues about which you have strong feel-
                     ings (e.g., abortion, prayer in schools, congressional reform, term
                     limits for members of Congress, forced busing, required minimum
                     racial hiring standards, mandatory AIDS testing, sexual harass-
                     ment). Write a persuasive purpose statement for each of those top-
                     ics. Your instructor will divide the class into groups and you will
                     evaluate each other's purpose statements.

6

Developing the Speech: Supporting Materials

Chapter Outline

Learning Outcomes

After reading this chapter, you should be able to:

Identify the types of supporting materials and explain their role in the development of a speech.

Describe the vehicles for support used in public speeches.

Explain why it is important to consider the accuracy, currency, and presentation of supporting materials.

Identify the different types of visual, audio, and audiovisual aids that speakers use.

*I*t is important to remember that a good relationship between the speaker and the listener is best achieved when the listener clearly understands the intent of the message. The speaker develops the message by defining terms, offering clarifying examples, explaining abstract concepts, presenting proven statistics, and restating ideas. This development is done through the use of supporting materials.

When gathering information to develop a speech, be aware that you can use **supporting materials** to back up your major and subordinate points. Supporting materials should clarify your point or offer proof—that is, it should demonstrate that your claim has some probability of being true. Some forms of support are more useful for clarity, whereas others are more useful for proof.

6.1   Types of Supporting Materials

The most commonly used supporting materials are illustrations, specific instances, expositions, statistics, analogies, testimony, and humor.

Illustrations

Examples that explain a subject through the use of detailed stories are called **illustrations**. They are intended to clarify a point, not offer proof. They may be hypothetical or factual.

Hypothetical illustrations ask the listener to imagine a situation or a series of events. The speaker usually begins by saying something like "Suppose you were . . ." or "Let us all imagine that . . ." Hypothetical illustrations might be used, for instance, by a medical technician to take listeners on a theoretical trip through the circulatory system. This passage from a speech uses a hypothetical illustration to support the point that laws are necessary:

> Suppose that America were a land without laws. People would then have no restraints. They would be free to murder their neighbors, steal from shopping centers, drive as they wished, and destroy the property of others. Chaos would reign, and human beings would soon be forced to return to a situation in which only the fittest would survive. This might lead to the establishment of laws so that individuals could live in harmony with their neighbors.

In contrast, **factual illustrations** refer to a real situation or event. They might be introduced by a statement such as "When I came to school this morning . . ." or "As the president recalls, . . ." A factual illustration might be used by a woman describing her experience during childbirth or by an earthquake survivor who tells the story of his rescue. One speaker developed a speech on safety codes with a factual illustration intended to vivify her point that the dangers she was describing were real, not just theoretical. The scenario could happen, and it did happen. She stated:

> Where Memorial School stands today, Jefferson School once stood. One day a devastating fire struck Jefferson School. Many students and teachers struggled frantically to escape the ravaging flames, but the fire quickly burned out of control. Eighty students and four teachers lost their lives in that tragic fire, and hundreds of others were seriously injured; they carry their scarring and crippling wounds to this day. The new Memorial School can never eradicate the memories of those who died during the tragic fire. As a mother whose daughter was killed in that fire, I can attest to the horror—a nightmare caused by this city's lack of safety codes regarding the sealing off of school doors. In order to keep intruders out, chains were placed on the exit doors. Those doors not only held intruders outside, they held the victims inside.

A speaker must select illustrations carefully so they will be relevant to listeners. For example, a funny story about Uncle Henry that does not relate directly to the point is best saved for another time. To be interesting, illustrations should be presented concisely. In addition, if the story goes on and on, listeners will have difficulty following or remembering the point the speaker is trying to develop.

Think back to some of the more memorable speakers you have heard. They probably used a number of relevant, interesting stories to support their points. This technique offers listeners a chance to identify with and respond to the speaker's perspective. As a result, they can better understand the points being made.

Specific Instances   Condensed examples that are used to clarify or to prove a point are called **specific instances**. Because they are not developed in depth, you can say a great deal quickly by using them and can provide listeners with evidence they can relate to your point.

If you want to develop the idea that speech communication is an interesting major for college students, for example, you could support your point with specific instances of careers that employ communication majors: speechwriting, teaching, research and training in business and industrial communication, political campaigning, health communication, and public relations. These are all careers that should be familiar to your listeners. If you add an unfamiliar example, such as human cybernetic processing, without explaining it, you run the risk of losing your listeners while they try to figure out what you mean. Be sure to use specific instances that your listeners will understand.

Exposition   An **exposition** gives the necessary background information to listeners so they can understand the material being presented. Sometimes speakers will want to define specific terms, give historical information, explain how they themselves relate to the topic, or explain the form the presentation will take. For example, a speaker who wants to explain the advertising campaign for marketing a particular product may find it necessary—during introductory remarks or within the speech itself—to clarify such terms and phrases as "bandwagoning," "plus-and-minus factor of surveying," and "Nielsen average rating."

An audience may need historical information as well. For listeners to understand the outcome of the Watergate investigation, for instance, they may need to know the specific events that led to the decision to launch the investigation. Similarly, in discussing the plays of Tennessee Williams, the speaker is wise to give a biographical history because many of Williams's plays draw on his personal life.

Listeners may also need a bridge between the speaker and the topic to understand why the speaker is discussing the subject or to establish the speaker's expertise. For example, a student nurse who is explaining the nursing program she recently completed should share her educational background with the audience. A woman who has undergone surgery for breast cancer will want to make that fact clear to a group of radiation technicians when explaining the emotional impact that treatment can have on a patient. A basketball coach who has worked with a star player would be an excellent source of information about the player's talents and dedication to the sport and the team.

Explaining the process the presentation will follow or the results the speaker wants to achieve may also he helpful to listeners. The speaker might distribute or display an outline of the major points to be made, or verbally explain what he will be doing and will want the audience to do as the speech proceeds.

A speaker discussing the organizational structure of the U.S. Information Agency might provide this exposition:

> The United States Information Agency is designed to tell America's story to people in other countries. The agency is made up of special offices that serve this purpose through their work in film, production, radio and television support, publications, and Voice of America broadcasting. Their effort is reinforced through the Overseas U.S. Information Services posts in prime locations throughout the world. The effectiveness of these services is assessed through an office of research. The key to the success of the various branches of the agency rests with the people who work in the services. They are committed to telling America's story professionally.

Statistics　　Any collection of numerical information arranged to indicate representations, trends, or theories is an example of **statistics**. Communicators use statistics to compare amounts ("The normal intelligible outdoor range of the male human voice in still air is 200 yards, while female screams register higher readings on decibel meters than male screams")[1] and to provide data ("The most recent census indicates the population of Ecuador is 8,053,280 people").[2] We will see more on the use of statistics a little later in this chapter.

Analogies　　A speaker often uses an **analogy** to clarify a concept for listeners—that is, the speaker compares an unfamiliar concept to a familiar one. Analogies often take the form of a comparison or a contrast. A comparison attempts to show the specific similarity between two things, whereas a contrast highlights specific differences between things. For example, in discussing the human cortex, an analogy could be drawn between human information processing and a computer process. This comparison is not intended to indicate that the cortex and the computer are one and the same but to show that if a reader understands the functioning of a computer, he or she may also understand the basic operation of the cortex. A company manager, for example, may compare the firm's employees to the members of an athletic team. Each group has important members who function in specific capacities; each member wishes to contribute to the final product—success.

For an analogy to be effective the speaker must demonstrate a connection between the two items compared. In addition, if the listeners are not familiar with the object, idea, or theory being used as the basis for the analogy they may be confused. Comparing one unfamiliar idea to

On Listening

Just as the speaker must select supporting materials carefully, so too should listeners analyze the speaker's evidence before accepting it as valid support for the argument presented. The listener should examine evidence for clarity (how clear and intelligible it is), accuracy (how precise and factual it is), and reliability (how trustworthy and dependable it is).

Some basic questions can guide the listener in assessing the speaker's evidence.

1. Is the evidence clear?
2. Is the evidence consistent with other known evidence?
3. Is the evidence consistent with the speaker?
4. Is the evidence timely?
5. Is the evidence applicable to the argument?
6. Is the evidence pertinent to the argument?
7. Is the source of the evidence reliable?
8. Is the source of the evidence competent in the area cited?
9. Is the source of the evidence free to report all findings?
10. Is the source of the evidence suppressing or distorting facts?
11. Is the source of the evidence sincere?

See Andrew D. Wolvin and Carolyn Gwynn Coakley, *Listening* (Dubuque, Iowa: William C. Brown, 1992), p. 350.

another unfamiliar idea may do little to clarify the concept. President Bush confused some individuals when, during the 1988 election, he made references to a "thousand points of light." Some people did not see the connection between lights and his idea of an active citizenry. In fact, the phrase was so bewildering to some that many comedians included it in their routines.

Speakers should also be careful not to overextend an analogy. A college president once developed an inaugural speech by comparing the school to a football team. The analogy compared faculty members to team players, students to spectators, the president to the coach, and on and on. After a while, the listeners lost track of the initial comparison and stopped paying attention, and the intended effect was lost.

Exercise care in selecting analogies, since comparisons that do not really hold up may weaken your speech. Historians, for instance, are reluctant to draw historical analogies because the social, political, and economic forces of one era may not be comparable to those of another. Thus, despite the claims of many doomsayers, the crises and upheavals in the world today and those during the decline and fall of Rome may not be truly analogous.

Testimony   A direct quotation (an actual statement) or a paraphrase (a reworded idea) from an authority is known as **testimony**. Speakers provide testimony in communication to clarify ideas, back up contentions, and reinforce concepts. Thus a speaker may use testimony if the authority is more knowledgeable about the topic or if the speaker believes that the opinion of an authority will make listeners more receptive to a particular idea.

An **expert** is a person who through knowledge or skill in a specific field gains respect for his or her opinions or expertise. We turn to lawyers, mechanics, economists, architects, and scholars to answer questions and give advice about their areas of expertise. We trust their opinions because they have acquired knowledge through personal experience, education, training, research, and observation. We also respect people who have academic degrees or licenses, who have received accreditation, or who are recognized by peers as leaders in their fields. For example, Neil Armstrong, the first human being to walk on the moon, can offer expert testimony regarding the appearance of the lunar surface. Likewise, Dr. Michael Gottlieb, the noted AIDS virus researcher, would be regarded as an expert on the effects of AIDS on the immune system.

In presenting the views of experts, a speaker should be careful to quote accurately, indicate the time and circumstances under which the information was supplied, and provide the source of the material. The testimony should be relevant and no longer than necessary. Listeners have difficulty handling lengthy readings of testimony and tend to tune them out rather quickly.

The direct quotations you select should be true to the source's original intention. Testimony taken out of context is not only misleading and confusing but also a dishonest way of using support. Before you accept testimony as support, assess it by asking the following questions:

1. Is the material quoted accurately? Advertisers for plays or movies are sometimes guilty of using only those quotes or parts of quotes that contain praise. For example, a statement that originally read, "The movie was effective if you like a weakly developed plot, poor acting, and confusing dialogue" could in a movie ad become "The movie was effective. . . ." Those little dots make all the difference; they indicate that something has been omitted, and in this case the omis-

sion totally changes the meaning. For the same reason, be alert to phrases such as "in part," "seemed to indicate," and "implied." These, too, are signs that not all the evidence is being presented.

2. Is the source biased because of position, employment, or affiliation? A quotation by the chairperson of the board of directors of a major tobacco company that cigarette smoking may not lead to cancer should be suspect because of the speaker's biased position. As listeners we must be careful not to blindly accept sources that serve the speaker's points of view. Debaters, politicians, researchers, speakers, and journalists are often guilty of manipulating listeners through this practice.

3. Is the information relevant to the issue being discussed? For example, in attempting to prove that vitamin C is not beneficial in protecting against the common cold, a speaker might say, "Vitamin C, as contained in oranges, can cause more harm than good. Take a dozen oranges, peel them, and crush them into a pulp. They will be in exactly the same state as they would be if you swallowed them. Pour the juice into a goldfish bowl, and place the fish in the bowl. Within minutes the acid in the juice may cause the goldfish to die." This statement has no relevance to the issue being discussed.

4. Is the source competent in the field being discussed? For example, what qualifies an actor to recommend changes in college administration procedures? What makes an athlete competent to recommend cars, insurance, credit cards, or soft drinks? Unless the speaker can show that these people are qualified experts in these areas, quotations from them should not be accepted as authoritative.

5. Is the information current, if currency is important? An advertisement for a musical production at a university theater raved: "*Chorus Line,* the best damn musical I've seen in years." Yes, a drama critic in a major newspaper did write that in reviewing the play. Unfortunately, unsuspecting readers may not realize that the statement described the original New York production of *Chorus Line,* not the performance being staged by the university students.

Humor

Humor, the quality of being funny or witty, is useful strategy for gaining and holding the audience's attention. Humor has often been the key that unlocks an audience's receptivity. The apt, well-timed, and confidently executed opening puts listeners at their ease.[3] For instance, humor was creatively used by a speaker who knew that his audience had already sat through an evening of speeches. He started out his presentation by saying, "I realize that I'm the fourth speaker you've listened to tonight, so I'd like you to know I use one rule for giving speeches. The mind

Humor helps to hold the audience's attention.

can only absorb what the seat can endure, and your seats have been enduring for a long time."

Research shows that:[4]

◆ Relevant humor in informative discourse will probably produce a favorable audience reaction toward the speaker.

◆ Humor that is self-disparaging may further enhance speaker image. Laughing at oneself publicly shows that you have a good sense of humor, do not take yourself too seriously, and are warm and human. However, overdoing it might harm your speaker credibility.

◆ Relevant humor in a speech can enhance the interest of the speech. This is especially true if the speech does not contain many other factors of interest, such as suspense, animated delivery, concreteness, and specificity.

◆ Relevant humor seems not to influence the effectiveness of persuasive speeches either negatively or positively.

◆ Humor may or may not make a speech more memorable. Humor may increase the interest, but evidence suggests that it does not necessarily increase immediate recall of the subject matter.

◆ The use of satire as a persuasive device may have unpredictable results. Research shows that satire, under certain conditions, can be persuasive, but inconsistently so. This is especially true when it is used by amateur speakers, since they may tend to use it at inappropriate times. In the hands of a professional satirist, satire may be an effective tool. Research showed, for example, that satire by humorist and newspaper columnist Art Buchwald "changed attitudes toward labor unions and our policy of nonrecognition of China."[5]

What are you looking for in using humor? Ask yourself the following questions:

1. Is the item funny?
2. Would you feel comfortable saying it?
3. Is it performable humor?
4. Will it offend the audience, if offense is not your purpose?
5. Is it appropriate to the tone of the speech?
6. Is it appropriate for the topic and purpose of the speech?

A person who effectively uses humor during a speech "never loses sight of his or her reason for being there. The laughs are supportive or illustrative of the occasion, the audience or the speaker. They show a speaker involved with his/her listeners and in tune with them."[6] In addition, care is taken not to offend the audience, unless offense is intentional and has a purpose. The 1992 Democratic presidential hopeful Senator Bob Kerrey found himself in hot water because of a joke he made about lesbians in a conversation before a speech that was recorded by C-Span and made public. The results were protests and demonstrations; Kerrey apologized, but many believe that he lost a number of followers because of his untimely use of humor. Ironically, the very next evening Vice President Dan Quayle's press secretary, David Beckwith, at a Bush/Quayle campaign fund-raiser, referred to Kerrey's joke and said, "The good news is that the lesbians are upset with Kerrey. The bad news is that they'll be coming our way to support us." Again, a poor choice of humor, and more negative reactions.[7]

Where does apt humorous material come from? Sometimes it is professionally written by a speechwriter or humorist specifically for the occasion. The problem with such material is that it is expensive. The best sources for most public speakers are humor books.[8] The speaker, too, is a fruitful source of humor. Humorous observations or experiences can be clever inclusions, and since they are personal, the audience can relate to the speaker's use of them.

Here are some hints for effectively using humor in a speech:

◆ Practice your humorous lines as you do the rest of your speech.

◆ Don't announce that you have a joke or a humorous story to tell. The worst thing you can do is say, "That reminds me of a funny story," because then you are challenging the audience. You're saying, in effect, "I'm going to make you laugh," and your listeners are likely to fold their arms across their chests in an attitude of "Oh yeah?"

◆ Don't attempt humor unless you are comfortable telling funny stories. If you thoroughly believe that you can't tell a joke, don't. You won't fool the audience, you will be uncomfortable, and it will show.

◆ Don't use puns, unless for some reason you want to elicit groans from your audience. Puns are the antithesis of what you are striving to achieve. A pun says, "Look how clever I am." It separates you from your audience.

6.2 Vehicles for Presenting Supporting Materials

Speakers often use attention devices, restatement, and forecasting as a means of presenting and focusing supporting materials.

Attention Devices

Attention devices focus the listener's concentration on one stimulus over all others in the environment. When you consider the amount of stimuli that are continually bombarding us, it is no wonder that speakers have difficulty gaining and maintaining the attention of their listeners. This task is made even more difficult by the fact that listening involves a process of tuning in and tuning out throughout the message. Some research suggests a person can concentrate for no more than sixty seconds.[9]

Because we can attend to any one stimulus for only a short period of time, a speech must be sufficiently compelling to ensure that listeners will tune back in to it. To accomplish this, try to choose **concrete supporting materials**, which are specific rather than general or abstract. Abstractions are usually not interesting to listeners. The speaker who explains the process of lunar landings to a nontechnical audience will probably find that an abstract discussion of the principles of velocity and stress will not hold the audience's attention. Instead, the speaker should use concrete illustrations from past Apollo landings.

You should also choose **familiar supporting materials**, which refer to ideas or objects about which the audience already has some knowledge. For example, a speaker who wants to describe a new economic program might refer to the daily effects inflation has on a household budget. Familiar examples help enable listeners to comprehend concepts that may be new to them.

To be a compelling speaker, you must work to be **vivid**—distinct and graphic—in your presentation. Lively descriptions, a colorful choice of language, and a vigorous style can all encourage listeners to pay attention to your message. A speaker addressing a group of potential airline flight attendants might stress the importance of cabin safety with some vivid descriptions of past accidents. You may also wish to use **novelty** by treating the subject in a unique or surprising fashion. One speaker chose a novel opening for his speech by saying, "I'm much like you in many ways. I have two arms, two legs, two hands, two eyes, and two ears. I wear clothes, go to school, and enjoy good food. I'm different from you, however, because I'm on methadone. You see, I'm a heroin addict."

Another device is **suspense**, whereby you develop expectation and uncertainty in your audience. A series of questions might create suspense: "What has three professional theaters under one roof? What is endowed with expensive Italian marble, Scandinavian crystal chandeliers, and other gifts from all over the world? What is designed to be a living memorial to a great American president? The Kennedy Center in Washington, D.C." Material that demonstrates **conflict**—strife and confrontation—is another effective attention device. A speaker might use conflict to interest listeners in a local political issue: "We have to decide today whether we are going to use our tax revenues to hire more teachers or more police officers. Both alternatives have advantages and disadvantages. Let me explain them to you."

Above all, speakers should be careful to use a variety of devices that are relevant to the subject of the speech and to the listeners. Effective speakers seek out materials that contain such devices to capture and maintain the attention of their audience.

Restatement

Have you ever been on the receiving end of a message and found yourself totally confused because of the amount of material it involved? Speakers often forget that listeners may not be able to sift through the information as it is presented. Therefore, to avoid confusion summarize each segment of a presentation by **restatement** before proceeding to the next one. Effective restatement is accomplished by rewording key points so that major ideas stand out for the listeners without becoming boring or repetitious. Internal summaries are not always necessary; but if material is complicated, a speaker is wise to use this method of clarification. For example, a speaker might restate the sentence "The United States should adopt a more aggressive foreign policy" with "Our nation, then, needs to pursue a more vigorous, definitive approach to its international relations." Care should be taken, however, not to use too many restatements because they can easily lose their impact.

Forecasting
To get the audience ready to focus on the next idea to be presented, speakers use forecasts. A **forecast** is a statement that alerts the audience to ideas that are coming. Sample forecast statements are "Let's now examine three ways in which bulimics purge food" and "By understanding the definition of *bulimic,* you can gain insight into why this is a psychological, not a biological, illness." The speaker would then proceed to develop the forecasted idea.

6.3 Supporting Materials—Accuracy, Currency, Presentation

No matter what supporting material you select to use, make sure it is accurate, current, and presented in a way that effectively and ethically develops the speech.

Accuracy of Materials
To make a statement and prove it with accurate support, begin with a **statement of declaration,** which proposes the major contentions of the speech. Then give the necessary exposition to clarify necessary terms, and develop the idea with illustrations, specific instances, statistics, analogies, and testimony. Without such clarification and development, the audience often will not understand the idea and will have little reason to accept your contentions. For example, a well-developed speech on bulimia included these statements and supporting materials:

Statement of declaration. "Bulimia is an eating disorder that involves binging and purging."

Exposition (definition of term): "Binging is the act of taking in as much food as possible, as much as 20,000 calories at a time."

Statistics: "This would be like eating 210 brownies or 5½ layer cakes or 18 dozen cookies."

Exposition (definition of term): "Purging is the evacuation of the food."

Specific instances: "The ways bulimics purge are by self-induced vomiting, use of laxatives (as many as 100 at a time), or ingestion of diet pills."

Before accepting statistics or any other information as truth and using them in your speech, ask yourself:

1. Who says so?
2. How does he or she know?
3. Is any information missing?
4. Did somebody change the subject?
5. Does it make sense?[10]

When information is accurately discovered, researched, or developed, has been properly interpreted, and is not out of date, it is a valid aid in reaching conclusions. Unfortunately, not all information and research, especially statistical studies, are accurately done, properly interpreted, or current. If you are going to refer to scientific studies in your speech, you need to be aware of the process of statistical surveying.

Statistical Surveying

Researchers and statisticians have developed methods for collecting data, called **statistical surveying**, that provide some degree of assurance that the resulting information will be correct.[11] Ideally, to find out everyone's opinion on a particular issue, everyone should be asked, but of course this is impossible for large populations. Thus, to make educated guesses about what people generally think about a subject, statisticians have devised methods of **random sampling**, which allow them to survey less than the entire population. These methods recognize the probability of error, so a speaker should indicate the possible margin for error when reporting the statistical results of a survey.

Be wary of studies in which people are allowed to call in their response to a radio or television station. In this sort of survey the population cannot be controlled—that is, the same people may call in over and over, or they may not be representative of the entire population. Also be suspicious if the number of people questioned is very small. Asking ten people at your college or university a question and then publishing the results as representing the entire school does not constitute a valid survey. Sometimes, too, a surveyor might be trying to get a specific result and may keep testing until reaching the desired conclusion, or may ignore results that do not agree with the goal. For this reason, be wary of statistics that are taken out of context, that are incomplete, or that do not specify the method used to collect the data.

Currency of Data

Studies and surveys done in the past may have been perfectly accurate at the time they were conducted. This does not mean, however, that they are accurate now. It is important that you use the latest data and not allow yourself to be influenced by information that is not up to date. When you give statistical information, always note when it was collected. When you receive it, be sure to ask for such information if you have any doubts. Some material, such as the generally accepted year of 1492 as the date for Columbus's arrival in the Americas, doesn't have to be from a 1992 source. However, if you are tracing the development of the AIDS epidemic, having current information from this year is imperative. As a public speaker, it is your responsibility to make sure that your conclusion is based on accurate and current information.

Presentation of Data

In using information in a speech, especially statistics, remember that a listener can retain only a limited amount of material. Long lists and complex numbers may go right over your listeners' heads if you do not help them visualize the information. For example, a long list—such as the figures representing the cost of each material used to produce a piece of machinery—can be written on a chalkboard or poster or can be projected on a screen. In this way, listeners view as well as hear, and they can refer to the numbers as needed.

Complicated numbers can be treated in the same manner. Consider, for example, the difficulty of learning geometry, algebra, or accounting without supplemental visual aids that assist the oral presentation. A number such as $1,243,724,863 is difficult to comprehend even if it is written down, but the phrase "approximately $1.25 billion" is within the grasp of an audience.

If statistics are important enough to be included in a presentation, they are important enough to be clarified. Technical subjects in particular require visualization. Speakers are responsible for determining the best way to convey the message to listeners. Here is an example of one way to use statistics effectively to support the thesis that there is a great deal of illegal immigration into the United States from Mexico: "The Immigration and Naturalization Service reported more than 1 million arrests for illegal crossings of the Mexican border in the fiscal year that began last October 1—a 40 percent rise over the same period a year earlier."[12] The fact that there were 1 million arrests means little to the audience. But the interpretation of this data—that this was 40 percent more than last year—conveys the message that illegal immigration is rising.

Be careful not to misuse information accidentally or intentionally. This can happen when only part of the information is present, the information is misinterpreted, or the information is used to prove something it was not intended to prove. Consider the following statements: "There were 51,000 rapes in the United States in a given year." "Two children die each day in the United States as a result of child beating." "College expenses will rise around 8 percent for resident students and 6 percent for commuting students next year." These are all numbers, statistics. But are they valid? How should we interpret these statistics?

There may have been 51,000 rapes reported to the police departments in the United States in a year, but was that the total number of rapes committed? Were all rape cases reported to the police? Who determined the number of children's deaths? On what basis can we predict rising college expenses? These numbers may be statistics, but if you do not quote their sources and explain how they were compiled, an audience may feel there is good reason to question their accuracy and therefore their value.

6.4 Supplementary Aids

Many speakers find the use of **supplementary aids**—visual, audio, and audiovisual—valuable in supplementing the oral segments of their presentations. Nevertheless, a speaker should ask three questions before deciding to use such aids: Is the aid relevant to the presentation? Will listeners better understand the material through the use of an aid? Will the aid create potential problems for me? Aids are intended to facilitate listener understanding, not function as decorative touches; they are to help, not hinder.

The supplementary aid is relevant if the speech cannot be given effectively without it. Listeners need to see the brushwork of Vincent van Gogh in order to appreciate how he achieved his visual effects. The audience needs to hear examples of country and western music in order to compare it with rock and roll. Watching a demonstration of how a particular piece of machinery works makes it easier for listeners to understand its application.

Visual aids that are not carefully chosen can be a drawback. The speaker who brought his pet puppy to class in order to illustrate how animals can be trained did not expect the dog to become frightened by the crowd and proceed to bite a student. Even if the puppy performed exceedingly well, where do you keep him after the speech if you are one of the first speakers?

In the classroom, supplementary aids are often used to teach particular techniques. For example, nurses sometimes learn how to give shots by inserting needles into grapefruits; firefighters study methods of ladder placement on film; and law-enforcement students listen to recorded interrogations as a supplement to discussions of methodology. All these aids are intended to supplement the speaker's voice.

Visual aids, such as this children's book illustration, sometimes can convey ideas better than words alone.

Visual Aids

Visual aids appeal to our sense of sight. They can include real objects, models, photographs, pictures, diagrams, charts, cutaways, and mockups.

Real Objects

To demonstrate the process of swinging a hammer, why not use a real hammer? Why not use an actual form to show how a traffic ticket is filled out, or bring in samples of the chemicals that are mixed to produce a particular product? All these are examples of using **real objects** as visual aids.

Models

At times, it is impossible to use real objects. In such cases, a **scale model** (in exact proportion to the dimensions of the real object) or a **synthetic model** (not in proportion but nevertheless representational) may be used. For example, although a Boeing 747 jet cannot be brought into an aviation classroom, a scale model certainly can be.

Photographs, Pictures, Diagrams, and Maps

Visual representations such as photos, pictures, or diagrams can be effective in reinforcing a message or even in providing new information to listeners. A photograph of a crime scene might be shown to a jury if the members of the jury cannot visit the scene themselves. General Norman Schwarzkopf, who led the American effort in Operation Desert Storm, made extensive use of photos and maps in his press briefings about the military maneuvers in the Persian Gulf War.

Charts   A **chart** is a visual representation of statistical data that gives information in tabular or diagrammatic form. For example, by visually displaying increases and decreases in sales, a speaker can more easily discuss the general sales trend as a whole. By the same token, a pair of columns comparing the number of doctors available to a hospital with the number of doctors needed presents a visual image of the problem.

Cutaways   A **cutaway** is a model that shows the inside of an object, which an audience would otherwise have to imagine. To show the seating plan of an airplane, for instance, a segment of the body is peeled away to reveal the interior. To show the layers of materials used to construct a house, a wall is cut in half so that we see the aluminum siding, the insulation, the studding, the wallboard, and the wallpaper.

Mockups   A **mockup** is a model constructed in sections. It is typically used to show how an object is put together. For example, in a speech explaining the plans for the new student activities building on your campus, you might use a mockup to demonstrate the process of construction. One room of the model might come off, revealing what will be on the second floor of the building; the second floor might be removed to reveal the layout of the first floor, and the first floor might be removed to reveal the basement. You would show the various segments of the building as your speech progresses.

   You could use the same principle in a step-by-step speech on how to do something. Let's say you want to illustrate outlining techniques. On an overhead projector, place a transparent sheet on which is written the Roman numeral I and the first major heading. Now explain the use of the Roman numeral. Then place another sheet on top of the original that shows points A and B under this heading. Now discuss the secondary level of an outline. Continue to add sheets and discuss the remaining levels of the outline. Use of this mockup visually illustrates the outlining procedure as you describe it orally.

Audio Aids   **Audio aids** such as records, tape recordings, and other sound duplication mechanisms may be the only way to demonstrate a point accurately to listeners. For example, a discussion of composer Andrew Lloyd Webber's music in the plays *The Phantom of the Opera, Evita, Jesus Christ Superstar,* and *Starlight Express* can be enhanced by allowing the audience to hear excerpts. Likewise, playing a recording of Martin Luther King, Jr.'s

"I Have a Dream" speech is an excellent way to demonstrate King's style of oral presentation.

Audiovisual Aids

Audiovisual aids such as films, videotapes, and audiotapes combined with slide shows mix sight and sound. Thus a video of a senatorial candidate making a victory speech at party headquarters on the election night allows the audience not only to hear the performance but also to see the reaction of the people who worked for the candidate's election. Showing a videotape of an executive's speech is an excellent way to illustrate that person's vocal and physical mannerisms. A presentation that combines audiotapes with slides, in which the pictures are synchronized with a prerecorded oral text, would make the step-by-step procedure a nurse uses in preparing a patient for surgery much more vivid.

Summary

This chapter described the types of supporting materials to be used in developing a speech. The major ideas presented were:

◆ Supporting material can be used to develop the major and subordinate points within the body of the speech. Supporting material should clarify the speaker's point or demonstrate that the point has some probability of being true.

◆ Supporting material includes illustrations, specific instances, exposition, statistics, analogies, testimony, and humor.

◆ Three means for presenting and focusing supporting material are attention devices, restatement, and forecasting.

◆ Using visual, audio, and audiovisual aids is often a valuable way to help the listener understand the message.

◆ Types of visual aids include real objects, models, photographs, pictures, diagrams, charts, cutaways, and mockups.

Key Terms

supporting materials
illustrations
hypothetical illustrations
factual illustrations
specific instances
exposition
statistics
analogy
testimony

expert
humor
attention devices
concrete supporting materials
familiar supporting materials
vivid
novelty
suspense
conflict

restatement
forecast
statement of declaration
statistical surveying
random sampling
supplementary aids
visual aids
real objects

scale model
synthetic model
chart
cutaway
mockup
audio aids
audiovisual aids

Learn by Doing

1. Find a humorous story that you could use in a speech about the educational system of the United States, women's rights, or sports.
2. What analogy could you use to explain each of the following?
    a. The growth cycle of a plant
    b. A tornado
    c. Living with a cat or a dog
    d. Attending a university or community college
3. Select one of the following purpose statements. Identify some supporting material that would be needed to develop the speech.
    a. To inform the audience why competency testing is being used as a determination for high school graduation by discussing the three major reasons for its use.
    b. To inform the audience why I believe that the theory of color therapy is valid by examining the research and findings by color therapy investigators.
    c. To persuade the audience to fill out and sign living wills by listing five reasons for them to do so.
4. What supplementary aid would be appropriate for a speech on these topics?
    a. A comparison between the population figures of the United States, Canada, China, India, and Brazil
    b. A demonstration of how to operate a Macintosh Power Book 140 computer
    c. The western migration of the pioneers across North America
    d. The interior and exterior design of Oriole Stadium at Camden Yards
    e. An explanation of the step-by-step construction of Oriole Stadium at Camden Yards, which will allow the audience to understand the stages of the construction
    f. An explanation of the physical parts of the brain so the audience can see its three-dimensional structure
    g. The difference between the vocalizations of a dolphin and a whale

    h. The performance of the Cleveland Ballet's production of *The Nutcracker*

5. Select a newspaper or magazine article that bases its conclusions on the use of statistical surveying. Evaluate the statistics by using the information on statistical surveying in this chapter.

Notes

1. Norris McWhirter, *Guinness 1984 Book of World Records* (New York: Sterling, 1984), p. 28.

2. Rob Rachowiecki, *Ecuador* (Berkeley, Calif.: Lonely Planet Publications, 1986), p. 13.

3. Bob Orben, "How to Spruce Up Those Dull Speeches," *Enterprise, the Journal of the National Association of Manufacturers,* April 1978.

4. A summary of Charles R. Gruner, "Advice to the Beginning Speaker on Using Humor—What the Research Tells Us," *Communication Education,* 34 (April 1985), 142–145.

5. Ibid., 145.

6. Orben, 1.

7. Cheryl L. Coward, "Gays Angered by Lesbian Jokes Told by Politicians," *Washington Blade,* November 22, 1991, p. 1.

8. Sources include: Bob Orben, *2500 Jokes to Start 'Em Laughing* (Comedy Center, Inc., 700 Orange Street, Wilmington, Del. 1981), *Reader's Digest Treasury of American Humor; Encyclopedia of Humor, The Comic Encyclopedia, The Speaker's Handbook of Humor, Podium Humor, Treasury of Humor, Jokes and How to Tell Them, How Speakers Make People Laugh,* and *Stories for Speakers.*

9. D. A. Norman, "Memory While Shadowing," *Quarterly Journal of Experimental Psychology,* 21 (February 1969), 85–93.

10. Darrell Huff, *How to Lie with Statistics* (New York: Norton, 1954), pp. 123–142.

11. Two excellent sources on statistics are Herbert Arkin and Henry Hill, *Sampling in Auditing: A Simplified Guide and Statistical Table* (Price Waterhouse and Company, n.d.); and D. A. Johnson and W. H. Glenn, *The World of Statistics* (St. Louis: Webster, 1961).

12. "Haul of Illegals Hits All-Time High," *U.S. News & World Report,* October 3, 1983, p. 11.

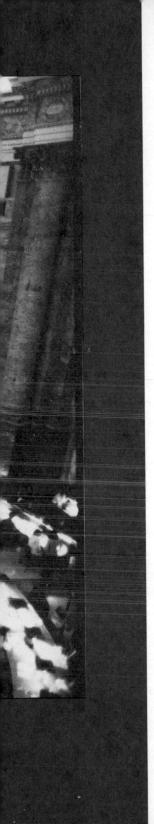

Sources of Supporting Materials

7

Chapter Outline

After reading this chapter you should be able to:

List and describe the research sources available for use in developing public speaking messages.

Identify basic reference sources used for obtaining overviews, concepts, data, and other types of information necessary for the development of public speeches.

Explain the value of using and the method for finding research sources such as books, magazines, newspapers, journals, indexes, government publications, publications from special-interest groups, and nonprint media.

Record research information.

⩭ 7.1   Sources of Information

Some of the information we use to develop messages is based on **personal knowledge**—personal experiences, observations, or learning acquired through sources such as school, the media, and reading. As we are exposed to information, we retain a certain amount of it. This knowledge forms the core of our basis for communication. We select words and examples from this storehouse, and we use it to organize messages.

Many times, however, to develop a message fully, we need information that is not part of our personal core of knowledge. In such cases, we must find **outside knowledge**—information from sources outside of our own experiences and direct observations. A research chemist, for example, could probably give a speech describing the company's major products. But what if she were asked to give a detailed presentation on the company's budget or to tell the complete history of the organization? Most speakers would find such topics difficult to handle without more knowledge. Sources of outside knowledge include books, magazines, newspapers, special journals, indexes, government publications, and the publications of special-interest groups. (See Figure 7.1.) Additional sources include nonprint materials such as tape recordings, records, films, videotapes, charts, and models, as well as interviews or correspondence with knowledgeable people in a particular field.

Be aware that there is a difference between doing research for a specific speech and gathering information about a topic. In doing purposeful research, you know exactly what you are looking for based on the speech goal, topic, and method, and you selectively pick material that

Figure 7.1

Quick Guide to Basic Reference Tools

For Overviews and Conceptual Information

◆ *Encyclopedias.* Use for historical, conceptual, and factual information written by experts, and for bibliographies (at the ends of articles) of works by important authors.

◆ *Handbooks.* Use for more detailed overviews of subjects, usually in single volumes devoted to narrow fields, with articles written by experts, often with bibliographies at the ends of sections. (To locate in the card catalogue or computer index, look under *handbooks, manuals,* or the specific title of the handbook or manual.)

◆ *Dictionaries.* Use for definitions of terms you do not understand and for synonyms of key words. Many dictionaries specialize in one subject only. (To locate in the card catalogue or computer index, look under *dictionaries,* then a specific title such as "Education.")

◆ *Annual Reviews.* Use for recent overviews of significant developments in a subject field, and for bibliographic information. (To locate in the card catalogue or computer index, look under *yearbooks.*)

For Data

◆ *Fact Books.* Use for hard information on names, places, and dates in a concise format. (Listed under *almanacs* in the card catalogue and computer index. Examples: *Facts on File, Information Please Almanac.*)

◆ *Statistical Sources.* Use for statistical support and documentation of your ideas. (Listed in the card catalogue and computer index under *statistics* and then the subject heading, for example, "Statistics—Labor Supply.")

◆ *Biographical Sources.* Use to verify the credentials of authors and to get information about people. (To locate in the card catalogue or computer index, consult personal names under subject headings or the name of the occupational group of the person.)

Springboards to More Information

◆ *Bibliographies.* Use to identify other books, parts of books, films, and magazine articles on a subject. (To locate in the card catalogue or computer index, consult the subject heading followed by the words *bibliography, biobibliography, discography,* or *film catalogue.*)

◆ *Indexes.* Use to locate more information, usually but not always limited to periodicals. Indexing is done for research reports, government publications, and parts of books, plays, poetry, or songs. (To locate in the card catalogue or computer index, consult the subject heading followed by the words *indexes, abstracts,* or *bibliography.*)

---

will help develop the specific outcomes of the speech. By contrast, in gathering information, you are looking for general material that might lead you toward a specific speech goal, topic, and method. For example, if you knew you wanted to give a speech about phobias, you would start gathering information about anything that had to do with phobias. From this accumulated information you should then be able to develop a purpose statement. However, if you already had developed a purpose statement, the search would be different. Let's assume your purpose statement is "To inform the audience about phobic diseases by listing, defining, and giving examples of agoraphobia, speechophobia, xenophobia, and claustrophobia." You would specifically restrict your search to finding a definition of phobic diseases, and definitions and examples of agoraphobia, speechophobia, xenophobia, and claustrophobia.

Speakers must also assess the validity of the information they locate. All sources of information reflect certain perceptions and biases. Consequently, it is wise to try to determine the bias of a source and to interpret its information accordingly.[1] When doing research for a presentation, it is a good idea to find several agreeing authoritative sources so that your supporting details will be credible to your listeners.

Books

Personal, academic, and public libraries are the fount of much information; nevertheless, you must know how to find the materials you need. In academic and public libraries, books are shelved according to a numerical system and can be located by looking through the card catalogue, the **computer output microfiche (COM),** or the library's electronic computer catalogue under the title, the author's name, or the general subject. The code number indicates where the volume is shelved.

Unfortunately, not all subjects are easy to locate. For example, an average library's card catalogue or computer search system would probably reveal no information if you looked under the title "Arapesh." To learn which books contain material about this subject, you would need some additional information. By looking in the encyclopedia, you would discover that the Arapesh are a primitive mountain-dwelling people of New Guinea whose society was investigated by anthropologist Margaret Mead and discussed in her book *Sex and Temperament in Three Primitive Societies.* Based on this information, you could look in the COM or card catalogue under such subjects as anthropology, Margaret Mead, New Guinea, and *Sex and Temperament in Three Primitive Societies.* You could then check the indexes of the books you find or do a computer search for references to needed facts.

Books are of great value in supplying information, but they can quickly become out of date. It generally takes at least a year for the average book to move from the author's final draft through the printing process and onto the shelves of a library. This is in addition to the time the author has taken to write the book. Some subjects change little, and in these areas books are a good research source. But for quickly changing subjects, more up-to-date sources are needed for a thorough investigation.

Be aware that just because someone wrote a book does not mean the person is an expert. Also realize that some authors may be biased and unethical. This often necessitates your ascertaining such factors as the author's political, social, or religious views. Books get published because the author has been able to convince a publisher that the material should be put into print, or because the publisher has determined that there is a need for such material.

Magazines Most magazines are designed to print recent information quickly. Sources such as *Time, Newsweek,* and *U.S. News & World Report* are published weekly, so their information is current. Researchers must be aware, however, that because these sources gather their data so quickly, some inaccuracies may occur. In addition, the editorial staffs of magazines—like the authors of books—sometimes have political and ideological biases, such as being politically conservative or liberal, that may temper what they write or influence what subjects they cover.

To find information in magazines, start with the *Readers' Guide to Periodical Literature,* a publication that indexes magazine articles by subject, title, and author. Remember, however, that not all magazines are listed in this guide. Check inside the cover of the bound volumes to see which magazines are listed. Many libraries also indicate which magazines they subscribe to so that researchers can narrow their choices to those publications. Besides using the *Readers' Guide,* you may undertake a computer search of magazine sources.

Further periodical listings may also be found in the *International Index* or in indexes to special magazines that report on particular areas, such as computers, nursing, or dental care. Business information can be found in the *Business Periodicals Index,* and educational concepts in the *Education Index;* the arts are covered in the *Humanities Index,* and psychology and sociology are in the *Social Sciences Index.*

Newspapers Newspapers, like magazines, contain current information that is published daily, weekly, or biweekly. Again, as is the case with magazines, because of the speed with which newspapers are written and printed, you must be aware of the possibility of error. In addition, understand as you read that not all parts of newspapers play the same role. News stories report events that have happened or are happening. Editorials reflect the beliefs of individual writers. These materials are not the same. News stories, it may be assumed, are based on research and facts; editorials are the opinions of the writers.

Many libraries do not keep past issues of newspapers, but some store newspaper information on microfilm. Some newspapers, such as the *New York Times,* have indexes similar in format to the *Readers' Guide to Periodical Literature.* In some libraries, computer searches for newspaper sources are possible.

On Listening

As a listener, you should be aware of how much the source of a piece of information can influence the way you perceive a message. Since individuals have differing capacities to observe and transmit information, sources may very well distort evidence, even unintentionally. Many information sources, the press, government agencies, pressure groups, and professional scholars, have biases that can limit the credibility of the information they produce.

Try to assess the biases of the information sources a speaker uses. Realize that "ideology, national or other group interest, individual self-interest, career involvement, unconscious partisanship, exile mentality, reaction against one's past, and desire for power are some of the biases which distort perception."[1]

[1]Robert P. Newman and Dale G. Newman, *Evidence* (Boston: Houghton Mifflin, 1969), p. 72.

Journals   Professional organizations often publish journals reporting research and theories in their specific fields. The Speech Communication Association, for example, publishes such journals as *Communication Education,* the *Quarterly Journal of Speech, Communication Monographs,* and *Critical Studies in Mass Communication.* Thus, students interested in finding out about some area of speech communication can refer to these journals. Similarly, students of law enforcement can find topics directly related to their field in such publications as *The Training Key,* a brochure circulated by the International Association of Chiefs of Police, and the *Journal of Law and Criminology.*

You can locate professional journals in various ways. Libraries have catalogues that list various organizations and their publications. Checking the footnotes in a textbook on the subject of interest will often give you clues to professional journals related to that field. Writing to or calling a professional organization is another way to find out about such publications.

Indexes   Encyclopedias, atlases, and bibliographical guides are all indexes that provide descriptive information in certain categories. In trying to find bibliographical material about the author Carl Sandburg, for instance, you are wise to consult *Who's Who Among North American Authors. Who's*

Who in America, another index, is also a possible source for this information.

Remember that an index gives you a minimal amount of information. Thus, if you want in-depth material about Carl Sandburg, a more fruitful approach is to search the subject index of the card catalogue or the electronic catalogue to locate such sources as *Carl Sandburg,* by G. W. Allen, and *Carl Sandburg, Lincoln of Our Literature,* by N. Callahan.

When using encyclopedias, you do well to recognize that many of them are expensive to produce and therefore are not completely reprinted each year. As a result, some material in encyclopedias may be out of date as well as limited.

Government Pamphlets

The U.S. government publishes pamphlets, available at minimal cost, on a variety of subjects. These can be found at bookstores inside federal buildings in many major cities of the United States. If there are no such outlets in your area, write to the Superintendent of Documents, U.S. Government Printing Office, in Washington, D.C., and ask for information about the specific topics you wish to research. Because it takes time for the information to be processed, plan ahead if you want to use this source. Also be aware that many libraries have government pamphlets in their research sections.

Publications from Special-Interest Groups

Special-interest groups such as the American Cancer Society, the Coalition for Rural Development, the American Chemical Society, and the American Society for Training and Development publish information regarding their research and programs. A telephone call or a letter to such an organization often brings a prompt response with the requested materials. Information about these groups can be located in the telephone book or in *Gale's Encyclopedia of Associations.*

If you use information from a special-interest group, remember that the organization has probably been founded to put forth a particular philosophy, or may have a bias because of its sponsorship or mission. For example, Planned Parenthood is an organization that provides people with birth control and abortion counseling. If you are looking for information about those topics, Planned Parenthood would be a good source; however, if you are looking for an unbiased, objective viewpoint on abortion, it probably would not be a valid source. Similarly, publications produced by Jewish organizations such as B'nai Brith, while being good sources of information about the realities of contemporary Jewish life, would not necessarily be good if you were seeking unbiased information about the Arab-Jewish conflicts in Israel.

Nonprint Media   Much information is also available from nonprint media. In fact, libraries and audiovisual departments of colleges and universities often have tape recordings, records, films, filmstrips, and videotapes from commercially and noncommercially prepared sources covering a variety of topics. These sources are usually catalogued in a manner similar to that used for books and periodicals. Some nonprint materials are available for general circulation, but others must be used on the premises.

Interviews   Researchers use interviews to find information that is not available from written or audiovisual sources or to supplement other types of research. What better way is there to find out how the budget of your college is developed, for example, than by talking to the treasurer or the budget director? Interviews can be conducted in a variety of ways. If the person you wish to interview is not available for a face-to-face or a telephone session, you can submit a series of questions to be answered either through writing or tape recording.

Here are some specific suggestions for conducting an informational interview:

Prepare for the interview. Determine what information you need. Select someone who is an expert on the topic. You can find the names of people by asking friends, instructors, or relatives about anyone they know or know about who is knowledgeable in the specific field. Consult such sources as professional directories, which are available in many libraries, and refer to the yellow pages of the telephone book. Call resource lines such as doctors' and counselors' services, governmental offices, or members of a college faculty. Call the local newspaper and talk to reporters or editorialists who may be able to lead you to an expert in the field. Prepare questions that will give you specific information that relates to your topic. Frame the questions so you get the exact material you desire. If, for example, you are interviewing a human resource manager for your speech about the nonverbal aspects of employment interviewing, you could ask, "What specific clothing should a male college graduate wear when interviewing with a Fortune 500 company?" This question would be more likely to yield useable information than the question, "What can you tell me about job interviewing?"

Make the initial contact recognizing that many people lead busy lives. Realize that people usually can't and won't drop everything because you have a speech due tomorrow. Few people will see you on the spur of the moment. Give yourself enough lead time to call or write and set up the appointment. Depending on the person and the position he or she holds, you may need to work through a secretary, an agent, or some other source to make the contact. Do not be discouraged if your first choice is

Interviews can be used to find information that is not available from written or audiovisual sources or to supplement other types of research.

not available; keep trying until you locate a viable source. Be sure when you do locate a source that you set an exact date, time, and location for the meeting. Even if the person agrees to supply information, he or she may not want to do an in-person interview. Some people prefer that you submit the questions you will be asking in advance, or might want to write their answers for you rather than be interviewed in person. If the person is going to respond in written form, include a self-addressed, stamped envelope with your questions.

Much of the success of an interview is often based on the initial contact. Be prompt, dress appropriately, have the necessary equipment you need (writing tool, paper, tape recorder with active batteries, if you plan to use one). When you enter the office, or wherever the interview is to take place, identify yourself by name and follow the greeting by introducing the topic.

Give any necessary background information. Explain to the person you are interviewing what your topic is, why you are interviewing her or him, what you expect to find out, and what you will do with the information.

Even if you have already discussed these issues when making the initial contact, you might consider going over them again to remind the interviewee.

Ask purposeful questions. You are interviewing this person because he or she has information you want. Don't waste time. Ask direct questions that elicit the specific information you are seeking. Follow up any unclear or incomplete answers by asking for specifics and examples. Ask a single question at a time, not a whole series, since multiple questions are confusing. If the interviewee gives short answers, ask for an explanation. For example, say you are interviewing an academic department chairperson about why there are fewer classes offered this semester than last, and she answers, "The budget." You might follow up by asking, "Specifically, what about the budget brought the need for the change?" Ask for examples, clarifiers, details, statistics, and illustrations so you have material to develop your speech.

Listen to what is said and how it is said. Take notes or ask if you can tape-record the interview. If you are taking notes, be sure they are accurate. To make sure you have recorded the material correctly, you may want to repeat major ideas back to the interviewee by stating, "Therefore, what you are saying is . . ."

Ask for any written material that might be available about the topic. Organizations often have materials such as pamphlets, press releases, books, or directories that they have prepared, which will make your search for information easier.

End the interview by thanking the person. Besides the personal expression of appreciation, it is also customary to send a thank-you letter to the interviewee.

⯐ 7.2 Computer Searches

Traditionally, a researcher would obtain information by going to a library and looking in the card catalogue or the *Readers' Guide* or asking the reference librarian what sources were available. Recently, however, there has been a marked change in the nature of information gathering in many libraries and on college campuses. In many libraries, computer output microfiche (COM) or **electronic catalogues** accessed through on-line computers have replaced traditional card catalogues. Because of the wide use of computers, the COM or electronic catalogues may be accessed from places outside the library. Besides COM, some libraries have their catalogues on magnetic tape that requires a special computer terminal for access.

The computer search is a **computer-based retrieval system** that allows the researcher to compile a bibliography or a set of facts relevant to a

Computer searches can pro-
vide information quickly from
a wide variety of sources.

specific topic. Searches may be used for a variety of purposes, including
gathering research or references, compiling a reading list, acquiring statistical information, or simply keeping abreast of developments in a field.
Naturally, a major advantage to this method is the time saved, as a
computer retrieves in minutes information that otherwise takes much
longer to compile. The search is also quite comprehensive and can locate
references that the most careful conventional searches may not. Another
feature is the timeliness of the material, since these data bases are frequently updated.

   Data base searching is done by the use of services from BRS Information Technologies, DIALOG, or Lockheed Corporation. These three
commercial vendors of computer services are often tied into long-
distance telephone services (TYME, TYMNET, or Telenet Communications Corporation) that allow subscribers with special equipment, usually
a modem, to search for and store information. These data bases can be
accessed from classrooms, dorms, homes, or faculty offices. A charge is
made by the minute for the use of the service.[2]

☰ 7.3   Recording Your Research

As you do your research, keep a record of where all the information
comes from so you can refer to the source to find additional information,
answer questions about the source, or give oral footnotes during a

Figure 7.2
*Recording Bibliographical
Information and Notes*

1. Tannen, Deborah. <u>You Just Don't Understand</u>.
   New York: William Morrow, 1990.

2. Bate, Barbara. <u>Communication and the Sexes</u>.
   New York: Harper & Row, 1988.

3. Pearson, Judy Cornelia. <u>Gender and Communication</u>,
   2nd ed. Dubuque, Iowa: William C. Brown, 1992.

<u>Topic</u>: Change Male-Female Communication Patterns
<u>Source</u>: 1-122

<u>Information</u>: "Habitual ways of talking are
hard to change. Learning to respect others' ways
of talking may be a bit easier. Men should
accept that many women regard exchanging
details about personal lives as a basic
ingredient of intimacy, and women should
accept that many men do not share this view."

speech. When you write a term paper, footnote **quotations** (material written or spoken by a person in the exact words in which it was presented) or **paraphrases** (someone else's ideas put into your own words). Do the same in public speaking, except orally. For example, in a speech concerning male-female communication, you might make the following **oral footnote** to present information from a source:

> Deborah Tannen, in her book, *You Just Don't Understand*, stated, "Habitual ways of talking are hard to change. Learning to respect others' ways of talking may be a bit easier. Men should accept that many women regard exchanging details about personal lives as a basic ingredient of intimacy, and women should accept that many men do not share this view."[3]

In some instances, you may also feel that it is necessary to establish the quoted author as an authority. In this case, you might preface your oral footnote by saying,

> Deborah Tannen, an internationally recognized scholar, has received grants from the National Endowment for the Humanities and the National Science Foundation and is a professor of linguistics at Georgetown University.

There are many ways to record both the bibliographical information and the notes that result from your research. As Figure 7.2 shows, one method is to use a running bibliography that lists the names of the authors, the titles of sources used, and the places, publishers, and dates of publication. The list is numbered so that you can easily refer to it when taking notes.

As you do your research and record your information, label your notes with the number of the source instead of repeatedly writing out the bibliographical material. Notes can be taken on three- by five-inch or four- by six-inch cards or on sheets of paper. Figure 7.2 shows how a typical footnote reference to the passage quoted from Tannen's book would appear on a card. The source of the quote is labeled as 1–122 (source 1 on the bibliography, page 122). Because the material is directly quoted, it has quotation marks around it. If you paraphrase material, quotation marks are not used, but it should be made clear that the material is from another source and not original to you.

If you use sheets of paper instead of cards, identify the source in the left-hand margin. Later, cut the paper into strips and arrange them as you organize your speech.

Summary

This chapter discussed the sources of supporting materials for a speech. The major concepts discussed were:

◆ The sources of information available to a speaker are personal experiences, personal observations, and accumulated learning, plus information derived from research and interviews.

◆ Research information may be found in books, magazines, newspapers, journals, indexes, government publications, and publications from special-interest groups. Additional information can be found in nonprint media and interviews.

◆ A computer-based retrieval system allows a researcher to compile a bibliography or information about a topic from a computer data base.

◆ When doing research, you should keep a record of where your information comes from.

◆ An oral footnote indicates the source of the information included in a speech.

◆ A quotation is material written or spoken by a person in the exact words in which it was originally presented.

◆ To paraphrase is to put someone else's ideas into your own words.

Key Terms

personal knowledge
outside knowledge
computer output microfiche
 (COM)
electronic catalogues

computer-based retrieval
 system
quotations
paraphrases
oral footnote

Learn by Doing

1. Select a controversial subject (e.g., abortion, mercy killing, legalization of marijuana) and identify a person who is an authority on it. Interview this person using the interviewing suggestions presented in this chapter, and then give an oral presentation to the class on the result of the interview. You should clearly state the interviewed person's stand concerning the issue and the reasons for the stand. After all the presentations have been made, a class discussion will be held on the value of the interview as a means of collecting relevant data for a speech.

2. Use the information collected from the interview in activity 1 to research the same topic. Look for the views of other authorities on the subject.

3. Find the following:
   a. The name of one book in your college library that contains information about the life of Harriet Tubman, and some information from the book using the bibliographical form explained in this chapter
   b. A magazine article about nuclear-waste disposal
   c. The longitude and latitude of Hempstead, New York
   d. Three encyclopedia notations about the White House
   e. The definition of the word *cacophony*, citing a dictionary
   f. The name of one of the journals published by the Speech Communication Association
   g. The population of the United States according to the 1990 census
   h. The birthplace of Carl Sandburg
   i. The name of a U.S. government pamphlet about the space program
   j. The gross national product of the United States in 1992
   k. The name of the person who wrote the musical *Miss Saigon*
   l. The subject matter of the play *As Is*

4. Use the format explained in the chapter to record three note cards for a speech with the purpose statement "To inform the class about the effects of the Salk polio vaccine." Two cards should have quotations, and one a paraphrase. No more than one card can come from a book.

5. Locate and footnote three sources of testimony concerning the effects of smoking on human beings.

Notes

1. See Robert Newman and Dale Newman, *In Evidence* (Boston: Houghton Mifflin, 1969), for insight into the types of bias present in many different sources of information.

2. For a discussion of computer searches, see Carolyn Wolfe and Richard Wolfe, *Basic Library Skills*, 2d ed. (Jefferson, N.C.: McFarland, 1986), pp. 113–118.

3. Deborah Tannen, *You Just Don't Understand* (New York: William Morrow, 1990), p. 122.

Structuring the Speech

Chapter Outline

Learning Outcomes

After reading this chapter, you should be able to:

Explain why it is important to carefully structure speeches.

Structure a speech to meet the needs of the listeners.

Explain what makes an effective introduction, central idea, body, and conclusion for a speech.

Give examples of attention getters for the introduction of a speech.

Identify the purpose and the various types of orienting materials.

Explain the purpose of the central idea of a speech.

Describe several different methods of issue arrangement for the body of a speech.

Describe the different ways to conclude a speech.

Identify and illustrate the various types of overall organization for a speech.

L isteners have limited attention spans, and they are always tuning in and tuning out on speakers' messages. Consequently, it is important to present a consistently structured message so that listeners will easily get back "on track" when they tune in again to the speech. In addition, most listeners have difficulty following the idea flow of a speech that does not have a clear step-by-step structure. If a speech is well ordered, the chance of its being successful increases.

In structuring your speech, you must make decisions about the type of introduction, the statement of your central idea, the method of arranging the issues in the body of your speech, and the type of conclusion to use. A well-structured speech ties together these four elements—introduction, central idea, body, and conclusion—in a unified overall organization. The three basic approaches to overall speech organization are the partitioning, unfolding, and case methods, which are discussed in detail later in this chapter.

8.1 The Introduction

The purpose of the **introduction** is to gain the listeners' attention and orient them to the material that will be presented.

Attention Material Speakers can use many types of introductory devices to gain the audience's attention, such as personal references, humorous stories, illustrations, references to the occasion or setting, rhetorical questions, action questions, unusual or dramatic devices, quotations related to the speech topic, and statements of the theme. We'll look more closely at some examples of these attention getters below.

Personal References Introductions containing personal references give the speaker's reasons for undertaking a presentation on a specific topic. For example, to introduce a fund-raising appeal, a speaker might describe his personal experience of receiving aid from the Muscular Dystrophy Association. Or a heart specialist might share her medical background and training with the audience before making comments about the health hazards associated with being overweight.

Humorous Stories Humorous stories are often an effective way to start a presentation. Make sure, though, that the humor fits the audience and the occasion, is relevant to the material that follows, and sets the desired tone. Realize that a story or joke that is quite funny in one speaking situation may be totally inappropriate in another. For example, a slightly off-color joke may be received positively in an informal speech setting but negatively in a formal speech setting.

Try to imagine how your listeners will receive humor. The purpose of the introduction is to gain an audience's attention and provide a bridge into the body of the speech. An audience is likely to believe that a humorous story told in the introduction has something to do with the topic of the speech and may become confused if the rest of the speech is not related to the story. Say, for example, a speaker begins a presentation with the following anecdote: A railroad agent in Africa had been bawled out for doing things without orders from headquarters. One day headquarters received a telegram from the agent which read, Tiger on platform eating conductor. Wire instructions. From this story an audience might logically expect the speech to be about following directions, making creative decisions, or working as a railroad agent.

Remember that humor sets a light tone. Speakers who want to give a serious presentation may have difficulty attaining a somber tone if the introduction has led the audience to anticipate something lighter. Telling a series of jokes at the start of a speech may give an audience the impression that the presentation will contain only humor. (For a more in-depth discussion of humor, see Chapter 6.)

Illustrations Illustrations in the form of stories, pictures, and physical objects help make ideas more vivid because they allow listeners to visualize the topic to be discussed. For example, a medical technician could clearly illustrate

Garrison Keillor's humorous stories about Lake Wobegon, Minnesota, have entertained listeners across the country.

the success of a new skin-grafting process for burn victims by showing slides of patient results. Similarly, a speaker who is going to talk about the need for well-equipped police cars might begin a speech with the following illustration: "Picture yourself stuck on a dark road some night with car trouble. Suddenly you see the headlights of a car. It could be almost anyone. But wouldn't you feel better if it turned out to be a police officer with all the repair equipment you needed?"

References to the Occasion or Setting

In referring to the special nature of the occasion or setting for the presentation, a speaker tries to build a strong bond, an alliance, and empathy with the audience. When this is accomplished, audience members will be responsive listeners because they will regard themselves as participants in the occasion. Speakers might refer to mutual experiences, common beliefs, or mutual needs. For example, in addressing an Independence Day company picnic, a speaker may refer to the founding of the nation and how both the speaker and the audience have benefited from the acts of our forefathers.

Rhetorical Questions A rhetorical question is a question the speaker does not expect the audience to answer directly. For example, a speaker might begin a speech on self-defense training by saying to the audience, "Have you ever asked yourself what you would do if someone tried to rob you?" In this case, the speaker does not intend to count how many audience members have or have not asked themselves this question. Instead, the speaker's purpose is to get the audience thinking about the topic and to build curiosity. Although they are sometimes overused, rhetorical questions can be an effective method of encouraging the audience to ponder a topic. Many times a speaker asks a second rhetorical question to further direct the audience's attention.

Action Questions Speakers use action questions as a means of involving audience members in the presentation and stimulating them to think and respond. For example, a speaker once started a presentation by asking, "How many of you have ever been involved in an auto accident? Will you please raise your hands?" After the hands went up, the speaker said, "For those of you with your hands up, do you remember that instant when you knew the accident was going to happen and you couldn't do anything about it?" After a pause, the speaker went on. "For those of you who haven't experienced that feeling, it's one of total helplessness." In a few brief sentences the speaker had involved the audience in a constructive way and was able to move easily into the next segment of the speech.

Unusual or Dramatic Devices Unusual or dramatic devices get the attention of the audience because of their unexpectedness or shock value. In one dramatic opening, a speaker trained as a lab technician set up equipment and drew blood from a student volunteer to show how blood is analyzed. Another speaker, in illustrating the influence of predetermined assumptions, asked for a volunteer who felt knowledgeable about rock music groups. The speaker wrote the names of three rock groups on the board and played short cuts from three songs. The volunteer identified which song was by which group. He was wrong in all three cases. The speaker stressed that she had selected pieces that were not typical of the groups, and therefore the "expert" was misled by his predetermined assumptions.

Quotations Related to the Speech Topic Speakers sometimes begin by quoting the words of a famous person, reading an account of a specific event, reciting a section of a poem or play, or reading a newspaper editorial. To introduce a presentation on the differences between the ways males and females communicate, for example, a speaker might say the following:

> Deborah Tannen is a sociolinguist on the faculty of Georgetown University. She is noted for her studies on male and female communication. In her book *You Just Don't Understand,* she states, "If women speak and hear a language of connection and intimacy, while men speak and hear a language of status and independence, then communication between men and women can be like cross-cultural communication. Instead of different dialects, it has been said they speak different genderlects."[1]

Such an introduction gains the audience's attention and indicates the general trend of the speech to follow.

Quotations must be relevant to the subject of the speech. But even when they are relevant, quoted ideas become meaningless if they are not presented effectively. The greatest mistake most speakers make in providing quotations is to read them too quickly, without stressing the appropriate words. Quotations are most effective when read meaningfully, slowly, and loudly enough to be heard. In addition, the speaker should establish the background and credibility of the source so that listeners understand the validity of the quotation.

Statements of the Theme   Many untrained speakers start out their presentations by saying, "Today I am going to tell you about . . ." Although this type of statement of theme is direct, it is not a particularly interesting or effective opener. A more creative theme statement will hold the audience's attention. For example, a mechanic started his presentation to a group of women at a YWCA by saying, "I don't like changing tires, and you probably don't either. However, if you get stuck some night on a lonely road and there's no way to call the auto club, and no one else around to change your tire, you'll probably thank me for spending the next couple of minutes telling you the five steps that can make tire changing easy."

Orienting Material

Orienting material, the second part of an introduction, is designed to give the audience the background necessary to understand the basic material of the speech. It ties in to the central idea, provides needed information, establishes personal credibility for the speaker, and demonstrates that the subject is important to the listeners. Orienting material might supply the historical background for an issue or a problem, define special terms, describe the speaker's relationship to the topic, and point out the audience's stake in the topic.

Historical Background   To present a topic fully, speakers often must explain what led up to present events. For example, a speech intended to persuade the audience to vote for a renewal of a school tax levy ought to include the pertinent facts about the history of the levy.

Definition of Terms   If special terms are going to be used during the entire speech or as the basis for the speech, the introduction is the place to define them. In a speech about agoraphobia, for example, the definition of this term (the fear of being out in public) should be given as orienting material so the audience understands it early in the presentation. This does not preclude defining other terms later. Only those terms that occur throughout the speech have to be included in the orienting material.

Speaker's Personal Relationship to the Topic   Speakers can sometimes gain credibility by describing their own personal tie to or experience with the topic. The fact that the speaker has a personal connection to the topic is of interest to most listeners. For example, a speaker intending to demonstrate the steps in mouth-to-mouth resuscitation could describe his Red Cross training and background as a lifeguard, which included lifesaving techniques. Such documentation establishes the speaker's authority to speak about the subject. If the speaker is introduced by someone who mentions this personal connection, then it is probably not necessary for the speaker to repeat it.

Importance to the Listeners   The most critical role of orienting material is to tie the subject to the listeners in some way. Listeners pay attention to ideas and issues they feel are relevant to them, so it is imperative that the speaker make that link at the outset. One good strategy is to show the importance of the topic based on the interests of the audience: "Look around you—many of you have just filed your income tax forms and wonder whether you will be audited." It may also be useful to connect the topic to a larger segment of the population to illustrate the importance of the subject both to the immediate listeners and to the general public: "The Internal Revenue Service reported that 106,853,000 income tax forms were filed in 1991. Your tax form was one of them."

≡ 8.2 The Central Idea

The purpose statement, which is designed to help the speaker prepare a speech, can also serve as the basis for developing a **central idea**—the overall point of the speech. The central idea explicitly gives the goal of the speech; at the same time, it implies what type of response the speaker wants from listeners.

If, for example, the purpose statement of a speech is "To inform the audience of the complex process employed in compiling information for *The Guinness Book of World Records*," then the central idea is "The process of collecting information for *The Guinness Book of World Records* is complex." If the purpose statement is "to persuade listeners that they should vote for the school-bond issue on November 2," then the central idea is "We should all vote for the school-bond issue on November 2." The importance of actually stating the central idea in a speech cannot be overemphasized. An audience that is not given the central idea may be frustrated and might never be sure what the exact point of the speech really is.

The central idea should be presented as a statement because a speaker who uses a question ("Should the federal government provide financial aid to private educational institutions?") is not indicating to the listeners what the main point really is. A speaker who presents the point as a statement ("The federal government should provide financial aid to private educational institutions") is clarifying which persuasive stand will be advocated. Notice also that the statement is concise and contains the overall idea.

8.3   The Body

The **body** of a message develops the major points of the speech and any subpoints that pertain to the speaker's central idea. When a speech lacks this sort of organization, listeners may become so confused that they simply give up trying to understand the message. Perhaps, for example, you had a history instructor who started a lecture by talking about the causes of World War I, then inexplicably wandered into a discussion of the marriage customs of Greece, and then commented on the Equal Rights Amendment. By the end of the class, you were no doubt confused and came away without a complete message or a well-defined idea.

To avoid confusing the audience, speakers can organize the major points and subpoints of a speech in a variety of ways. These methods of sequencing are called **issue arrangement**. The issue arrangement of a speech is dependent on two factors. One is the method of development you have specified in your purpose statement. If, for example, the purpose statement indicates that you will be developing the speech by "listing and discussing the step-by-step process of . . . ," you will probably want to use chronological issue arrangement. The second factor that determines the type of issue arrangement you use is the overall form of organization you choose for your speech. As discussed later in this chapter, the partitioning, unfolding, and case methods of organization each have patterns of issue arrangement that fit them best.

Issue arrangement can take six forms: spatial arrangement, chronological or time arrangement, topical arrangement, causal arrangement, comparison-contrast arrangement, and problem-solution arrangement. Issue arrangement for major and subordinate points may be a mixture of these forms as long as they are consistently handled.

On Listening

One of the greatest challenges facing us as listeners is to maintain concentration on a speaker's message. Because we have such limited attention spans, it is difficult, even with the most compelling speaker, to focus on a speech for any great length of time. As a result, speakers are wise to structure their messages to be readily listenable.

But the reality of our lives as public listeners is that most speakers are not readily listenable. Consequently, we must take matters into our own hands and work at concentration in order to sort through the speaker's verbal and nonverbal messages. One technique that many listeners find helpful is to identify the main points and keep a mental "flow chart" of these points as the speaker progresses. Since we listen so much faster than the normal conversation rate, we have plenty of time to recapitulate, to create mental summaries of what the speaker has said, and even to anticipate what he or she will say next.

Some listeners rely extensively on taking notes to structure their understanding of a speaker's presentation. This can assist you in focusing on the message and help you be more mentally disciplined as a listener. But note taking can distract from listening, and it is possible to rely on it too much. Do you ever listen to a friend with a pen in hand? Probably not, since you are actively paying attention to what your friend is saying! Try not taking notes as you listen to a speech. Instead, raise your energy level and work at focusing your attention on the speaker and the message. Create mental summaries as the speech develops. When the speech is over, try to summarize these points again and even write them down if necessary. Review your mental summary again later to ensure that the speaker's points are in place in your long-term memory and that you can recall and use them as needed.

Concentrating can be a challenge if the speaker isn't well organized or structures information in a format that isn't consistent with the way in which you yourself think. But developing mental discipline can improve your listening and help you recall information. As we are all required to handle vast amounts of information, this listening challenge is one we need to meet.

Spatial Arrangement

Many people organize information automatically, even though they are not aware of it. Suppose some friends of yours are visiting you at your college. They have never been on campus before, and they ask you to tell them about the institution. You start by describing the building located on the south end of the campus and then proceed to talk about all the other buildings, citing their locations from the south to the north. You have organized your presentation according to **spatial arrangement**. In other words, from a set point of reference (the southernmost building), you proceeded to explain each building in terms of its geographical location. This is a common method for giving directions, for routing merchandise in a store or factory, or for talking about where you went on your vacation.

In using spatial arrangement, a speaker sets a point of reference at some specific location and then proceeds to give directions starting from the established reference point. Thus the organization is based on keeping to a set order following a pattern: left to right, north to south, or from the center to the outside. To illustrate, spatial arrangement might be used for the body of a speech with the purpose statement "To inform the audience of the financial tax base of Ohio by examining the state from north to south." Accordingly, the body of the outline for a speech may look something like:

III. Body
    A. Northern Ohio
        1. Toledo
        2. Lorain/Elyria
        3. Cleveland
        4. Youngstown
    B. Central Ohio
        1. Mansfield
        2. Akron
        3. Canton
    C. Southern Ohio
        1. Cincinnati
        2. Dayton
        3. Columbus

The major headings in the body of this speech are developed spatially from north to south, and each of the subdivisions is developed from west to east.

Chronological or Time Arrangement

Chronological or time arrangement orders information from a beginning point to an ending one, with all the steps developed in numerical or time sequence. Recipes are often given in time sequence, for instance, as are reports of chemistry experiments or the charts of patients in a hospital. By telling what happened—or what should happen—first, second, and so on, the speaker presents a pattern that allows the audience to understand the ideas.

For example, chronological arrangement can be used to develop the body of the speech with the purpose statement "To inform the audience of the major accomplishments of the Reagan administration by identifying those accomplishments from 1981 through 1988." The outline for the body of such a speech might read:

Accomplishments of the Reagan administration
A. Accomplishments of the first term
    1. 1981
    2. 1982
    3. 1983
    4. 1984
B. Accomplishments of the second term
    1. 1985
    2. 1986
    3. 1987
    4. 1988

Topical Arrangement

A speaker who uses **topical arrangement** explains an idea in terms of its component parts. For example, a speaker might organize a talk on dogs (the general topic) by discussing cocker spaniels, poodles, and then collies (the component parts), developing ideas about each breed completely before going on to the next one. The three parts of this speech could be further organized by covering each breed's temperament, size, and coloring. In this way, the speaker would organize the ideas by classifying dogs (the general topic) according to specific identifiable characteristics (the component parts) and by developing each subsection according to an identifiable pattern of information.

Topical arrangement lends itself to certain subjects. For example, if you wanted to explain to an operating-room technologist the instruments to be used, the procedures to be followed, and the responsibilities of each member of the medical team, you would discuss all aspects of one component before proceeding to the next. To illustrate this process of organization, an outline of the main headings and subheadings of the body of a speech whose purpose statement is "To inform the audience about Siamese cats by discussing their coloring, vocal characteristics, and behavior patterns" would be:

Characteristics of Siamese cats
A. Coloring patterns
    1. Seal point
    2. Chocolate point

        3. Blue point
        4. Lilac point
    B. Vocal characteristics
        1. Does not meow
        2. Sounds like a baby crying
        3. Talks back
    C. Behavior patterns
        1. Crawls into any opening
        2. Plays with small objects
        3. Jumps onto high surfaces
        4. Likes warm surfaces
        5. Is extremely curious

Causal Arrangement

To write an accident report, a police officer uses a method called **causal arrangement**. This is the process of showing how one event made another event happen—in other words, how a cause (the first event) led to an effect (the second event). Thus, the officer would determine what series of events took place and then would demonstrate how these events caused an end result: "Car X was proceeding south on Main Street and failed to stop at the corner of Main and Canal streets for the red traffic light [*series of events—the cause*]. Car X proceeded into the intersection and was struck by Car Y [*end result—the effect*]." An alternative way to use causal arrangement is to begin with the effect (Car X was struck by Car Y) and then to explain what caused it (Car X was proceeding south on Main Street and failed to stop at the corner of Main and Canal streets for the red traffic light). This second method is a good one to use when there is a specific observable result that can be fully understood only by determining what brought it about.

    To illustrate cause-to-effect organization, the body of a speech whose purpose statement was "To inform the audience that a series of identifiable events result in the disabling fear known as agoraphobia, by listing and discussing these events" would be:

Series of events resulting in agoraphobia
A. Cause—Sequence of events
    1. First event
        a. Physical symptoms such as heart palpitations, trembling, sweating, breathlessness, dizziness
        b. No apparent cause for the physical symptoms
    2. Second event
        a. Duplication of physical symptoms in a place similar to the site of the first event
        b. Increasing awareness of fear of going to certain places

    3. Third event
       a. Symptoms occurring when person thinks of going to a place similar to the site of the first event
       b. Feeling of being out of control when thinking of leaving the safety site (usually the person's home)
  B. Effect—Agoraphobia
    1. Personality changes
       a. Frequent anxiety
       b. Depression
       c. Loss of individual character
    2. Emotional changes
       a. Impassiveness
       b. High degree of dependence on others
       c. Constant alertness

Note that this outline lists the events leading up to the final result and discusses the final result last. The alternative arrangement, called effect-from-cause organization, would give the final result first and then list the events leading up to it.

Comparison-Contrast Arrangement

Suppose a friend asks you to explain the similarities between a community college and a four-year college. Your explanation will probably follow the **comparison method** of organization, in which you would describe how two or more things are alike. You would probably talk about the similarities in curriculum, staff, facilities, activity programs, and costs. If, however, your friend asks you about the differences between the two types of colleges, you would use the **contrast method**, developing your ideas by giving specific examples of how these institutions differ. By combining these two methods into the **comparison-contrast arrangement**, you could discuss both the similarities and the differences. You might set up the body of a speech with the purpose statement "To inform the audience of some of the similarities and differences between state-sponsored two- and four-year colleges in Ohio" as:

Similarities and differences between two- and four-year state-supported Ohio colleges
A. Similarities
    1. Are governed by the Board of Regents
    2. Receive state funding
    3. Offer general studies courses
    4. Must receive permission to add new curricula
    5. Are governed by a board of trustees appointed in part by the governor

B. Differences
1. Two-year colleges: funded in part by their local communities; four-year colleges: not funded by communities
2. Two-year colleges: offer associate degrees; four-year colleges: offer bachelor's and advanced degrees
3. Two-year colleges: have certificate and two-year terminal programs; four-year schools: no certificate or two-year terminal programs
4. Two-year colleges: less expensive

Problem-Solution Arrangement

Speakers use the **problem-solution arrangement** when they are attempting to identify what is wrong and to determine how to cure it or make a recommendation for its cure. This method can be used to think through a problem and then structure a speech. A speaker discussing the problem of child abuse, for instance, may wish to begin by analyzing the problem: the influence of family history, the lack of parental control and/or knowledge, and the different types of child abuse—physical, sexual, mental, and emotional. Such an analysis may then lead to a consideration of various solutions, such as stricter legislation mandating penalties for child abuse, stronger enforcement of child abuse laws, improved reporting procedures, and greater availability of social services to parents and children alike. The key to effective problem-solution arrangement is to come up with solutions that will be workable, desirable, and practical for the people who will implement them.

An alternative form of the problem-solution method is the **see-blame-cure-cost method**. In this four-step organizing technique, the evil or problem that exists is examined (see), what has caused the problem is determined (blame), solutions are investigated (cure), and the most practical solution is selected (cost).

When you develop a message using problem-solution arrangement, always clearly state the problem, its cause, the possible solutions, and the selected solution. This allows your listeners to share a complete picture of your reasoning process. If the message is well developed, listeners will understand why the selected solution is best, how it will work to solve the problem, what it will or will not do, what the costs will be, how long it will take to work, and what is needed to implement it.

This method of organization is particularly useful for speeches that seek to confront and solve the problems of life, business, industry, and government. It can be used to decide among treatments or procedures to follow, products to buy, or machines to use. Consider, for example, this outline for the body of a speech with the purpose statement "To inform the audience why I believe that the solution to the acid rain problem is to require coal-burning companies and smelting plants to build taller smokestacks, use scrubbers, and wash their coal before using it":

Solution to acid rain problem
A. Problem
   1. Acid rain is caused by substances such as sulfur oxides and nitrogen oxides.
   2. Acid rain falls anywhere that is downwind of urban or industrial pollution.
   3. Acid rain has significant negative effects.
      a. It decreases the fertility and productivity of soils.
      b. It causes freshwater lakes and streams to become barren of fish, amphibians, invertebrates, and plankton.
      c. It deteriorates such materials as stone, marble, and copper.
      d. It affects human health through the contamination of the water we drink and the fish and wildlife we eat.
B. Solution
   1. Coal-burning companies and smelting plants should be required to build taller smokestacks to disperse the pollution.
   2. Scrubbers, traps in smokestacks that can catch 90 percent or more of the sulfur oxides emitted, should be required for all industrial users of smokestacks.
   3. All coal burned by industrial users should be washed before it is used.

A more detailed outline of this speech might include subdivisions under each of the statements of solution to explore whether it is workable (developing why the suggestion will solve or help solve the problem), desirable (explaining why the suggestion will not cause greater problems), and practical (indicating how the suggestion can be put into practice).

Here is an outline to a problem solving speech with the purpose statement "To inform why, by listing my reasons, I believe the use of a waterbed can aid in overcoming common sleeping problems":

Solution to several common sleeping problems
A. Problems
   1. Insomnia (difficulty in falling asleep)
   2. Chronic backaches
   3. Sleeping discomforts caused by pregnancy
   4. Concerns for unborn child
   5. Bedsores caused by confinement to bed
B. Solution—Use of a waterbed
   1. It increases ease in falling asleep because of flotation feeling.
   2. It has the same soothing effect as sleep-inducing drugs without the medicinal side effects.

3. It provides longer periods of sleep with less movement.
4. It eliminates sore muscles and swollen joints, thus reducing stiffness.
5. Its heat reduces tension, which reduces stress.
6. It increases comfort during pregnancy by allowing the user to lie in a stomach-down position.
7. Its flotation and heat act like a second uterus for the unborn child.
8. Even body distribution on the surface of the mattress reduces bedsores.

Arrangement for Major and Subordinate Points

Speakers usually use one method of issue arrangement for the major points, always keeping in mind that other methods may be used as necessary to present the subordinate points. For instance, in a presentation on the causes of World War II, a speaker may decide to organize the major points with a chronological arrangement and use a spatial arrangement for the subordinate points. The outline would be:

Body
A. Events in 1935
    1. England
    2. France
    3. Germany
    4. Russia
    5. Japan
B. Events in 1936
    1. England
    2. France
    3. Germany
    4. Russia
    5. Japan
C. Events in 1937
    1. England
    2. France
    3. Germany
    4. Russia
    5. Japan

No matter which pattern you select to develop the major points of your message, use that pattern consistently for each major heading. Likewise, be consistent in your handling of the subordinate points. Otherwise your audience will be confused by sudden changes or shifts in sequence and will fail to follow the presentation.

☰ 8.4 The Conclusion

Whatever the purpose of the speech, the presentation should end with
a **conclusion**, which is usually a summary and a clincher. A summary
should restate the major points of the speech so that the listener can
recap what has been covered. A clincher should leave a final message of
intent.

The Summary

The **summary** of a speech restates the main points of the body of the
speech. It is a redundancy device intended to allow the audience to hear
the important issues once again, for the last time. The simplest way to
accomplish the summary is to repeat the major points of the body in the
order in which you presented them.

The Clincher

A **clincher** is a device used to make a final appeal to the audience and
to ensure that they remember your message. Some common clincher
techniques are personal references, humorous stories, illustrations, rhetorical questions, action questions, unusual or dramatic devices, and quotations.

A *personal reference* might be appropriate for a heart specialist who
established his expertise at the start of the speech and wants to reestab-
lish his authority in the conclusion. Another speaker may find it appropriate to end the presentation with a *humorous story* that summarizes the
ideas. As mentioned earlier, humorous stories should always be appropriate to the central idea of the speech.

A young person who had become dependent on drugs might end a
speech with an *illustration* of how difficult it was for her to turn away
from the drug scene. A speaker who posed *rhetorical questions* or *action
questions* at the beginning of a presentation can conclude by answering
them. For example, the speaker who asked audience members what they
would do if they were robbery victims might restate the major alternatives presented in the message. The speaker who asked the audience
members to raise their hands if they had ever been involved in an auto
accident might summarize the experience of losing control of a car.

One speaker concluded a speech about the necessity for proper dental
hygiene by passing out a small cup of disclosing solution and a small
mirror to each member of the audience. She then asked them to rinse
out their mouths with the solution, which turns plaque and other substances on or between the teeth bright red. This activity effectively demonstrated the importance of proper brushing and the value of *unusual*

or *dramatic devices* for concluding a speech. *Quotations* can also memorably restate the major theme of a presentation. For example, a speaker might summarize a speech against the death penalty by reading the vivid description of an execution presented in Truman Capote's book *In Cold Blood*.

8.5 The Overall Organization of a Speech

The three basic approaches to overall speech organization are the partitioning, unfolding, and case methods. Whichever type of overall organization you choose, you should realize that to remember a message, listeners require repetition of key points. They do not have a chance to run through the message a second time to grasp points that were not clear originally. A reader can reread a passage, but a listener cannot relisten unless the speech has been recorded (and even then, it may not be played back immediately). Consequently, you need to be obvious in stating your main points—the central idea and the issues in the body—and in providing transitions and internal summaries that assist listeners in following the sequence of your speech.

Speakers who can build in **redundancy**, repetition of their points, can foster listening comprehension of their messages. Television commercials use the technique of redundancy by extensively repeating material to reinforce the message in the viewer's mind. Politicians use redundancy in developing campaign slogans that can be repeated at many speaking occasions.

The Partitioning Method

The **partitioning method of organization** depends on a great deal of repetition and is the most direct ordering of ideas for listeners to follow. The sequence requires adherence to this outline:

I. Introduction
    A. Attention material
    B. Orienting material
II. Central idea
    A. Statement of central idea
    B. Restatement of central idea
    C. Division (listing of issues by some method of issue arrangement)
        1. First main issue
        2. Second main issue
        3. Third main issue (and so on)

III. Body (Transition: forecast of the first issue)
　　A. First main issue
　　　　1. Discussion of first main issue through examples, illustrations, and explanations
　　　　2. Discussion of first main issue through examples, illustrations, and explanations (and so on)
　　(Transition: restatement of first main issue and forecast of second issue)
　　B. Second main issue
　　　　1. Discussion of second main issue
　　　　2. Discussion of second main issue (and so on)
　　(Transition: restatement of second main issue and forecast of third issue)
　　C. Third main issue
　　　　1. Discussion of third main issue
　　　　2. Discussion of third main issue (and so on)

IV. Conclusion
　　A. Summary (restatement of issues and central idea)
　　B. Clincher

When using this type of organization for a speech, you start with the introduction and lead into your central idea. Then you state the central idea, restate it, and divide it by listing the main issues you will cover in the order in which you will cover them. This restatement and division constitute what is called the **partitioning step**. For example, a speaker whose central idea is "there are several problems with the use of radiation therapy" may use this partitioning step: "To understand these radiological difficulties, we will look at the harmful effects of radiation therapy and the poor quality of radiation facilities in hospitals."

From the partitioning step, you move into the first issue of the body of the speech with a transition that forecasts the first issue. For example, the speaker might say, "Turning, then, to our first point, let us consider the harmful effect that radiation therapy has had." If such a direct statement may be unacceptable to listeners because of opposition to the idea, the speaker can use an indirect forecast: "We can begin with a look at the effects of radiation therapy." This forecast should lead into a discussion of the main points of the issue. Restatement is also important. As new material is added, the speaker should hold the audience's attention and clarify the main points by repeating them in different words. This enables listeners to keep the main points in mind and not to get lost in the supporting details.

When moving from one issue to the next in the body of the speech, a speaker is wise to use clear bridges between ideas. These bridges, called **transitions**, provide the listener with a connection between the points.

Thus, a good transition consists of two parts: the *restatement* of the previous issue and the *forecast* of the next one. For example, a speaker presenting a talk on marine biology provided a transition between two issues by stating, "From the evidence presented, it appears that the problems of water pollution are massive. How, then, can we tackle these problems?"

Use of the partitioning method requires careful transitions, each containing a summary and a forecast, from one issue to the next. There should be only a small number of issues in the body of the speech. The more issues developed, the longer the speech will be—and a long speech may strain the listening process. Once the last issue in a partitioned speech has been discussed, the presentation concludes with a summary that restates the central idea and the main issues. This summary gives listeners a chance to review the points that have been discussed.

Successful partitioning requires the repetition of major points. It follows this format: "I tell the audience what I'm going to tell them, then I tell them, and then I tell them what I've told them." This outline develops a speech according to the partitioning method of organization:

Purpose statement: To inform the audience of the alternatives an intake counselor has by listing and discussing the options.

    I. Introduction
        A. Attention material: Each of us probably makes hundreds of decisions every day. We decide what to eat, what to wear, what television program to watch, what time to go to bed.
        B. Orienting material: In my work as an intake counselor with the Department of Juvenile Services, I must make decisions that can seriously affect a child's life. An intake counselor gets the police report when a juvenile commits a crime, calls in the parents and the child to decide what actions should be taken, and counsels them. An investigation of such work can help you to understand some of the procedures that local governments use to combat the problems of juvenile delinquency.

   II. Statement of central idea
        A. Let us consider the alternatives an intake counselor has.
        B. The counselor can make three major decisions.
        C. These decisions are:
            1. Send the case to court.
            2. Close the case at intake.
            3. Place the child on informal supervision for forty-five days.

 III. Body
      (One decision that a counselor may make is to send the case to court.)

A. The law states that you must send the case to court if:
1. The charge is denied.
2. The juvenile has a prior record.
3. You notice signs of trouble with the family.
4. The case is like Tommy's. Tommy had been picked up for breaking and entering . . .

(Thus a case may be sent to court. A counselor may also decide to close a case at intake.)

B. There are several reasons for closing the case at intake:
1. The child admits guilt.
2. The incident was a first offense.
3. The parents are supportive and the home life is stable.
4. An example of a case closed at intake was Henrietta's . . .

(As a result, a case may be closed at intake. A counselor may also decide to put a juvenile under informal supervision.)

C. Supervision for forty-five days is warranted if:
1. The child or the family is in need of short-term counseling.
2. The procedure is not used often.
3. The court has never ordered this in the past.
4. The case is like Lynn's. Lynn . . .

(Through informal supervision, some children can be helped.)

IV. Conclusion
A. Summary: The basic decision is to arrange court appearances, stop the action at the beginning, or supervise the client.
B. Clincher: The goal of the whole intake process is to provide whatever is best for the child so that the child will have proper care, treatment, and supervision.

Even though partitioning organization can be used for a speech with any purpose, it is especially well suited to informative speaking and informative briefing. Because the aim of such a speech is to increase the listener's comprehension of a particular body of information, a clear structure and repetition of the major points are warranted.

The Unfolding Method

The **unfolding method of organization** can be used for a speech with any purpose, but if you want to persuade your listeners of something, you will find this format the most useful. An unfolding organization differs from a partitioned organization in one important way: It does not restate the central idea or include the division step. One possible sequence for an unfolding format is:

    I. Introduction
       A. Attention material
       B. Orienting material
   II. Statement of central idea
 III. Body (organized by some method of issue arrangement)
       (Transition)
       A. First issue
           1. Discussion of first issue through examples, illustrations, and explanations
           2. Discussion of first issue through examples, illustrations, and explanations (and so on)
       (Transition)
       B. Second issue
           1. Discussion of second issue through examples, illustrations, and explanations
           2. Discussion of second issue through examples, illustrations, and explanations (and so on)
       (Transition)
 IV. Conclusion
       A. Restatement
       B. Clincher

The unfolding format may be appropriate for an audience that initially agrees with the central idea and issue that the speaker plans to develop. At other times, however, a speaker may want to use variations of this format. For example, if prior analysis leads you to conclude that you are going to face a hostile audience, a group unsympathetic to your purpose statement, you will want to approach your listeners more subtly, moving from particular facts to a general conclusion. If members of the audience oppose your stand, it does not make sense to alienate them by stating your central idea early in the presentation. Instead, present the body of your speech first. Lead them through the main points, moving from areas of shared agreement into areas of controversy. If you arrange the main issues subtly and word them carefully, you may be able to establish acceptance of your purpose statement just before you reach the conclusion. This variation of the unfolding format would be:

    I. Introduction
       A. Attention material
       B. Orienting material
       (Transition)
   II. Body (organized by some method of issue arrangement)
       A. Discussion of first issue
           1. Examples and illustrations
           2. Examples and illustrations (and so on)

    B. Statement of first issue
(Transition)
    C. Discussion of second issue
        1. Examples and illustrations
        2. Examples and illustrations (and so on)
(Transition)
III. Statement of central idea
(Transition)
IV. Conclusion
    A. Restatement
    B. Clincher

For instance, if you are trying to persuade a group of people to vote for a candidate, and you know the audience is not committed to that candidate, you are wise to develop your position by stating the issues, stands, and actions of the candidate; stressing the positive aspects of your candidate; and building strong support. After establishing this argument, then state the central idea by revealing the voting action you want from the audience.

The unfolding method of organization is more flexible than the partitioning method because it lends itself to a variety of formats. For example, you can place the statement of the central idea anywhere in the speech as long as it comes before the conclusion. Your transitions do not have to restate and forecast issues; they simply have to establish clear connections. Furthermore, with this method you do not have to restate all the issues and the central idea in the conclusion. Remember, however, that a good conclusion should summarize your presentation in some way.

As a speaker, you want to maintain a clear framework for your listeners so that the speech moves forward sequentially. Remember that the speech is of no value if at the conclusion the audience does not clearly understand your central idea. This outline develops a speech according to the unfolding method of organization:

Purpose statement: To persuade each member of the audience to donate his or her body to science by listing and discussing the reasons for donation.

    I. Introduction
        A. Attention material: Picture a three-year-old girl attached to a kidney machine once a week for the rest of her life. Picture a little blind boy whose world is blackness or a father who is confined to his bed because he has a weak heart.
        B. Orienting material: Such pictures are not very pleasant. But you can do something about them.

II. Statement of central idea: You should donate your body to science.

III. Body
   A. Scientists need organs so that others may live normally.
      1. List of organs that can be donated.
      2. The need for speed in transplanting organs. (Thus specific organs can be used.)
   B. Your body can be used as an instrument for medical education.
      1. Who can donate and how.
      2. The need to eliminate shortages.
   (As a result, your entire body can continue to serve a useful purpose.)

IV. Conclusion
   A. Summary
      1. Organs are needed so that others can live normally.
      2. Your body can be used for medical education.
   B. Clincher
      1. I am a benevolent person who believes that everyone is born with a benevolent nature. I know that you and I will help those less fortunate than we are. I am a potential organ and cadaver donor through my will. A donor's card, like the one I carry, can be obtained through any medical foundation. I cannot overemphasize the need for body and organ donations.
      2. Don't, as the saying goes, wait "for George to do it." You do it! Take immediate action to become an organ and cadaver donor.

The Case Method

In some respects, the **case method of organization** is less complex than the partitioning and unfolding methods because here the speaker discusses the central idea without breaking it into subpoints. As a result, this format is especially suitable for speeches designed to amuse, entertain, or present a single issue. If, for example, your central idea is that "kids say the funniest things," then the body of a speech organized using the case method would include a series of examples of children's clever sayings connected by clear transitions. Here is the format for a speech developed by case organization:

I. Introduction
   A. Attention material
   B. Orienting material
   (Transition)

II. Central idea
    (Transition)
III. Body
    (Organized in a sequence)
    A. Example—a case
    (Transition)
    B. Example—a case
    (Transition)
    C. Example—a case (and so on)
    (Transition)
IV. Conclusion
    A. Summary
    B. Clincher

When you use case organization, be careful not to develop subpoints in the body of the speech so that they become main points in themselves. The danger of subdividing is that you may not develop each subdivided point fully, and your listeners may become confused. If, for example, your central idea is that "kids say the funniest things" and you say in one of the transitions, "Kids say funny things at school and at camp," you have subdivided your central idea into two issues.

This outline develops a speech according to the case method of organization:

Purpose statement: To inform the audience of some ways in which left-handers are discriminated against by listing some examples.
  I. Introduction
      A. Attention material: Have you ever pondered the design of a butter knife or the structure of a gravy ladle?
      B. Orienting material: These structural problems are important to all of us who are afflicted with a key social problem—left-handedness. (As a left-handed person I believe that . . .)
  II. Statement of central idea
      A. Left-handers are discriminated against.
      B. Let's look at some examples.
  III. Body
      A. Example: Tell a story of the difficulties encountered when using scissors.
      (Transition: Another experience I've had . . .)
      B. Example: Tell a story of the problems with school desks designed for right-handed people.
      (Transition: This experience points out another one . . .)

     C. Example: Tell a story about the problems with words such as "gauche" and "southpaw."

    (Transition: So you see . . .)

IV. Conclusion

    A. Summary: Left-handers are discriminated against all the way from the way items are designed to the names they are called.

    B. Clincher: To add insult to injury, recent research suggests that left-handedness may result from brain damage at birth. But, then, we're in good company. Eleven presidents of the United States have been left-handed!

A consistently structured speech is an advantage to both the speaker and the listeners. The speaker is assured of developing a presentation that is clear and that accomplishes its goal. In addition, since the speaker has taken the care to develop a sequential speech and to consider the audience and its needs, the listeners are able to easily follow the flow of ideas.

Summary

This chapter investigated the principles of structuring a message. The major ideas presented were:

◆ A public communication message is usually divided into four parts: introduction, central idea, body, and conclusion.

◆ The introduction contains the attention material and the orienting material.

◆ The central idea describes the purpose of the presentation and specifically states its main theme.

◆ The body develops the major points of the presentation.

◆ The conclusion summarizes the presentation and may also contain a motivating statement.

◆ Attention material can include personal references, humorous stories, illustrations, references to the occasion or setting, rhetorical questions, action questions, unusual or dramatic devices, quotations related to the theme, and statements of the theme.

◆ Orienting material gives an audience the background necessary to understand the basic material of the speech.

◆ Orienting material may include historical background, definition of terms, the speaker's personal relationship to the topic, and the topic's importance to the listeners.

◆ The central idea should be presented as a statement.

◆ The method of ordering the points and subpoints in the body of a speech is called issue arrangement.

◆ Issue arrangement takes one of six forms: spatial arrangement, chronological or time arrangement, topical arrangement, causal arrangement, comparison-contrast arrangement, or problem-solution arrangement.

◆ A summary restates the major points of the speech.

◆ Clinchers can include personal references, humorous stories, illustrations, rhetorical questions, action questions, unusual or dramatic devices, and quotations.

◆ The basic approaches to overall speech organization are the partitioning, unfolding, and case methods.

Key Terms

introduction	see-blame-cure-cost method
orienting material	conclusion
central idea	summary
body	clincher
issue arrangement	redundancy
spatial arrangement	partitioning method of
chronological or time arrangement	organization
topical arrangement	partitioning step
causal arrangement	transitions
comparison method	unfolding method of
contrast method	organization
comparison-contrast arrangement	case method of organization
problem-solution arrangement	

Learn by Doing

1. Your instructor asks for a volunteer and gives him or her a card that has a picture drawn on it. Each member of the class has a sheet of paper and a pencil. The volunteer tells the class how to draw the picture exactly as it appears on the card. No one is allowed to ask any questions. When the volunteer has finished giving directions, the members of the class compare their drawings with the original. After the activity, the class discusses the following questions:

   a. Would it have helped if the volunteer had given a general overview of what to draw before beginning to give directions? How does this question relate to what you have read in this chapter about the purpose of an introduction?

   b. Did the volunteer's instructions have a conclusion? How might a conclusion restating the major points have helped you?

   c. Were there any words used in the directions that caused noise to enter into the communication? What were they? How did they cause problems?

   d. Was the structure of the directions clear?

2. Do activity 1 again. This time, the next volunteer builds on the positive things the first volunteer did and makes improvements based on the discussion.

3. A speaker informs the class about an unusual topic—something about which the audience has no knowledge. Sample topics are the language of bees, the structure of a glacier, or organic architecture. Be sure the speech has a clear structure and lasts no more than five minutes. Be sure this presentation is a well-organized speech following the basic elements of speech development discussed in this chapter.

4. Select a subject that you are expert in. Present a speech to your classmates in such a way that when you finish, they too will have a thorough understanding of the topic. Take no more than six minutes to deliver it. Be sure this presentation is a well-organized speech following the basic elements of speech development discussed in this chapter.

5. Prepare a speech of no more than five minutes informing the class about a controversial theory. Sample topics are: "The Loch Ness monster exists"; "Vitamin C prevents and cures the common cold"; "Rational emotive therapy can alter behavior"; "Homosexuality is neurological"; and "Alcoholism is an inherited disease." Explain the theory and the various arguments concerning the theory. Be sure this presentation is a well-organized speech following the basic elements of speech development discussed in this chapter.

6. You are going to give a speech about your education (elementary, high school, college). The speech is to be presented to your college speech class. Write a purpose statement for the speech.
   a. Prepare an attention-getting introduction for the presentation that uses each of these introductory devices:
      1. Personal reference
      2. Humorous story
      3. Rhetorical question
      4. Unusual or dramatic device
   b. What orienting material would be needed for this speech?
   c. Write the purpose statement as a central idea.
   d. What would be the major points for the body of the speech?
   e. What would be an appropriate clincher for the speech?

Notes

1. Deborah Tannen, *You Just Don't Understand* (New York: William Morrow, 1990), p. 42.

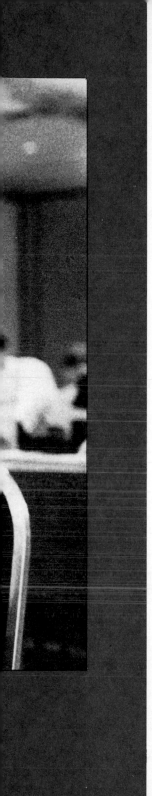

Formats for the Speech

9

Chapter Outline

**Learning
Outcomes**

After reading this chapter, you should be able to:

Identify the four modes of speech presentation.

Explain how to develop an impromptu or ad lib presentation.

Describe the advantages and disadvantages of the extemporaneous mode.

Describe the advantages and disadvantages of the manuscript mode.

List some ways of preparing effective oral language.

Describe the advantages and disadvantages of memorizing a speech.

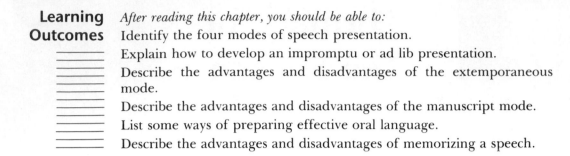

After analyzing the audience, developing a purpose statement, doing whatever research is necessary, and deciding on the supporting materials to use, speakers have to select the mode of presentation. There are four basic modes of presentation: impromptu and ad lib, extemporaneous, manuscript, and memorized.

9.1 The Impromptu and Ad Lib Modes of Presentation

In **impromptu speaking** there is very little time for preparation, and the speaker organizes ideas while he or she is communicating. Some speech theorists distinguish this mode from **ad lib speaking** in which a speaker has no time to organize ideas and responds immediately when answering a question, volunteering an opinion, or interacting during interpersonal communication. The impromptu mode gives the speaker a short period of time to decide what to say, whereas the ad lib mode requires complete spontaneity. For example, when a teacher asks a question in class and gives the students a minute or so to think of the answer, the students are using the impromptu mode.

Thus, the impromptu and the ad lib modes are both characterized by the short period of time used to prepare an answer and by the lack of or minimal use of notes. Their advantage is that they allow the speaker to appear natural and spontaneous and thereby encourage listeners to believe that the speaker is revealing his or her real feelings. Spontaneity has its costs, however. The speaker has no chance to develop an organized and well-analyzed statement or to research statistics, examples, or illustrations to explain the ideas clearly. Still another liability is the speaker's tendency to ramble or use unnecessary phrases such as "you know" and "stuff like that" to gain thinking time or gloss over nonspecific information. The lack of preparation can also result in uncertainty.

Putting together an impromptu speech requires quick work and immediate decisions. The process is the same as preparing for any other type of speech, except that there is less time to organize the material. Unless you know in advance that you are going to be asked to speak, you are not going to have the opportunity to do any research. Therefore, everything to be included must come from your own personal knowledge. As you try to organize your thoughts, keep the following in mind:

1. Ask yourself what topic you wish to present.
2. Word a purpose statement that represents the topic.
3. List the major headings that develop the purpose statement. (If paper is available, jot them down. Write these in the vertical middle of the sheet of paper so you have time to add the introduction and the statement of the central idea later. Skip spaces in between each of the major headings so that if you have time available for developing subpoints, you will be able to write them in.)
4. Arrange the major headings according to one of the methods of organization (spatial, chronological, topical, causal, comparison-contrast, or problem-solution). Use the list you developed for step 3 to jot down the order of each heading next to the item.
5. Decide on an introduction. Most ad lib speakers tend to use a rhetorical question or a reference to the theme, but often you can think of a story (an illustration), a dramatic device, or another introductory device. Because you probably will not have time to write out the whole introduction, jot down several key words so you will remember what you want to say.
6. Formulate your central idea. This should be no problem because it parallels your purpose statement.
7. The easiest form of conclusion is simply to restate the major points you made. If you can think of a clincher, all the better. (Below the list of major headings, write down several words that will remind you of the planned conclusion.)
8. If you have time, go back to see if you can think of any examples that back up the major ideas you want to present. If you have examples, write them in at the appropriate place. If not, try to think of some as you speak, making sure that you clarify or define any words that may be unfamiliar to your listeners.

In extemporaneous speaking, speakers take time to think about personal information they have that would help develop a well-thought-out speech and, if necessary, do research.

☰ 9.2 The Extemporaneous Mode of Presentation

People who know in advance that they will be giving a presentation most often use the extemporaneous mode of speaking, developing a set of aids, such as notes or outlines, to assist them in presenting their ideas. In **extemporaneous speaking**, speakers take time to think about personal information they have that would help develop a well-thought-out speech and, if necessary, do research. Teachers and clergy, for example, frequently are extemporaneous speakers.

The extemporaneous mode offers many significant advantages: enough time to structure the presentation and find the information needed to develop the central idea; the security of having notes or an outline to refer to throughout the speech; the use of quotations, illustrations, and statistics in written form for backing up ideas; the opportunity to develop solid analytical information; the opportunity to go over the materials before presenting them; and a more spontaneous and natural oral presentation and physical presentation than are likely in the manuscript or memorized mode.

Unfortunately, the extemporaneous mode has some disadvantages as well. For example, speakers who do not allow sufficient time for preparation and rehearsal may lose their train of thought during the presentation and have to grope for words. Speakers who refer to materials too frequently during the speech or have too many notes may fail to interact with the audience. Furthermore, because extemporaneous material is never written out word for word, a speaker will not have a permanent record of the speech.

To avoid having an excessive number of notes, you should limit the quantity to those needed for security without being overdependent on them. In determining just what is essential, you are wise to consider this analogy. The first time you drive to a particular site, you may need an in-depth set of directions, complete with route numbers, road markers, and indications of the exact mileage. On your second trip you need less information, and by the third trip you need almost none. So it is with your use of notes and outlines. You should have enough information to feel comfortable and free to navigate through the presentation with no fear of getting lost. The only way to discover the extent of your readiness is to take several oral test drives through your speech to ascertain how much prepared information you really need to have with you in the form of notes.

Developing a Speech Outline

As an extemporaneous speaker you need to determine if you wish to use an outline while presenting the speech. An outline helps you make sure your speech develops your purpose statement and gives you a presentational aid while you speak. Many speakers start out with a **planning outline**, a brief framework used to think through the process of the speech. It contains the major ideas of the speech, without elaboration. It is your means of thinking through the things you wish to say and putting them in a structural order. A sample planning outline is:

Purpose statement: To inform the audience about organ transplants by discussing the parts of the human body that are commonly donated, the need for donations, who can donate, and the process of becoming a donor.

I. Introduction
   A. Attention getter—story of Debbi, who died in an accident
   B. Orienting material
      1. Definitions of organ donor, transplant
      2. History of donations
II. Statement of central idea—parts of the human body that are commonly donated, the need for donations, who can donate, and the process of becoming a donor

III. Body
    A. Parts of the human body that are commonly donated
    B. Need for donations
    C. Who can donate
    D. The process of becoming a donor
IV. Conclusion
    A. Restatement—parts of the human body that are commonly donated, the need for donations, who can donate, and the process of becoming a donor
    B. Clincher—contribution of Debbi and her family

At this point you will need to decide whether you are going to proceed with generating a **developing outline**, which expands the planning outline by adding the details that will flesh out the speech. You will need to add the attention getter and orienting materials; expand the major topics of the body with examples, illustrations, and analogies; determine the internal summaries and forecasts; list the major ideas for restatement; and settle on the clincher. In order to do all this, it helps to know the form for constructing an outline and some general rules that relate to the format.

The purpose of the outline format is to interconnect the various parts of a speech. Traditionally the outline contains Roman numerals for major headings, and letters and numbers for subordinate points.[1] The format is:

I. Major heading
    A. Major point   (level 1)
        1. Subordinate point   (level 2)
            a. Subordinate point   (level 3)
                (1) Subordinate point   (level 4)
                    (a) Subordinate point   (level 5)

There is controversy over the general principles of outlining etiquette. Experts espouse "rules" that they feel must be followed. Others disagree with those regulations. If you are presenting the speech in an academic setting, the course instructor will probably give you specific rules for outlining. Here are some generally accepted, but not universally agreed on, suggestions for developing a speech outline.

1. *Block information on your paper for clarity of ideas.* One of the major fears speakers have is that they will get lost in the middle of the presentation. In order to avoid this possibility, use consistent indenting in your outline, so that each major head is flush with the left margin, each major point is indented five spaces, each level 2 subordinate point is indented ten spaces, and so on. If you use this form you should be able to visually find your place as you proceed through the

speech. Note the consistent indenting used in the outlines presented in this text.

2. *On the outline, use sentences, phrases, words, or a combination of sentences, phrases, and words.* As a speaker you will need to determine what you desire to have in front of you while you speak. If you feel most comfortable writing whole sentences on your outline, then do so. Be careful, however, that you don't put down so much material that you read rather than speak to the audience, or get lost in the reams of material. Some speakers like to write out their introduction and conclusion in sentence form, include the text of quoted materials, and use phrases and words for the rest of the outline. Some speakers, wishing to ensure that they speak rather than read, use only short phrases or words on the outline to clue them to their next idea. Though some sources will advise you to use only sentences or only phrases, your comfort and the usability of the materials should dictate what form you decide on.

3. *Use parallel wording for the major points of the body of the speech.* One purpose of the outline is to allow you to be sure your ideas cover the topic sufficiently and are all given equal weight. Word your major points so the relationship among your ideas is clear. For example, using the planning outline for the speech about organ donations, parallel wording for the main points would be:

    A. The most commonly donated human organs
    B. The need for donations of human organs
    C. Who can donate human organs
    D. The process of becoming an organ donor

    All these major points clearly relate back to the purpose statement and develop the major theme of the speech.

4. *Use subordinate points to support the preceding major point.* The purpose of subordinate points, at any level, is to flesh out the preceding idea by adding clarifiers, examples, illustrations, analogies, or quotations. Some outlining purists contend that "for every A there should be a B and for every 1 there must be a 2." In general, this makes sense. If you are subdividing an idea, or breaking it into parts, then by definition you must have at least two subideas. This does not mean, however, that if you are supporting an idea with an example you must have two examples. Again, the important thing to remember is that the purpose of an outline is to help you develop a clear and organized speech.

5. *Decide whether to include speech structure labels.* The planning outline for the speech about organ donations indicates the formal segments of the speech (introduction, central idea, body, conclusion, and each subordinate heading). Many speakers prefer this, as it helps

them keep track of where they are in the outline and make sure that all the necessary parts of the speech are present. If these headings are distracting to you, you may choose to omit them in the final outline you take before the audience as your presentational aid.

6. *Include internal summaries and forecasts.* Many speakers use an **internal summary**, which summarizes each major point before proceeding to the next major point, and make transitions in the form of **forecasts**, which tell the listener what is coming next. Speakers who wish to do this often write out their summaries and forecasts and place them on the outline in brackets between one major point and the next. For example, here is how the first major point of the speech on organ donation would appear with an internal summary and a transition:

III.   Body
   A.   The most commonly donated human organs
      1.   Cornea
      2.   Kidney
      3.   Heart
      4.   Lungs
      5.   Pancreas
      6.   Liver
      7.   Bone
      8.   Skin
      (Internal summary: The parts of the human body that are commonly donated are the cornea, kidney, heart, lungs, pancreas, liver, bone, and skin.)
      (Forecast: Let's now examine the need for these tissues and organs.)
   B.   The need for donations of human organs

Again, if you find the speech structure labels "internal summary" and "forecast" distracting, you may want to leave them out.

7. *Write notes in the margins to remind yourself of necessary information.* Some speakers like to alert themselves to things as they speak. For example, if you tend to speak rapidly, you might want to write "Slow Down!" in the margin in red ink. If during practice you keep forgetting to show the chart you want to use, indicate in the margin the point at which you want to display it. Though marginal notes are not an official part of the outline, they are yet another device to make the speech effective and to help you feel comfortable and gain confidence.

Practicing with the Outline

Preparing your **presentational outline**, the material you will take before the audience as your presentational aid, is among the final steps in polishing your speech. After you have completed the developing outline, practice using it. You may find that there is too much material or so much detail that you get lost in all the words. You may find that you know the material fairly well and don't need lengthy outline entries.

As you practice, cross out unneeded material and add necessary ideas. When you feel comfortable—the speech is about the right length and you are speaking easily with the amount of material you have— transcribe the presentational outline. Practice with it to make sure it is right and write down any marginal notes you need. At this point you are prepared to give an extemporaneous speech.

≡ 9.3 The Manuscript Mode of Presentation

Usually speakers adopt the extemporaneous mode because it allows them to interact freely with the audience and adapt to feedback. There are times, however, when a speaker finds it necessary to prepare an exact word-for-word presentation—for example, when the speaker will be quoted, must meet specific time requirements, or must have exact word selection. A business executive who makes a statement for the company, a police officer who reports an arrest of importance to the community, a nurse responsible for reporting the condition of a patient—all must be sure their statements are exact.

Some people find it necessary to hand out copies of their speeches to the newspaper, radio, and television media for reproduction after the oral presentation. This is true for political candidates as well as labor representatives and the officers of boards of education and corporations. In all these cases, the material these speakers present must be quoted word for word. Similarly, radio and television announcers write down their exact remarks so they can fit their presentation into precise time slots. Speakers who have been asked to talk for only a certain predetermined time at a meeting or conference also find it useful to script their presentations.

In the **manuscript mode** of delivery, the material is written out and delivered word for word. This mode of speaking has the advantage of providing accurate language, solid organization, and a permanent written record of the speech. But this mode also has some disadvantages. It is very difficult for a speaker who reads from a manuscript to adapt the speech during the presentation to suit the audience. As a result, the speaker is very dependent on prior audience analysis. Another problem with the manuscript mode of delivery is that it requires the ability to read effectively from the written page. A good manuscript speech should be conversational and animated, and the speaker should use extensive eye contact, vocal inflections, and physical actions to maintain rapport with listeners.

One method for establishing eye contact with the audience while following the manuscript in an unobtrusive way is called **eye span**. This involves training your eyes to glance down quickly, allowing you to pick out a meaningful phrase and deliver it to the audience. As you reach the end of the phrase but before you have finished saying it, glance down again and grasp the next phrase to say. (It is helpful, in using eye span, to underline key words and mark off phrases.) Television newscasters who do not have a TelePrompTer available often use this method to maintain contact with viewers, looking into the camera as they speak.

Adjusting from a Written to an Oral Style

Effective manuscript presentation requires an effective oral style. Remember that writing a speech for the listening ear is quite different from writing an essay for the reading eye. Because your listeners will hear your words only once, your choice of language, materials, and structure must be designed to achieve instant understanding. To understand this, find an essay that you wrote for English class and read it aloud. You will probably discover that it sounds stilted because of its complex sentences and other features of written language style. For example, a phrase such as "as seen above" may be perfectly acceptable in writing, but in a speaking situation it may cause the audience to look at the ceiling.

Even though written language and spoken language are meant to develop the same ideas and to accomplish similar communication objectives, there are some distinct differences between the uses of the language and the form in which the language is presented. Therefore in preparing a speech in which you are going to use a manuscript, you must be sure to prepare the material as spoken, rather than written, language. One is meant for the ear and the other for the eye.

Preparing the Manuscript

Effective oral language is designed for instant intelligibility by the listener. Unlike the reader who has the opportunity to reread a passage, the listener has only one opportunity to receive, understand, and interpret the oral message unless he or she has used an audio- or videotape recorder and can replay passages for review. When composing something that will be heard, rather than read, you must write as though you are speaking, not reading. To do this, write the way you would talk, say the material aloud as you are writing, and practice reading the material aloud. In addition, be aware of these pointers:[2]

1. *Use the active voice, not the passive voice.* ("The manager wrote the report" rather than "The report was written by the manager.")

Profile: Brendan Sullivan, *attorney*

"Every moment of glory in the courtroom is the product of hundreds of hours of hard work."

For trial lawyer Brendan Sullivan, as this comment suggests, there is absolutely no substitute for painstakingly thorough preparation. Unlike speakers who simply preach "practice, practice, practice," Sullivan unwaveringly preaches "first, prepare, prepare, prepare!" In other words, practice is useless—particularly in the courtroom—until you have mastered your material.

For speakers, hard work and uncompromising preparation will likely be read by an audience as confidence—and confident speakers are convincing speakers. Sullivan, a graduate of Georgetown University Law Center and a familiar TV face during Oliver North's Iran-Contra trial, rigorously follows his own advice, spending hours—often at night and on weekends— readying his cases. The result of his dedication? Not one of his clients since 1973 has gone to jail. Not one.

Sullivan's outwardly mild-mannered appearance belies the impassioned eruptions he sometimes allows to surface in the courtroom. The intensity of his words and delivery helps show judges and jurors his sincere, steadfast belief in the arguments he presents. Though Sullivan is convinced that preparation is of the utmost importance, he would never sacrifice skillful delivery. In court, he seeks a delicate balance in which he can sway his audience's emotions while maintaining his credibility.

"Do not read to your audience," Sullivan advises. A flat, lifeless recitation of text prevents you from connecting and relating to your listeners. It's also boring. (Besides, speakers should be so well prepared that a simple outline provides all of the prompting they need.)

The seemingly basic ability to effectively deliver a spoken message is, in fact, a skill to be honed in oneself and respected in others. This fact Brendan Sullivan understands.

2. *Keep sentences short.* The reading eye cannot comprehend a sentence much more than 17 to 20 words long. The listening ear has an even shorter attention span.

3. *Amplify rather than describe.* Long descriptions are boring to listeners; instead, show them your point in a brief verbal or even a visual segment. Use supplementary aids if they are appropriate.

4. *Use short, simple words.* Remember that while readers have the privilege of going over your material again, listeners do not have that option.

5. *Use repetition.* Memorable speakers are those who repeat words and phrases stylistically. They have realized that it sometimes takes more than one hearing for the receiver to grasp their meaning.

6. *Write to reflect your audience's personality.* Adapt your word choice and style of language to your listeners.

7. *Write for one member of the audience.* A good way to personalize your manuscript is to think about one person as you put it together.

8. *Avoid abstract language.* Keep your language concrete and clear. Avoid using vague or technical terms that the audience may not understand.

9. *Avoid referent problems.* Be careful not to use the pronoun "they" to refer to one person. Also, be very specific as to the referent for a pronoun. If you mention one man's name and then another man's name, do not use "he" to refer back to one of them. The audience may become confused about which person you are referring to.

10. *Watch the context of your sentence.* Planned humor is an excellent device to get and hold attention, but unplanned humor that emerges from the way sentences are worded can be embarrassing.

11. *When you are finished, stop.* A short, to-the-point presentation often has the greatest impact. The classic example of this is Lincoln's "Gettysburg Address," which was only three minutes long.

12. *Avoid using "you" when referring to yourself.* If audience members are expected to apply the material to themselves, then "you" is appropriate, but if the reference is to an experience you yourself had, or to something you are going to do, then use "I."

13. *The word "we" is more involving than the word "you."* Because saying "we" gives the audience the idea that you are including yourself, it establishes a common bond between you and your listeners.

14. *Unless precision is absolutely necessary, round off any numbers you use.* It is difficult to comprehend a number such as $1,124,569.68. Rounding this off to "a little more than $1 million" makes it much easier to grasp.

15. *Avoid using words and phrases not intended for listening, including phony fancies and verbs turned into nouns.* Phony fancies are fuzzy words or expressions a speaker might use in order to sound important, impressive, or knowledgeable. A few examples include "for the purpose of finding" rather than "to find"; "in reference to," "of the order of magnitude," or "pertaining to" rather than "about"; "prior to" rather than "before"; and "procure" rather than "get." Some expressions that start out as verbs end up as nouns if you add too many words. Examples include "he tends," which becomes "he exhibits a tendency to"; "I appreciate," which becomes "allow me to express my appreciation"; and "let us consider," which becomes "let us take into consideration."

16. *Be appropriate.* Language must be adapted to the components of communication—the speaker, audience, topic, and occasion. Build your speech with language you are comfortable using. The purpose of language is to convey a message, not impress the audience. The use of "big" words, technical terms, and acronyms to represent ideas may give the impression that you are well versed in the subject, but

if the audience fails to understand the message, the end goal of the presentation—understanding—is lost. Your strategy in word selection centers on analyzing the components of the speaking situation and selecting words that best convey the message orally.

17. *Be clear.* Clarity is based on the selection of simple, specific expressions—words that allow for understanding because they are aimed at the audience's level of knowledge. To achieve clarity, do not speak down to the audience, but use language the audience understands. Compare the following pairs of statements in terms of ease of understanding:

    a. A joyful feeling of contentment is not a commodity that can be obtained through the normal channels of currency exchange.
       Money can't buy happiness.
    b. A basic writing implement, used judiciously, has the potential for greater impact than an ancient, double-edged weapon.
       The pen is mightier than the sword.

    In addition, clarity is achieved through the use of a grammatical style that does not confuse. What is really meant by each of these church-pulpit announcements?

    > This being Easter Sunday, we will ask Mrs. Johnson to come forward and lay an egg on the altar.

    > This afternoon there will be a meeting in the north and south ends of the church, and children will be baptized at both ends.

18. *Use phrases that are easily remembered.* Many memorable phrases are clear ideas with profound meanings that were expressed with simplicity. Two examples of such messages are President Franklin Delano Roosevelt's appeal for national unity in the face of the Depression of the 1930s when he said, "We have nothing to fear but fear itself," and John F. Kennedy's inaugural call for a national referendum of dedication when he said, "Ask not what your country can do for you; ask what you can do for your country." Many bumper stickers and highway advertising signs express ideas in catchy phrases by employing in a few well-chosen words: "Born to Shop," "Save the Whales," and "If You Can Read This, Thank a Teacher."

19. *Be vivid.* Vividness is the use of words that express forceful ideas and that create an emotional or sensory experience for the listener. Advertisements that stress "lemon scents," "fluffy softness," and "bone-chilling cold" create vivid sensory images. Vividness allows the audience to become involved in the ideas being expressed. Selecting words or images that incite strong emotions creates vividness. For example, a commercial against drug use showing a dead body in a morgue, an identification tag hanging from one toe, followed by a voice stating, "Drugs kill!" presents a vivid message.

It takes considerable experience to retrain your writing style so you can produce a speech that is appropriate for the listening ear. Just because you are a great writer does not mean you can prepare a great speech. Indeed, great prose writers often do not make great speech writers because, as one expert noted, "Public speaking must be recognized as a separate art. . . . The words may be the same, but the grammar, rhetoric and phrasing are different. It is a different mode of expression—a different language."[3]

9.4 The Memorized Mode of Presentation

In the **memorized mode**, a speech is written out word for word and is then committed to memory. Public speakers seldom use this mode of communication because it is potentially disastrous. After all, even if the speaker commits the information to memory, forgetting any one idea can lead to forgetting everything. Whereas speakers who use the extemporaneous or the manuscript mode can refer to information, those who memorize their speech have no notes available for reference. Furthermore, memorizers may be so concerned about getting the exact word in exactly the right place that the meaning of the words becomes secondary.

The few advantages of the memorized mode include the ability to select exact wording and examples, to look at the audience during the

An important point about listening is that we shouldn't always think in terms of "listen to." "Listen with" is also a significant part of the experience.

A speaker's listeners interact with one another as well as with the speaker. The listeners' interactions should be a meaningful part of the communication process and a source of satisfaction and growth. Couples, or groups of friends, often enjoy attending speech events together and then discussing their individual responses. Indeed, "listening with" other people can be a true growing experience as you come to understand more about yourself and how you respond and more about your listening partners.

Recognize that each individual has a different listening style, just as each speaker has a different speaking style. It is interesting to consider why your listening style and, indeed, listening preferences may be so different from those of your listening partners.

entire speaking process, and to time the presentation exactly. For this reason, some speakers like to memorize their openings and closings to ensure that they can comfortably get started and finished. But the manuscript mode provides these same advantages and is less fraught with danger. Thus the disadvantages of memorized speaking usually so overshadow its advantages that few people choose to use this mode.

Summary

This chapter examined the formats for speeches. The major ideas presented were:

- The speaker can use four basic modes of presentation: impromptu or ad lib, extemporaneous, manuscript, and memorized.
- Impromptu speaking requires you to present your ideas with little preparation.
- Ad lib speaking allows you no time to prepare.
- In the extemporaneous mode of speaking, you develop a set of speech aids, such as notes or an outline, to assist during the presentation.
- In the manuscript mode of delivery, you write the material out and deliver it word for word.
- In the memorized mode, you write the speech out word for word and then commit it to memory.

Key Terms

impromptu speaking
ad lib speaking
extemporaneous speaking
planning outline
developing outline
internal summary

forecasts
presentational outline
manuscript mode
eye span
memorized mode

Learn by Doing

1. The class sits in a circle. The instructor throws a ball to someone in the circle and then passes an envelope to the same person. The person selects one of the statements from the envelope, takes several minutes to prepare, and gives a two-minute presentation on the topic. But before speaking, the first person tosses the ball to someone else, who will be the second speaker. While the first person is speaking, the second person selects a topic and prepares a speech. Each speaker, in turn, tosses the ball to the next speaker. This pro-

cess continues until all members of the class have spoken. The envelope may contain these statements:

a. "I did something that I was proud of."
b. "I made a promise and I kept it."
c. "I believe that college is necessary."
d. "The thing I like best about my college job is . . ."
e. "The thing I like least about my college job is . . ."
f. "The person I respect most is . . ."
g. "The place I visited that I liked most was _____ because . . ."
h. "If I had $1 million, I would . . ."
i. "If I had three wishes, they would be . . . and I would . . ."

2. Most of the time when you give impromptu speeches you know about the topic a little bit ahead of time. To practice impromptu speaking, list on a three- by five-inch card three topics you think you could speak about for a minimum of two minutes. Your instructor will collect the cards and select one of the topics for you to give an impromptu speech on. You will have two minutes to get ready. You may use any notes you can prepare within that time.

3. Prepare a speech of three to five minutes using the extemporaneous mode. Choose a subject you feel strongly about (a pet peeve, a belief that someone holds that you cannot accept, a political candidate you support, etc.). All students will present their speeches on the same day. On that day, the class is divided into groups of three to six. Present your speech to the other members of your group. After all the presentations, each listener makes two positive comments about the first speaker's presentation and suggests one improvement. The second speaker's presentation is then discussed, and so on. After this practice day, you will each present your speech to the class as a whole. Before the whole-class presentation, adjust your presentation according to the analysis your group members have given you.

4. The instructor brings to class a shopping bag filled with miscellaneous items (a comb, an eraser, a panda bear, a feather, a ball, a block, and so on). The class is seated in a circle. The bag is handed to one student, who reaches into it without looking and pulls out an item. The instructor reads one of the following statements and gives the student about one minute to think, and the student gives a speech of at least two minutes.

a. "I would like to be a (name of the object) because . . ."
b. "I would not like to be a (name of the object) because . . ."
c. "(Name of the object) reminds me of a time in my life when I found myself . . ."
d. "The (name of the object) I removed from the bag is similar to (name of another object) because . . ." It is different because . . ."

Alternatively, a student could choose an item and prepare a speech while the preceding person speaks. This will necessitate a delay while the first speaker prepares, but after that each person gets as long to prepare as the preceding speaker talks.

Notes

1. Andrew Wolvin, *Effective Speechmaking* (Washington, D.C.: Transemantics, Inc., 1977), p. 20. For an in-depth discussion of outlining formats, see Stephen D. Body and Mary Ann Renz, *Organization and Outlining: A Workbook for Students in a Basic Speech Course* (Indianapolis: Bobbs-Merrill, 1985).

2. Judson Smith, "Writing for the Eye and Ear," *Training* (March 1981), 67–68.

3. Louis P. Nizer, as quoted in Jerry Tarver, *Professional Speech Writing* (Richmond, Va.: Effective Speech Writing Institute, 1982), p. 100.

Oral and Physical Presentation

10

Chapter Outline

Learning Outcomes

After reading this chapter, you should be able to:

Clarify how to read from a manuscript.

Identify some oral and physical factors that lead to an effective presentation.

Use visual aids in a presentation.

Define *speechophobia* and identify some ways of dealing with it.

People who have captured their listeners' attention are apt to share certain qualities. These include confidence and ease, authority, conviction, credibility, sincerity, warmth, animation, enthusiasm, vitality, intensity, concern, and empathy. They also make effective use of eye contact, conversational tone, variety of pitch, pacing, projection, and phrasing.[1] For example, regardless of whether they approved of his politics, speech analysts generally agreed that early in his administration Ronald Reagan established himself as an effective communicator, a skill that helped him get some of his programs passed against great odds. As one critic observed, "He has a style that doesn't interfere with the content, and he seems to be able to make his listeners sit up and take notice."[2]

10.1 Verbal and Nonverbal Style

The listenable speaker is one whose presentation is readily received and understood by the listeners. The qualities that constitute you as a speaker—your verbal and nonverbal communications—represent your **speaking style**. Every individual's speaking style is distinctive and communicates much about the speaker as a person. Think of someone you know who is a public speaker—a politician, a religious leader, a teacher or professor. What is it that allows you to identify this person's distinctive speaking style? Usually it is the sound of the voice, the words chosen, the gestures and body positions. A **listenable speaker style**—a way of presenting material that commands audience attention—has three important qualities: clarity, conciseness, and colorfulness.

Clarity is clearness. Your selection of words and phrases should communicate your intent and be understood by listeners. Sometimes it is easy to get wrapped up in technical jargon, slang, and imprecise wording that confuses audience members if they do not have the same background as you. Remember, if the message is important enough for you to be taking the time to give it, then you need to select wording that enables the listener to receive it. Speakers who use abstract, unclear, undefined terms are practically asking the audience not to listen, and intentionally or unintentionally ensuring that the message will not be understood. For example, a speaker who presents an informative briefing on future campus development and refers to traffic jams as "pedestrian-vehicular conflict" is not being clear. A business major who gives a speech about "MBOs" and never defines the term will lose the audience's attention.

It is important to explain unusual terms, especially if your audience analysis shows that your listeners may not be familiar with the vocabulary. For example, in a persuasive presentation about the role individuals could play in saving our nation's forests, one speaker realized that his audience had little background in forestry. He offered a definition of the term *duff* in his orienting material, since the term would appear several times during the presentation. It helped the audience to know that "duff" is the layer of decaying pine needles, leaves, and branches that fall and collect on the ground in the forest.

Likewise, a speaker should strive for nonverbal clarity. Gestures, facial expression, and vocal inflections should enhance the presentation and reinforce the verbal message. A speaker trying to persuade listeners to attend a rally in favor of university tuition reform will fail to get the audience involved if the material is presented in an orally flat manner, with little facial enthusiasm, and few gestures. How we say something has a great deal of effect on how the listener receives the message.

Language that has **conciseness** is specific and to the point. Historically, speakers went on for hours. This is not the case today. Partially because of the influence of television, which presents and solves problems in half-hour time slots, including commercials, many listeners have become conditioned to brief, tightly organized messages. It is important, therefore, to get to the issues and make your points quickly. This lesson has been well learned by political speakers, who boil down their messages in an effort to create **sound bites**, 15- or 30-second messages that communicate the theme or main point of an entire speech. In his 1988 presidential campaign, George Bush's "No new taxes" was a tiny sound bite that became the major message of his campaign.

A speaker's nonverbal dynamics should also be concise. Vocal hesitations ("um," "uh," "er") and vocal fill-ins ("you know," and "stuff like that") do nothing to clarify the message, but do a lot to distract the listener. In the 1992 presidential campaign, candidate Paul Tsongas spoke haltingly, with a flat oral pitch, and slow pace. He was tagged as "boring," and this, probably more than anything else, caused him to find it necessary to withdraw from the race. Though his message may have been appealing, his slow measured pace turned listeners away.

Profile: Sandy Linver, *president, Speakeasy Inc.*

"The most effective speakers—the ones you sit up and listen to—are those who take the risk of being themselves."

In 1973, with this idea as a foundation, Sandy Linver started Speakeasy Inc., a consulting firm with offices in Atlanta and San Francisco that teaches speaking skills to business and professional people. The company's mission reflects her strong belief that "effective speaking doesn't depend on magic formulas or mechanical techniques. It depends on each individual's willingness to reach inside for the best of himself or herself and to reach out to share that with the audience." Linver is the author of two books, *Speak Easy: How to Talk Your Way to the Top* and *Speak and Get Results.*

What does Speakeasy offer its clients? "Whether it's a seminar or a consulting project, a speech rehearsal or a workshop, our goal is to give each individual we work with the skills and support to make the most of a communication situation." With its tantalizing array of workshops, private coaching and consulting services, and seminars, Speakeasy attracts an impressive list of clients, including IBM, The Coca-Cola Company, Arthur Andersen, and Gannett Broadcasting. Speakeasy offers programs with such fascinating and practical titles as "Talk So People Listen," "How to Face an Audience Without a Tranquilizer," and "Take Charge of the Q & A."

Crucial issues in contemporary organizational communication leap from the pages of Speakeasy's promotional literature:

◆ Data don't communicate. People do.

◆ You know you're better than your competition. But has your market got the message?

◆ Leaders not only have a vision—they have the ability to communicate their vision to those who can help make it a reality.

◆ Developing communication skills does more than grow your bottom line. It also grows your people.

This company does not mass-produce communicators. Its seminars and workshops are rigorous and intensely personal, and often are limited to as few as ten people per class. Using a variety of tools such as videotaping, coaching, critiquing, discussion, and written feedback, Speakeasy earns high marks for improving business communication in the boardroom, among workers, with customers, and with the media.

Colorfulness is language that helps the listener visualize the speaker's message. A good speaker tries to create word pictures that enhance the listening experience. Martin Luther King, Jr.'s "I Have a Dream" speech has become a lasting example of an effective speech because of the color of the language selected. This speech is also memorable for the gesture and vocal inflection style of the speaker. The Reverend Jesse Jackson in his oft-quoted "Rainbow Coalition" speech, used vivid language to make his point:

> Young America, dream. Choose the human race over the nuclear race. Bury the weapons and don't burn the people. Dream of a new value system. . . . Dream of lawyers more concerned about justice than a judgeship. Dream of doctors more concerned about public health than personal wealth. Dream of preachers and priests who will prophesy and not just profiteer. . . .[3]

How much more colorful this wording is than "We have to change our ways, get a new value system, and be responsible."

Now you might be thinking, "I'll never have to give that kind of speech." No, your words may never become national treasures, but the way in which you present your class speech, or a speech to co-workers or the local city council, can have as much effect, in its own way, as any national or international speech. If a speech is worth giving, every effort should be made to make it as effective and meaningful for the listener as possible. A listenable speaking style will help you do this and is a valuable skill for all communicators to work to develop.

10.2 Vocal Delivery

Audience members often have to be enticed to actively participate in a speech. They will tend to listen with attention when the speaker is dynamic and enthusiastic. The vocal elements of communication are pitch, volume, rate, quality, animation, and pause. **Pitch** is the tone of sounds, ranging from high (or shrill) tones of soprano to low (or deep) tones of bass. **Volume** is the fullness or power of the sound, ranging from loud to soft, and **rate** is the speed at which words are spoken. (Most people speak about 150 words per minute, the equivalent of one-half to two-thirds of a double-spaced, typewritten page.) **Quality** is the characteristic tone of a speaking voice, and **animation** has to do with the liveliness of the presentation. A **pause** is a temporary stop or hesitation. All these elements set the vocal level of speech.

A well-prepared speech can be enhanced by effective vocal delivery, but it can also be diminished by poor delivery. Speaking in a monotone—a flat, boring sound resulting from constant pitch, volume, and rate—or with a shrill pitch (much like fingernails dragged across a blackboard) will eventually cause the audience to tune out. Another distracting vocal trait is speaking at so rapid a rate that listeners cannot follow the ideas. Speakers who have a nasal sound to their voice or who speak too softly or too loudly may also have trouble keeping their audiences interested. Some people have physical problems that prevent them from articulating words correctly; others have extremely high or low vocal pitches or unpleasant tonal qualities. These problems can all be addressed by a speech therapist. Most aspects of vocal delivery, however, are skills that students in the communication classroom can develop on their own.

For example, if your vocal presentation lacks variation in pitch, try to raise and lower your voice as you speak. You can do this by tape-recording a presentation several times, trying different varieties of pitch. Follow the same procedure to correct speech that is too fast or too slow. Even if you do not think you have any vocal problems, tape-recording is an excellent way to observe your style of delivery. Remember, however, that sitting down with a tape recorder and speaking into it will not give you as accurate a tool for assessment as will using the recorder in a natural speaking setting. Once you have an accurate recording, ask yourself whether *you* would enjoy listening to you as a speaker. If the answer is yes, go right on fascinating people with your dynamic animation. If the answer is no, identify the vocal elements you have problems with and concentrate on making changes to correct them. If you feel incapable of adjusting your vocal delivery on your own, seek advice from your speech instructor.

⹀10.3 Pronunciation

As one observer has written, "To **pronounce** means to form speech sounds by moving the articulators of speech—chiefly the jaw, tongue and lips. There are many different and acceptable ways of pronouncing American English, because our language is spoken differently in various parts of the United States and Canada."[4] **General American speech**, defined as that spoken by well-educated Americans and Canadians of the central, midwestern, and western regions of North America, tends to be the most acceptable of the regional dialects. Nevertheless,

> speech in general and pronunciation in particular are appropriate if they are consistent with the objectives of the speaker in his/her role of communicator of ideas. The listeners, the occasion, and the speaker as a personality are some of the factors that determine appropriateness. Speech becomes substandard if the pronunciations are such that they violate the judgments and tastes of the listeners.[5]

Because your audience will evaluate you not only on the basis of what you say but also on how you say it, you should be aware of some common pronunciation problems and their causes. Then you can work toward making your use of oral English representative of the type of image you would like to portray. There are several common types and causes of pronunciation problems.[6]

1. *Sloppy or incorrect articulation.* If you say "air" for "error" or "dint" for "didn't," you are being lazy in your use of articulators. As you practice a speech you have prepared, be aware of words you mispronounce. Be conscious of dropping the "g" sound at the end of words ending in "ing," such as "going," "doing," and "watching." Also be aware of slurring words together. "Alls-ya-godado" is not an understandable substitute for "all you have to do." "Ja-know?" is not as clear as "Did you know?"

2. *Affectation.* In New England and southern speech, saying "eye-thuh" for "either" is generally acceptable, but in the western or midwestern

On Listening

One of the first scholars to study the behavior of listeners in an audience described that behavior in a classic work on audience psychology:

"It is unnecessary to suppose that, in the case of auditors, any super-individual mind or group consciousness is involved. The simple fact is that auditors, it would seem, are more likely to act in concerted fashion than is the case with spectators. Two reasons for this difference may be suggested.

"In the first place, the auditory appeal pursues each member of the congregation, more or less regardless of his bodily attitudes and adjustments. The ear hears, whether or not it be directed toward the spatial source of the sound. And the appeal is practically uninterrupted, since the ear cannot be closed as can the eye. Hence at every instant the auditors are quite likely to be assailed by the same features of the appeal, and the conditions are more favorable for concerted response, which, when it appears, will suggest unitary reaction.

"In the second place, the appearance of unitary response is in part due to the sympathetic suggestions exerted by each member of the group upon his neighbors. Signs of emotion, of interest and enthusiasm, or approval or resentment, of apathy or protest, of amusement, sorrow, or tenderness, on the part of a neighbor, tend reflexively to arouse similar feelings or attitudes in the observer. These signs are more likely to consist of facial changes, bodily attitudes, gestures, and other visible manifestations, than of clues that can be heard."

From H. L. Hollingsworth, *The Psychology of the Audience* (New York: American Book Company, 1935), pp. 15–16.

states this pronunciation may sound out of place. Some people pepper their speech with a "British" sound because they think it makes them appear more sophisticated. If used inconsistently, such overdone pronunciation comes off as affected and can be distracting. As you prepare to speak to an audience, avoid putting on an affected tone or overdoing the pronunciation of words such as "envelope," "tomato," and "ask."

3. *Ignorance of correct pronunciation.* Most of us have reading vocabularies that are far larger than our speaking vocabularies. Sometimes, when reading aloud, you might come across a word you understand the meaning of but that is not part of your speaking vocabulary. Other times, you might encounter a technical term or a name with which

you are unfamiliar. In preparing a public speech, you may want to use a dictionary to look up the pronunciation of words you are not in the habit of saying aloud. It is very difficult to fake your way through a word that is beyond your pronunciation abilities, and incorrect pronunciation tells the audience you have not prepared properly.

4. *Vowel distortion.* Some of us have grown up in oral language environments in which words are mispronounced because of vowel substitutions. Some examples of vowel distortion are "melk" for "milk," "sekatury" for "secretary," "minny" for "many," "jist" for "just," "Warshington" for "Washington," "punkin" for "pumpkin," and "git" for "get." In some cases, vowel distortion may be such a strong habit that the speaker needs the help of a speech pathologist to correct the problem. Being aware of these distortions allows some people to begin monitoring their own pronunciations and correcting themselves.

5. *Pronunciation outside the norm.* If we assume that general American speech is the norm, certain pronunciations are generally not considered acceptable in the communication marketplace of business, education, and the professions. "Asked" is not "axt," "something" is not "sumptin," and "picture" is not "pitcher."

10.4 The Physical Elements of Public Speaking

The physical elements of communication include personal elements such as gestures, movement, posture, and eye contact.

Gestures   **Gestures** are hand and body motions and facial expressions. Interestingly, researchers have determined that people who use hand movements when they talk appear freer, more open, and more honest to an audience.[7]

Each person uses a distinctive pattern of gestures while communicating; some use a great number of gestures, whereas others use only a few. Gesture patterns result from environmental influences and are often tied to the emotional involvement we feel as we are speaking. Emotional involvement also affects the vocal elements of delivery—the pitch, volume, and rate of speech. Broad gestures are often accompanied by loud volume and strong changes in pitch. To an audience, speakers who use few gestures sometimes seem personally uninvolved with the topic. At the same time, speakers who overplan and practice gestures usually appear to be insincere, automatic, and lacking in natural presentational style.

Billy Crystal used expressive hand gestures while he was host of the 1992 Academy Awards.

To be effective, gestures should be natural and complement the speaker's oral dynamics. As you begin to feel comfortable in presenting materials you will find yourself less conscious of what you are doing and simply start to do it. Just recall how you talk on the telephone or get involved in an animated conversation. You don't worry about your hands in those situations, so you should not worry about them during a speech. Forget them and they will take care of themselves. Your hands will be active when your body calls for their movement—unless you are gripping the lectern so tightly that you cannot let go, or have your hands jammed inside your pockets, or are playing with keys, money, jewelry, or the buttons on your clothing.

Movement   **Movement** (such as walking back and forth in front of an audience) is influenced by the emotional distance a speaker wants to establish, the amount of emotional energy within the speaker, and the speaker's need to stay near the lectern to refer to notes or use a microphone. A person who wants intimate interaction with audience members will move or lean toward them. But if the desire is to create a more formal feeling, the speaker will remain stationed behind the lectern, using it as a barrier. To avoid distracting their listeners, some speakers consciously limit the area they cover so that their movements do not become more interesting than their speaking. Of course, if a microphone is anchored to the lectern, the speaker must remain there. In addition, the arrangement of the audience may confine the speaker's space.

It is usually a good idea for a speaker to employ opening and closing pauses in the presentation. Because it takes an audience a while to settle down to listening, a speaker is wise to assume a comfortable position before the audience and pause for several seconds before starting the presentation. At the end of the speech, the speaker usually presents the last sentence emphatically—by raising or lowering the voice—to indicate that the presentation is over. The speaker should then pause again for several seconds before leaving the lectern.

Posture   The effective speaker devotes some attention to **posture**, for a forceful stance adds to the dynamic image that a speaker can convey through these nonverbal, physical dimensions. The speaker's posture should not distract from the speech itself. Speakers must be careful not to lean to one side or to shift their weight back and forth. Listeners can also be distracted by a speaker who puts one foot across the other or leans on the lectern.

Eye Contact   Establishing **eye contact** by looking into the eyes of your listeners as you speak is another key to effective speaking. In fact, eye contact is considered by some public speaking theorists to be one of the most important aspects of speech. It is your way of establishing credibility, as you can "look the audience in the eye," and ties you directly to your listeners. Audience members are likely to feel more involved in the presentation if you look at them. Maintaining eye contact also helps you receive feedback so you can adjust the presentation accordingly.

To use eye contact effectively, look directly at your listeners, not over their heads. Be sure to shift your focus so that you are not maintaining contact with just one section of the audience, and be especially careful not to overlook those in the front or back rows.

≡10.5 Reading from the Manuscript

Using a manuscript can be difficult because you must look at the audience at the same time that you are trying to read your material with animation and naturalness. To do this, you will have to work out some system of following the script unobtrusively so you can maintain eye contact with the audience without losing your place. Be careful not to move or flip the manuscript pages unnecessarily because this draws attention away from you and toward the manuscript. Also try to avoid falling into a monotone. Read according to the meaning by stressing important words and ideas, and vary your tone of voice so that you are speaking naturally. Some speakers run the index finger of their left hand down the side of the manuscript so they are continually pointing to the start of the next printed line that they will be reading. This way, when they look up, they can find their place when they return to the manuscript.

It also helps to arrange the script in a manner that keeps you from getting lost. Double- or triple-space the information; do not divide sentences by starting them on one page and finishing them on another; and do not write or type on the back of the pages. If useful, place virgules and underscores in the script so that you remember when to pause and what words to stress.

Virgules are slash marks used to indicate a pause or a stop. Usually, a / is used for a short pause, / / for a longer pause, and / / / for a full stop. **Underscores** are placed beneath a word or a phrase to indicate that it should be stressed. For example, the word *now* is to be stressed in the sentence: Do it <u>now</u>. Notice that the entire meaning of the sentence changes if the underscoring becomes: Do <u>it</u> now. If you feel that underscoring will help you to present the material in a meaningful way, be sure to use it. Usually a single underscore indicates a minor stress, and a double a stronger stress; a triple underscore represents the point at which you should increase the volume and the power of your vocal delivery.

10.6 The Use of Supplementary Aids

Effective use of supplementary aids such as visual, audio, and audiovisual material is often critical to the impact of a speech.

Using Visual Aids Here are some basic suggestions to keep in mind when you use visual aids in a speech:

◆ *Do not stand between the visual aid and the audience because you will block the view.* If an aid is important enough to use, it is important that the audience sees it.

◆ *Speak toward the audience, not toward the visual aid.* Focus your attention on the aid only when you want the audience to look at it.

◆ *Know the visual aid well enough so that you do not have to study it while you talk.*

◆ *Point to the particular place on the aid that you are discussing.* If, for example, you are speaking about the Yucatán peninsula and you have displayed a map, point specifically to this area of Mexico with your finger, a pencil, or a pointer. You know where the Yucatán is, but your listeners may not.

◆ *Use the aid at the point in your presentation where it will have the greatest impact.* Prepare the listeners for the aid by explaining what they are going to see (for example, "We are going to look at a chart that will demonstrate what has been happening to one business in this country during the last five years"). Then clarify what the aid is illustrating ("This chart shows the decline that has taken place in shoe production in the last twenty years. As you will note, production in 1973 was at this level, whereas the chart shows a decrease in 1993 to this level"). Finally, pull the ideas together ("Thus, a look at one industry, the shoe industry, can help us to see . . .").

◆ *If you do not need the aid for other parts of the speech, put it down, cover it up, or turn it over.* An exposed visual aid can distract listeners. Indeed, it may become so interesting that they will stop paying attention to your presentation. If you are going to refer to the visual aid throughout the presentation, keep it exposed; but once its purpose is completed, put it away.

Using Audio and Audiovisual Aids

Though not as commonly used as visual material, audio and audiovisual supplementary aids also must be carefully planned. Here are some suggestions for using them:

◆ *Be sure you are familiar with the operation of the equipment.* Know how to turn on and adjust the television, video recorder, tape recorder, overhead or opaque projector, or other aid.

◆ *Make arrangements for turning the lights on and off at the appropriate times.* It is extremely frustrating for an audience to be seated in the dark for long periods of time. Your credibility may suffer if you must pause in your presentation to ad lib a procedure for the lighting.

◆ *If you are using slides, plan whether you yourself will run the equipment or whether an assistant is needed.* If you need assistance, make prior arrangements.

◆ *Make prior arrangements for the equipment you need.* If you must have equipment, check to make sure that it is available and that it will be present when you arrive.

◆ *Make sure the materials you are going to use are compatible with the equip-*

ment. Not all audio, visual, and audiovisual equipment is compatible. Make sure that your materials will work with the available equipment.

☰10.7 Speaker Anxiety

Very few speakers escape the "butterflies." There is no cure for them except to realize that they are beneficial rather than harmful, and certainly never fatal. Actually, the tension usually means that the speaker is keyed up and so will do a better job. Edward R. Murrow, considered by many to be among the finest television news commentators, called stage fright "the seat of perfection," and Mark Twain once comforted a fright-frozen friend about to give a speech by saying, "Just remember they don't expect much."[8]

Even normally brave people are frightened by public speaking, a condition known as **speechophobia**. U.S. astronaut Sally Ride, the first female crew member of a space shuttle mission, followed her historic accomplishment by "giving an average of one speech a day, traveling across the country and Europe. . . . In a question-and-answer period after her speech to the American Bar Association, a woman asked, 'Were you afraid?' 'I was a lot more scared getting up to give this speech,' she replied."[9]

Yet even with all these assurances that your anxiety is normal, you are probably still saying to yourself, "I don't want to get up. My knees knock, my stomach churns, my legs shake, and my mouth gets dry." In lieu of a cure, recognize that there are some positive and negative approaches to speaker anxiety.

Negative Affecters of Speaker Anxiety

Speakers who perceive the public speaking situation to be traumatic often have some false assumptions about what to do to help themselves. None of these actions, however, truly help people handle anxiety:

They avoid the experience of giving a presentation. The more you speak, the more comfortable you will get. Though the nervousness may not go away completely, it should let up as you get more practice.

They fail to prepare, assuming that the longer they avoid confronting the situation, the less time there will be to build up anxiety. If you are not prepared, your panic upon stepping up to speak will probably be greater than it would be if you had given your presentation some practical thought.

They take drugs or alcohol because they think it will relax them. All these substances will do is dull your reflexes, increase your likelihood of forgetting your material, and help you make a total fool of yourself.

**Positive Ways
of Handling
Speaker Anxiety**

No definitive research proves that there are guaranteed ways to completely overcome public speaker anxiety. We know that proper preparation helps. In addition, many seasoned speakers employ a few specific techniques that help them manage their nervousness. These include breathing techniques, expectancy restructuring, rehearsing, and stance.

Breathing Techniques

When it comes to relaxation, speakers find it helpful before beginning to take several deep breaths and expel all the air from their lungs.[10] Others like to shake their hands at the wrists to "get out the nervousness." Some people favor grabbing the seat of their chair with both hands, pushing down and holding the position for about five seconds, repeating this action about five times. This tightens and then loosens the muscles, which causes a decrease in physical tension.

Though traditionally many speakers try to shake off their anxiety, Gestalt psychology has suggested a different approach: that speakers get in touch with their feelings. Rather than pushing your anxiety away, advocates recommend, you should let it go as far as it can. What will typically happen is that your anxiety will reach a peak and then subside. If you are dubious, try the following experiment: Sit in a chair, and place your hands one inside the other with the palm of one hand resting on the palm of the other hand and the fingers of one hand wrapped around the back of the other. Force your hands together and keep forcing them. Do not let them move. Even though the force will make your hands start to shake, keep on forcing them together. Soon your whole body will probably start to shake. You will then reach a point where the shaking will stop and relaxation will set in.

There are two ways you can use the above exercises in speaking. If you perform the hand-in-hand activity immediately before you get up to speak, you will probably be physically relaxed by the time you greet the audience. Alternatively, think of the experience of getting up before the audience and let yourself feel the anxiety. Let it stay in your mind and imagine that you are going through the experience. Let yourself be as nervous as you can; psychologically push it as far as you can. Some people report that by imagining the upcoming experience in its worst way, the actual experience becomes much easier.[11]

**Expectancy
Restructuring**

Another way of managing anxiety is to change your expectations. We all tend to perform the way we expect to perform: **expectancy restructuring** is based on the idea that if you expect to do well, then you will do well. If you have negative expectations, you must change them to positive expectations. If you are afraid to get up and give a speech because you expect the experience to be negative, you may experience some or all of the negative side effects of that fear—sweating palms, quivering voice, and so forth.

To overcome this, first prepare a well-structured and well-supported speech so that you have confidence that the material will be well received. Then visualize the actual setting in which you are going to give the speech. Picture yourself getting out of your chair, walking to the front of the room, arranging your materials on the podium, looking at the audience, and giving the speech. As you see yourself presenting the material, look at various people. They are nodding their heads in agreement; they are interested and are listening attentively. You complete the speech and return to your chair, feeling good about yourself. The more you visualize this positive experience, the more you will expect to do well. Soon you will be expecting success, not failure.

Rehearsing It cannot be stressed enough: One of the best ways to relax is to be ready for the speech. This means starting to prepare far enough in advance so that you have enough material, the speech is well structured and well organized, and you have a chance to practice it. Some speakers try to convince themselves that they will do better if they just get up and talk, with little or no thought as to what they will be saying. This is a fool's contention; it is usually proposed by a procrastinator or a person who is not properly aware of the speaker's responsibility to audience and self. Yes, some speakers can get up and "wing it," but the normal mortal cannot. So prepare and practice!

There is no one best way to rehearse. For most people, sitting at a desk and going over the material by mumbling through the outline or notes constitutes a starting point. This will alert you to ideas that do not seem to make sense, words you cannot pronounce, places where you go blank because you need more notes, and passages that need more or fewer examples. Make the changes, and continue to orally review your notes until you are satisfied with the material.

Once you are satisfied with the material, try to duplicate the setting in which you are going to speak. In most instances, you will probably be standing behind a lectern. If so, practice with a lectern, put a box on a desk, or place a piece of cardboard over the bathroom sink. Stand and speak. This will get you comfortable with moving pages and looking up from the notes or manuscript; you will also find out whether your typing or writing is going to cause you reading problems.

Duplicate as closely as possible what you are going to do. If you are going to use visual aids, use them. If you are going to demonstrate some object, demonstrate it. The more familiar you become with exactly what you are going to do, the more likely it is you will be comfortable doing it. Remember, you practice typing sitting at a typewriter, you practice driving sitting behind the wheel of a car, and you practice a sport by duplicating the competitive setting. Do the same thing with your speech.

Stop practicing when you are comfortable with your material and have

Rehearsing your speech is one of the best ways to reduce speaker anxiety.

worked out the problems related to using notes and supplementary aids. Do not overpractice. You can never become perfect. You are striving to become as comfortable as you can in what is a stressful situation for almost all of us.

Stance   The way you stand can affect your presentation. Place yourself in a balanced and comfortable stance during the speech. Do not lock your knees, as this makes the whole body rigid, causes difficulties in breathing, and often results in shaking, a dry mouth, and vocal quivering. Try not to lean on the podium because this will cut off your ability to make gestures and discourage natural movement.

When you begin, put into practice what many speakers have found to be an effective stress reliever—the **triangle stance**. In the triangle stance,

Figure 10.1

Foot Placement to Relieve Speaker Anxiety

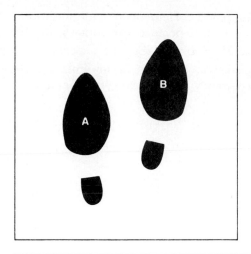

as Figure 10.1 shows, you place foot A at a slight angle and foot B at about a forty-five-degree angle, with your heel placed roughly even with the arch of foot A. Keep your feet about six inches apart. Shuffle your feet slightly until you feel comfortable and balanced. Place your weight on foot A and let your hip extend a bit. You will feel your other leg relax. This process allows you to breathe and gesture more easily. As you proceed through the speech, you can alter the stance by switching the foot positions, always remembering to put your body weight on the foot placed in back.

Look at the people in the audience who are alert during the presentation, nodding their heads as you speak. Concentrate on your material. Try to relax and do as well as you can . . . no one can ask for anything more! And if all else fails, remember that there have been no reported deaths from the shock of giving a speech.

Summary

This chapter examined the oral and physical elements of delivering a speech. The major ideas presented were:

- Listenable speaker style is characterized by clarity, conciseness, and colorfulness of verbal and nonverbal elements.
- The vocal elements of communication are pitch, volume, rate, quality, animation, and pause.
- To pronounce means to form speech sounds by moving the articulators of speech.
- Speakers should be careful to pronounce words clearly.

◆ The physical elements of communication include gestures, physical movements, posture, eye contact, and the use of visual aids.

◆ Speechophobia is the fear associated with giving a speech.

◆ Speaker anxiety can be minimized through breathing techniques, expectancy restructuring, rehearsing, and stance.

Key Terms

speaking style
listenable speaker style
clarity
conciseness
sound bites
colorfulness
pitch
volume
rate
quality
animation
pause

pronounce
general American speech
gestures
movement
posture
eye contact
virgules
underscores
speechophobia
expectancy restructuring
triangle stance

Learn by Doing

1. Some of the most commonly mispronounced words in general American speech are listed here. Look up each word in a dictionary or pronunciation guide. During a class session, you will be asked to pronounce these words and use them in sentences: *across, acts, actually, all, ambulance, any, asked, because, catch, doing, familiar, fifth, genuine, going, horror, hundred, introduce, just, library, next, nuclear, particular, picture, prescription, probably, pumpkin, recognized, sandwich, secretary, Washington, with.*

2. This instrument is composed of 6 statements concerning feelings about speaking in public.[12] Please indicate the degree to which each statement applies to you by marking whether you (1) strongly agree, (2) agree, (3) are undecided, (4) disagree, or (5) strongly disagree. Work quickly; record your first impression.

   ____ 1. I have no fear of giving a speech.

   ____ 2. Certain parts of my body feel very tense and rigid while I am giving a speech.

   ____ 3. I feel relaxed while giving a speech.

   ____ 4. My thoughts become confused and jumbled when I am giving a speech.

   ____ 5. I face the prospect of giving a speech with confidence.

   ____ 6. While giving a speech, I get so nervous I forget facts I really know.

To obtain your score: Add 18 to your scores from items 1, 3, and 5, and then subtract your scores for items 2, 4, and 6. This is your final score.

Interpretation: Scores can range from a low of 6 to a high of 30. Any score above 18 indicates some degree of apprehension. If your score is above 18, you are like the overwhelming majority of Americans.

Notes

1. Dorothy Sarnoff, "Self Esteem," *New Woman* (July 1983), 76.

2. "How to Speak Better in Public: An Interview with Sandy Livner," *U.S. News & World Report,* April 6, 1981, pp. 60–61.

3. Jesse Jackson, "The Rainbow Coalition" (speech presented at the Democratic National Convention, San Francisco, July 17, 1984), transcript reprinted in Lloyd Rohler and Roger Cook, eds., *Great Speeches for Criticism and Analysis* (Greenwood, Ind.: Alistair Press, 1988), p. 110.

4. Stuart W. Hyde, *Television and Radio Announcing,* 4th ed. (Boston: Houghton Mifflin 1983), p. 130.

5. John Eisenson, *Voice and Diction: A Program for Improvement* (New York: Macmillan, 1974), pp. 158–159.

6. Hyde, pp. 131–132.

7. M. L. Clark, E. A. Erway, and L. Beltzer, *The Learning Encounter* (New York: Random House, 1971), pp. 52–65.

8. George Plimpton, "How to Make a Speech," *Psychology Today* (October 1981), 58–59.

9. "Ms. Ride Yearns for an End to Her Speaking Schedule," *Norfolk Virginian Pilot,* August 3, 1983, p. A–2.

10. These activities and others were summarized in a presentation by Martin Freedman at the Eastern Communication Association Convention, Ocean City, Maryland, May 1980.

11. This discussion is based on information shared by Les Wyman at a workshop entitled, "Introductory Gestalt Workshop," at the Gestalt Institute, Cleveland, Ohio, February 1982.

12. This is a section of the Personal Report on Communication Apprehension (PRCA-24), from Virginia P. Richmond and James C. McCroskey, *Communication: Apprehension, Avoidance and Effectiveness,* 3rd ed. (Scottsdale, Ariz.: Gorsuch Scarisbrick, 1992), pp. 125–126. For a more comprehensive public speaking apprehension test, students should take the PRPSA (Personal Report on Public Speaking Anxiety), which is reprinted in the Instructor's Manual accompanying this text.

Informative Speech

11

Chapter Outline

Learning Outcomes

After reading this chapter, you should be able to:

Define informative speaking.

Discuss the need for informative speaking.

List and explain the types of informative speeches.

Describe the steps a successful informative speaker takes in developing a speech.

e live in an information age: "Knowledge is doubling at the rate of 100 percent every 20 months."[1] One social observer has suggested that the need for people who can retrieve and explain information will greatly increase in the future.[2]

Because time has become a precious commodity to most of us, we have to rely more directly on speakers in all sorts of settings to provide us with the information we need. We attend lectures to learn about social and political issues and participate in seminars to learn new skills and upgrade others. Job training is based on a great deal of oral instruction, and the classroom lecturer delivers most of the material necessary to master the content of many college courses.

Businesses have recognized this need for information disseminators. For example, The Boeing Company employs an information specialist to help employees present information in the best way possible. According to one specialist, "A factor vital to the health of any corporation is the constant exchange of accurate information. Although traditional, written forms of business communication remain important, the oral exchange of information occupies an increasingly important role in the functioning of today's companies."[3] More and more organizations are hiring consultants to do information training as the quick upgrading and changing of equipment and job needs take place. What occurs in these public speaking sessions is informative speaking.

≡11.1 Characteristics of Informative Speaking

Traditionally, **informative speaking** has been defined as discourse that imparts new information, secures understanding, or reinforces accumulated information. At present, however, controversies persist among communication theorists with regard to this definition. For instance, some theorists propose that all speaking is persuasive in nature—that is, that the traditional distinction between informative speaking and persuasive speaking is simply a matter of degree.

This text assumes that all communication contains elements of persuasion. Any audience must be persuaded to accept the information a speaker presents. (Indeed, even the act of using materials to gain attention is a persuasive act because the speaker is asking listeners to dismiss other competing stimuli.) However there is a distinction between informative and persuasive speaking that centers on the structure of the message and the particular appeals used in the persuasive speech. These are covered in the next chapter.

As in any other type of presentation, effective informative speaking depends on audience analysis. The speaker must consider the audience's present knowledge about the subject, the background information the audience possesses, and the extent to which definitions, understandable analogies, examples, and clarifiers need to be used. The speaker must also determine the appropriate language level, the attention devices to be used, and the structure of the message that will best fit the group. Research suggests that speakers often may think their listeners lack the necessary information, whereas the listeners themselves may not feel the same way.[4] Mindful of this discrepancy, the astute speaker determines the listeners' real needs and uses that information to develop the speech.

In an informative presentation, the speaker must always keep the purpose of the presentation firmly in hand. A clear purpose statement is essential. Consider the following three sample purpose statements:

"To inform by defining what the drug Rho-Gam is and to explain the reasons it has eliminated the need to give blood transfusions to some newborn children who have a problematic factor in their blood composition."

"To inform the audience what the Heimlich maneuver is, how it was developed, and how this technique can prevent people from choking to death."

"To inform the audience of what the Heimlich maneuver is and to teach them how to do the maneuver by demonstrating each step."

Note that the last two purpose statements have the same subject but different goals. The former explains the maneuver and its value. The latter explains the maneuver and then teaches the steps for performing it.

These purpose statements may sound rather formal, but they are stated in a manner that narrows the subject and indicates specifically what the speech will include. The purpose statement thus serves as a fence around the territory to be covered in a presentation and indicates how to "corral" the information. If you do not set up these sorts of boundaries, you may find yourself discussing many things but not achieving your desired outcome.

⹀11.2   Types of Informative Speaking

There are many ways to organize a discussion of the types of informative speaking. One classification scheme examines presentations about objects, processes, events, and concepts.[5] Specific types of informative speeches also can be identified by the setting in which they are typically used. Examples include informative briefings, technical reports, lectures, and question-and-answer sessions.

Speeches About Objects

Speeches about objects describe a particular thing in detail. The object may be a person, a place, an animal, a structure, a machine—anything that can be touched or observed. The speaker first identifies the object, and then discusses its specific attributes.

Here are two sample purpose statements for informative speeches about an object: "To inform the audience what a compact disc (CD) player is and to cite some specific factors to consider when purchasing one"; "To inform the audience why a dolphin is classified as a mammal and to describe some of the experimental work on identifying the language capabilities of this unique creature."

Speeches About Processes

Speeches about processes instruct the audience about how something works, is made, or is done so that the listeners can then apply the knowledge themselves. The end purpose may be either to gain understanding of the process or to be able to do something. This type of speech would be used to train people to operate a piece of equipment or to perform a manufacturing process. Sample purpose statements for informative speeches about processes are "To inform the audience of the step-by-step process of using the move feature of the *WordPerfect* word-processing program"; "To inform the audience of the step-by-step process employed by Chrysler Corporation in developing a design for an aerodynamic automobile"; "To inform the audience, through a demonstration, of the steps to follow when filling out the income tax short form."

Speeches about processes often lend themselves to chronological arrangement. In this method of organization, the speaker describes the first step of the process, then the second, then the third, and so on.

Speeches About Events

Speeches about events inform the audience about something that has happened, is happening, or is expected to happen. This type of presentation can be developed in many ways, but it tends to work well in a chronological, comparison-contrast, or spatial arrangement. Here are several purpose statements for informative speeches about events: "To inform the audience of the spread of the AIDS virus in the United States by examining the statistics for the years 1980 to 1992" (time sequence arrangement); "To inform the audience of the similarities and differences in the American and Russian revolutions based on their economic causes" (comparison-contrast arrangement); "To inform the audience of western migration in the United States by tracing the major stages of the pioneer movement from the East Coast to the West Coast" (spatial arrangement).

Speeches About Concepts

Speeches about concepts examine theories, beliefs, ideas, philosophies, or schools of thought. Much of the formal educational process consists of speeches about concepts. Possible topics for such speeches are explanations and investigations of business theories, philosophical movements, psychological concepts, and political theories.

Because many ideas about concepts tend to be abstract, a speaker must be sure to use precise language, define terms, give historical background, avoid undefined slang and jargon, and use appropriate clarifying support materials such as audio, visual, and audiovisual aids. Examples of purpose statements for informative speeches about concepts are "To inform the audience of the existential movement in philosophy by stating Jean-Paul Sartre's definition and application of existentialism in the play *No Exit*"; "To inform the audience about the theory that abused children grow up to be child abusers through an examination of three classic research studies"; "To inform the audience of the theory that musical theater composers Alan Jay Lerner and Frederick Loewe used the theme of the search for a perfect time, a perfect place, and a perfect love story as the basis for their musicals."

Informative Briefings

Most business, organizational, and technical communicators gain current knowledge in their fields as a result of **informative briefings**. The fundamental objective of an informative briefing is to share data and

Business, organizational, and technical communicators give informative briefings to share data and insights among people with common interests.

insights among people with common interests. The briefing usually involves delivery of information to the audience, followed by the exchange of data, ideas, and questions among participants.[6] This type of speech is used to explain organizational policies, procedures, and issues. For example, the sales manager of an automobile dealership might use an informative briefing to tell her staff about the new models, the head of a nursing unit might explain to his staff the procedures to follow when treating new patients, or a military commander might outline troop movements to the press.

As with any other kind of speech, preparation for an informative briefing requires careful audience analysis to determine what background and definitions are needed to ensure comprehension. It is not uncommon, given the nature of when and how briefings are used, for the audience to be quite knowledgeable about the subject. If the audience has considerable knowledge, the speaker does not have to cover the background material in as much depth as he or she would for uninformed listeners.

Technical Reports **Technical reports** are concise, clear statements explaining a process, detailing a technique, or discussing new elements either to people within a business or industry or to people outside it. Unfortunately, a majority of executives in corporate America are convinced that recent college and university graduates cannot give technical reports effectively. Executives surveyed said that fewer than 20 percent of the people they worked with were capable of giving a concise, clear oral report and that they had far greater difficulty training people to do this than to write a clear letter.[7]

One of the major factors in the development of a technical report is determining the proper format. The first rule of giving a report is to ask those who request the report what form they would like it to take. Find out how much time will be allowed and how much detail is required.[8]

Speakers who give technical reports must have a good sense of the audience. If the audience consists of nontechnical people, all technical words must be defined, and analogies familiar to the audience should be included to clarify the ideas presented. This does not mean the speaker has to water down the material so that it is no longer accurate. Instead, the speaker should be sure to define words, give examples, and present ideas in a variety of ways to make sure that listeners understand the concepts being set forth.

If your presentation includes technical drawings or a number of statistics, use handouts so that everyone can examine the materials. If the group is small, consider allowing audience members to ask questions as you develop your ideas so that they have the opportunity for immediate clarification where necessary. Be careful, however, to maintain control of the structure and the material as you answer questions.

When you structure a technical report that involves a recommendation, start with a statement of the proposal unless there is a compelling reason not to do so. (You may want to hold the recommendation until the end if you know the audience will be hostile to it or if you want to give complete background information before revealing your recommendation.) After you have made your proposal, explain how you arrived at it. Give just enough background to clarify but not so much as to make the presentation dull.[9]

Lectures Probably the most familiar type of informative speaking is the **lecture**, the formal presentation of material to facilitate learning. Lectures are an integral part of academic life, serving as the main vehicle for the presentation of information in almost all subject fields. Lectures are also used in many other settings—by guest speakers at Parent-Teacher Association, Kiwanis, fraternity, or sorority meetings; invited speakers at lunch or dinnertime seminars in corporate headquarters; or distinguished speakers at public arts, religious, or academic events.

To be effective, lectures should conform to the same characteristics we expect in other forms of informative speaking. A good lecture should be carefully adapted to the intended audience. It should be clearly organized with easy-to-follow transitions so that listeners can stay "on track." A memorable lecture is well developed, with supporting details to elaborate each major point. Like all informative speaking, lectures often tend to be heavy with explanations and consequently are considered to be dry. A variety of supporting materials (stories, statistics, analogies) enhance the explanatory details and involve the listeners more readily. Many lecturers also use humor to get and hold attention. The speaker also may involve the listeners by asking them questions, probing for information, and inviting inquiries during the presentation instead of waiting until the question-and-answer session.

Timing is an important consideration. Lecturers should always be aware of the time frame. An audience usually expects a lecturer to stay within a certain framework (such as a class period) or within the boundaries of what the audience can comfortably absorb.

Question-and-Answer Sessions   The **question-and-answer session** that follows many speeches is a type of informative speech itself.[10] It is an on-the-spot test of unrehearsed answers that measures the speaker's knowledge, alerts the speaker to areas in the speech that were unclear or needed more development, and gives the listeners a chance to probe for ideas.

In some instances, the question-and-answer session allows receivers to point out the weakness of the speaker's arguments or present alternative views. This occurs more frequently after persuasive speeches than after informative presentations. Some communication analysts wonder whether it is acceptable for a question-and-answer session to serve as a forum for the proposal of alternative concepts. If confronted by a hostile questioner, speakers themselves will have to determine whether they want to deal with the issue or remind the prober that the purpose of the session is to ask questions, not to give a counterspeech or engage in debate.

☰11.3   Developing the Informative Speech

Every informative speaker has a challenge—to get the audience to understand and retain the information presented. When we consider that

On Listening

It is possible to improve your ability to listen for comprehension. The following list identifies several characteristics of listeners who effectively comprehend speakers' messages.

1. The listener is honest with the speaker when he or she is not able to attend fully.

2. The listener maintains a diet of healthy food, which stimulates an active, energetic mind.

3. The listener takes measures to reduce stress, which diverts one's energy and attention.

4. The listener monitors his or her own listening behavior.

5. The listener works to control external distractions.

6. The listener works to control his or her own internal distractions through self-discipline and bracketing other concerns to go back to them at a later time.

7. The listener schedules a time each day to deal with concerns, reflections, and even daydreams.

8. The listener is energized by a desire to learn.

9. The listener does not fake attention but, rather, enters into the communication with honest concentration.

10. The listener creates penetrating, meaningful questions to ask the speaker.

11. The listener listens in order to share the speaker's message with another person.

12. The listener listens as if the speaker were speaking to him or her individually.

13. The listener practices the appropriate listening skills in each communication situation as an active participant.

See Andrew D. Wolvin and Carolyn Gwynn Coakley, *Listening* (Dubuque, Iowa: William C. Brown, 1992), pp. 237–238.

the typical listener remembers only about 10 percent of an oral presentation three days after hearing it, we recognize how great a challenge this is.[11]

Learning-theory specialists point out that the basis for retention and understanding is the establishment of relationships (associations and connections) between information and physical or mental activities. We learn through repetition (by hearing ideas over and over) and through experiencing (doing a task to see what it is).[12] We are more likely to remember things that have relevance to us. We remember information that will somehow make our life easier, that helps us to know something we did not know before, or that we will be rewarded for knowing. In other words, we will remember when we see a reason to do so. We also remember because an idea makes sense to us—the order in which concepts are presented makes the idea easy to understand, or the examples and other developing materials make the idea clear.

Understanding how people learn can assist you in planning your informative speech. Consider using supplementary aids to help your listeners remember your message. It is estimated that we learn 1 percent through taste, 1.5 percent through touch, 3.5 percent through smell, 11 percent through hearing, and an astonishing 83 percent through sight.[13] Once you know this, you will realize that your best chance of getting people to remember is to have them hear and see the content of your presentation. Such devices as slides, charts, illustrations, pictures, and models help to reinforce and clarify what you say.

Here are several pointers to keep in mind when developing an informative speech:[14]

1. *Order your ideas clearly.* Select a method of organization that helps your audience follow the step-by-step development of the speech.

2. *Use chronological arrangement if the speech lends itself to a progression (first, second, and third) or sequencing (years or ages).* Sample subject: explaining a science experiment that proceeds from step 1 to step 6.

3. *Use spatial arrangement if the speech has a geographical basis (for example, from east to west, from top to bottom, or from the inside out).* Sample subject: tracing the voyage of Christopher Columbus from Spain to the New World.

4. *Use topical arrangement if the subject divides into specific parts.* Sample subject: describing the life cycle, characteristics, and environmental effects of the gypsy moth.

5. *Use comparison-contrast arrangement when the topic illustrates similarities and differences.* Sample subject: comparing Nebraska's unicameral

(one-house) legislature with the two-house legislative system of all other states.

6. *Use the familiar to explain the new.* To present a new idea, use an analogy based on an idea the audience already understands. For example, you could explain how an FM radio signal travels by comparing it to the way a bow and an arrow work. The arrow goes as far as the bow projects it and then drops. If something gets in its way, however, the arrow stops moving. Similarly, the FM signal goes as far as its signal power allows it to move unless something, such as a building or a mountain, gets in its way and stops it. The analogy is one of the most impressive clarifying devices available to an informative speaker.

7. *Use vivid illustrations.* Descriptions, stories, comparisons, contrasts, and verbal pictures increase your chances of gaining and holding the audience's attention. A listener who can visualize an idea is more likely to remember it.

8. *Avoid being too technical.* If you have ever tried to follow directions for using a computer program when you knew nothing about computer language, or tried to repair a piece of electrical equipment using a technician's manual, you know the difficulty of understanding materials that may be fine for an expert but are not geared to the layperson. If your subject is at all technical, evaluate the vocabulary level of audience members. Based on their backgrounds and experiences, choose terms that are not likely to confuse, or clarify the technical terms you do use. Remember, the purpose of the speech is not to impress the audience with your vast vocabulary; the purpose is to accomplish the informative objective of the speech. Select words that will help, rather than hinder, your task.

9. *Personalize your message.* Audiences are more attracted to real examples than to fictional or hypothetical examples. If at all possible, use illustrations that allow your audience to identify with the plight of a victim, to understand and share in someone's joy, or to realize how an event changed someone's life.

10. *Do not speak down to your audience, but do not overestimate audience knowledge.* There is no set guideline for evaluating an audience's level of knowledge other than to learn as much as you can about what your listeners know specifically and generally. For example, many professors who grew up during the Kennedy era often forget that most students now in college were not even born at the time of JFK's presidency. Instructors who want to draw parallels between then and now usually must provide some historical background.

Alternatively, references to the Bush presidency might serve as appropriate illustrations for this type of audience.

11. *Use as much clarification and detail as you feel are necessary to ensure listener understanding.* If anything, err on the side of overexplanation. Most audience members appreciate a speaker who makes an effort to communicate clearly.

≡11.4 Developing the Question-and-Answer Session

Before you enter into a question-and-answer session, set the ground rules. Ask the program chairperson about the process to be used and the time limit, and specify any restrictions you wish to place on this segment of the speech. Some speakers like to call on the participants. Others prefer to allow the chairperson to entertain the questions. Some presenters want all questions written out beforehand and want to select the questions they will answer. If you have any restrictions, let the chairperson know before you give the speech, and inform the audience of the rules.

The most difficult part of many question-and-answer sessions is to encourage audience members to ask the first question. Once this hurdle is overcome, questions seem to flow naturally. To break the ice, you may want to have someone in the audience prepared to ask a question. Another technique is to ask a question yourself. This can be accomplished by stating, "I've often been asked my views concerning . . . ," and then proceeding to indicate your views.

Here are some additional suggestions for managing the question-and-answer session:

Before you answer a question, restate it so that everyone knows what it is. If the question is complicated, simplify it in the restatement.

Do not speak only to the questioner; speak to the whole audience.

Be patient. If you have to repeat material you have already covered, do so briefly.

If a question goes on and on, prompt the asker to summarize the question.

Keep your answers short. Restate the question, give your response, clarify any vocabulary if necessary, give an example if appropriate, and then stop. Following the response, some speakers ask the questioner whether the answer was satisfactory.

Back up your responses with examples, statistics, and quotations.

If the question is overly complicated or of interest only to the asker, suggest a discussion with the questioner after the speech or via correspondence.

If the question is irrelevant, indicate that it is interesting or thought provoking but does not seem appropriate to the presentation. Do not get sidetracked or pulled into a private debate with the questioner.

If you do not know an answer, say so. You can offer to find out the answer and report back accordingly.

Limit the discussion to one question per person, and avoid getting caught in a dialogue with one person. Others who have questions will become frustrated, and those who do not will get bored.

Be willing to be corrected or at least to recognize another person's viewpoint. Thank the questioner for the clarification or acknowledge that more than one point of view is possible ("That's an interesting idea" or "The idea can be viewed that way"). You may win the battle of words by attacking or insulting the questioner, but you will lose the respect of the listeners in the process. Indeed, it is futile to get involved in a battle of words with a heckler or a person with a preconceived attitude or bias.

Know when to end the session. Do not wait until interest has waned or people begin leaving. You can lose the positive effect of a speech by overextending the question-and-answer session.

☰11.5   The Informative Process in Action

It is helpful to study the process of preparing an informative speech. Figure 11.1 shows the steps a successful speaker took in developing a speech.

As you develop your own informative speeches, remember that this form of communication occupies a prominent place in today's information age. Because listeners must turn to information sources in increasing numbers, informative speakers must present information in a clear, meaningful, interesting way so that the message is understood and the audience wants to listen.

Figure 11.1

Outline for a Sample
Informative Speech

Purpose statement: To inform the audience that AIDS is a major health problem by explaining that it is a complex disease that has spread all over the world and by describing some of the things being done to solve the problem.

Attention material to arouse the listeners' interest

Orienting material to relate the topic to the listeners and get them involved

Central idea of the speech Partitioning step to reiterate the thesis and list the main points to be covered in the body

First main point Discussion of AIDS as a complex disease through explanations and medical information

Transition

Second main point Discussion of how AIDS has become a major world problem, with statistics and explanations

Transition

I. Introduction
    A. Attention material: My friend John is dying of AIDS. He's not like Magic Johnson, who has gotten all sorts of national attention since he discovered that he, too, is suffering from the disease.
    B. Orienting material: AIDS has become everyone's disease.

II. Central Idea
    A. AIDS is a major health problem.
    B. In examining this health problem, let's consider:
        1. What AIDS is.
        2. Why AIDS has become such a critical problem.
        3. What is being done to overcome this health crisis.

III. Body
    A. AIDS is a complex disease.
        1. AIDS is acquired immunodeficiency syndrome.
        2. It is caused by a virus that destroys the body's ability to fight illness.
        3. You can contract AIDS through unprotected sex with an infected partner or from sharing drug needles and syringes with an infected person.

    (As medical researchers seem to progress slowly in finding the key to treating this complex disease, AIDS is an increasing health problem.)

    B. AIDS has become a major problem in the world.
        1. Once viewed primarily as a disease among homosexuals, AIDS has spread to the heterosexual population as well.
        2. More than 118,000 Americans have died of AIDS. Victims are men, women, rich, poor, white, black, Hispanic, Asian, and Native American.
        3. College students are considered a major at-risk population by the Centers for Disease Control.
        4. The problem is not limited to the United States. AIDS has become a problem of worldwide proportions. Some liken it to this century's bubonic plague.

    (This major world health problem continues to mystify medical researchers who are striving to find ways to conquer the problem.)

<table>
<tr><td>

Third main point
Discussion of what is being
done to solve the problem
of AIDS

</td><td>

C. What is being done to solve this problem?
   1. Researchers believe that it may take years before a vaccine can be developed to treat AIDS.
   2. Scientists today are re-evaluating their theory as to the cause of AIDS, suggesting that one or more co-factors may be working with HIV (human immunodeficiency virus) to trigger AIDS.

</td></tr>
</table>

IV. Conclusion

Summary of major points

    A. Summary
       1. It is clear that AIDS is a very complex disease.
       2. AIDs has become a major world health problem.
       3. Though researchers are attempting to do something about AIDS, a vaccine and a true understanding of the disease are years away.

Clincher
Tie back to attention
material

    B. Clincher
       1. There may be no hope for my friend John.
       2. However, understanding the nature of this health problem may be helpful to the rest of us.

Summary

In this chapter on informative speaking, the key ideas presented were:

♦ Informative speaking imparts new information, secures understanding, or reinforces accumulated information.

♦ Informative presentations depend on audience analysis.

♦ Informative speeches may be about objects, processes, events, and concepts.

♦ Types of informative speeches are informative briefings, technical reports, lectures, and question-and-answer sessions.

♦ The challenge for an informative speaker is to get the audience to understand and retain the information presented.

♦ To develop an informative speech, order ideas clearly, use the familiar to explain the new, use vivid illustrations, avoid being too technical, personalize the message, and do not speak down to the audience.

♦ To present a successful question-and-answer session, the speaker should establish the ground rules for the session and be able to effectively answer the questions asked.

Key Terms

informative speaking	informative briefings
speeches about objects	technical reports
speeches about processes	lecture
speeches about events	question-and-answer session
speeches about concepts	

Learn by Doing

1. As a homework assignment, list two topics that you are interested in speaking about for an informative presentation on objects, processes, events, or concepts. In class, your instructor will match you with a partner. With the assistance of your partner, select a topic for a speech based on audience analysis (your class), setting (your classroom), and purpose (an informative speech of three to five minutes). After you have both selected your topics, meet with another group. Present a short informative speech indicating what topic you have selected and why this topic suits you, the audience, the setting, and the purpose. The speech should use a structure that includes an introduction, statement of central idea, body, and conclusion.

2. Bring to class an object or piece of machinery (e.g., a camera, food processor, or microscope) that members of your class may not know how to operate or that you have a different way of operating. Be prepared to teach someone else how to use the equipment. In class you will be placed in a group with four of your classmates. Decide the order in which you will present the material. Then, the first speaker should give a two- to four-minute presentation on how the object works. Then the second speaker should demonstrate how the object operates, then the third speaker, and so forth. Your success as a speaker is measured by whether the speaker following you can operate the object.

3. You are going to give a "what-if" speech. On each of three 3- by 5-inch notecards, indicate something that could go wrong immediately before, during, or after a speech (e.g., you drop your speech outline in a puddle of water just outside your classroom building; the bulb goes out in the projector halfway through your slide presentation; an audience member challenges your statistics during the question-and-answer period). The instructor collects the cards, shuffles them, and hands them out one by one. When you get your card, give a restatement of the possible occurrence and a contingency plan for dealing with the situation.[15] (This assignment may take place when a short amount of time remains at the end of any class period.)

4. All students present one-minute speeches in which they describe a pet peeve, something that bothers them in daily life. They should tell what the peeve is, why it is a peeve, and what they would like to see done about it, if anything.

5. Investigate some phase of a career you are interested in and present an informative speech on it. The presentation must include the use of a supplementary aid. Sample speech topics: a future audiologist explains the differences among several brands of hearing aids; an accounting major illustrates how a balance sheet is prepared; an aspiring musician demonstrates how music is scored.

Notes

1. Connie Koenenn, "The Future Is Now," *Washington Post,* February 3, 1989, p. B5.
2. Ibid.
3. Michael F. Warlum, "Improving Oral Marketing Presentations in the Technology-Based Company," *IEEE Transactions on Professional Communication,* 31 (June 1988), 84.
4. Richard Hoehn, *The Art and Practice of Public Speaking* (New York: McGraw-Hill, 1988).
5. These categories are based on those reported in James H. Byrns, *Speak for Yourself: An Introduction to Public Speaking* (New York: Random House, 1981), Chapters 14–17.
6. H. Lloyd Goodall and Christopher L. Waagen, *The Persuasive Presentation* (New York: Harper & Row, 1986), p. 105.
7. John T. Molloy, "Making Your Point, Not Burying It," *Self* (April 1981), 92.
8. Ibid.
9. These suggestions for structuring a technical report are based on Richard Weigand, as reported in *Communication Briefings* (January 1986).
10. This discussion is adapted from Maureen Haningan, "Master the Game of Q&A," *Working Woman* (December 1984), 34–35.
11. Hoehn, *The Art and Practice of Public Speaking.*
12. G. H. Jamieson, *Communication and Persuasion* (London: Croom Helm, 1985), pp. 5–16.
13. Hoehn, *The Art and Practice of Public Speaking.*
14. Ibid.
15. This activity is based on John Alfred Jones, "Preparing Contingency Plans for Public Speaking Situations," *Communication Education,* 30 (1981), 423–424.

The Persuasive Speech

Chapter Outline

After reading this chapter, you should be able to:

Explain how people are influenced by persuasive messages.

Explain how people are influenced by coercive messages.

Describe how speaker credibility, logical arguments, and psychological appeals can affect listeners.

Analyze a persuasive speech to ascertain its potential effectiveness based on logical arguments and psychological appeals.

Prepare a persuasive speech using credibility, logical arguments, and psychological appeals.

*E*very day we are bombarded with messages intended to convince us to take some action, reinforce some commitment, accept some belief, or change some point of view. And almost every day we also send such messages as speakers. The process of influencing the decisions other people make is complex and involves many communication variables. **Persuasion** is "the process by means of which one party purposefully secures a change of behavior, mental and/or physical, on the part of another party by employing appeals to both feelings and intellect."[1] It is an important process. Through persuasion, we affect others and they affect us.

Persuasion, which allows listeners to choose for themselves whether to change what they think or how they behave, should not be confused with coercion. **Coercion** is influence that leaves the listener no desirable alternative but to adopt the change of mental or physical behavior the speaker proposes. Despite the negative aspects of coercion, speakers sometimes use it when other persuasive methods fail, fully aware that backlash may occur. For example, in the early 1970s, in an effort to bolster and stabilize a sagging economy, President Richard Nixon gave a speech recommending that industries should freeze wages and prices on most consumer products and that corporations should voluntarily adopt wage-price guidelines appropriate to their particular products. When this persuasive approach did not work, Nixon made a second speech in which he set up a wage-price control board to force compliance with the guidelines. The public reaction to this second speech was strong and negative: union workers protested, big business objected, and the stock market faltered. Indeed, the reaction was so strong that some economists believe that the inflation and recession of the mid-1970s were a direct result of a negative backlash from these coercive economic policies.

≡12.1 Influencing Through Persuasion

The purpose of the persuasive process is to influence. A field representative from a data-processing company who stresses her product's lower cost and ease of operation is using persuasion to make a sale. A shift supervisor who tells a group of workers, "You have a choice—work nights or quit," is using coercion. This strategy may be effective in bringing about change, but it usually leads to resentment, discouragement, and lack of respect and trust on the part of the person who has been coerced. For this reason, parents, teachers, salespeople, managers, and others in a position of influence usually find that they receive more cooperation and more positive responses when they use persuasive techniques rather than coercive tactics.

Even influence that is not coercive can sometimes be dangerous, because powerful speakers can make people do what they may not want to do or endorse an idea they may not fully support. One of the best defenses against persuasive manipulation is for listeners to recognize that persuasion has the potential to be unethical or to distort the truth. Persuasive communication strategies are essentially amoral—neither good nor bad. It is only how particular speakers use these strategies, and to what ends, that gives communication a dimension of morality. By knowing this and by being equipped to recognize manipulative and coercive methods, you may be able to protect yourself as a listener from being "taken." Likewise, persuasive speakers have a responsibility not to manipulate their listeners' motivations to unethical ends.

Coercive speakers often use psychological appeals aimed at fear, hatred, social pressure, and shock that cause people to perform acts they may never have done if they had been able to step outside the situation and objectively evaluate the potential consequences. A particularly horrifying example of manipulation was Adolf Hitler's emotional appeal to the German nation to build a "master race." Many people responded to this appeal, thereby knowingly or unknowingly participating in the destruction of other human beings, and later deeply regretted their actions.

Persuasion is often accomplished through repetition, since one message seldom results in any real change on the part of receivers. As a result, individuals and organizations typically spend massive amounts of money waging persuasive campaigns for all sorts of consumer products, social causes, international efforts, and government projects. This approach to persuasion relies on systematic, repeated exposure to the message with the objective of enhancing retention by listeners.

☰12.2 The Process of Persuasion

The persuasive speaker makes a claim and backs it up with motivating reasons and emotional appeals that encourage the listener to accept it. To do this, you must plan your speech by analyzing the audience and presenting arguments that will find favor with your particular listeners. The **theory of field-related standards** suggests that not all people reach conclusions in the same way and thus may react differently to the same evidence or appeals. Therefore, in establishing your arguments, you may want to include as many different types of appeals as you can to cover the various thought processes of the audience members. For example, to establish arguments for why your listeners should vote for a particular candidate, you might describe the candidate's positions on several issues rather than just one. Specific types of psychological appeals are described at length later in this chapter.

Identifying **group standards**, the habits of thinking or the norms of a particular group, also may help you develop your arguments. For example, if you are speaking to a group of labor union members, you can assume that on labor-related issues they will have views that favor the union rather than management. If you are going to propose a change in the present style of plant operation, show how it will be good for the union and its membership.

Try to determine the **individual standards** held by certain people within the group who have influence over other members. If you can persuade these influential members to go along with the proposal, will the entire group then go along? Who are the leaders? Who holds the most influence? If possible, try to key your appeals to that person or group of people. For example, if labor leaders support a proposal, the union membership probably will also. If the president of a club agrees, so may the rest of the club. If the student body leader, or the captain of the football team, or the head of the interfraternity council accepts an idea, the members of that person's group are likely to accept the idea too.

To be persuasive, you must develop your materials so that listeners feel the solution, plan of action, or cure that you are presenting is reasonable. Two methods of reasoning that you might consider using are critical and comparative advantage reasoning. In apply **critical reasoning**, you establish criteria and then match the solutions with the criteria. Let's say for example, that you are developing a plan of action for solving

On Listening

"The major function of critical listening . . . is to detect problems in the message cues or the apparent intention of the speaker, which might make the communication experience defective or even dangerous. To say that there can be great power in the communication experience is also to say that listeners must be wary. The symbolic ecology of the communication experience can be contaminated too easily.

"For these reasons, critical listening has monopolized the attention of many oral communication teachers. It often emerges in discussions of how to protect ourselves from persuasive manipulation or control. The general semanticist Wendell Johnson . . . made a succinct case for this importance of critical listening:

> As speakers, men [sic] have become schooled in the arts of persuasion, and without the counter-art of listening a man can be persuaded—even by his own words—to eat foods that ruin his liver, to abstain from killing flies, to vote away his right to vote, and to murder his fellows in the name of righteousness. The art of listening holds for us the desperate hope of withstanding the spreading ravages of commercial, nationalistic, and ideological persuasion.

"In order to resist such possible abuses, critical listeners must understand the process of persuasion so that they can identify both spurious and authentic forms of evidence, proof, and argument. Critical listening skills most frequently taught in speech communication courses include the assessment of source credibility, analysis of inductive and deductive patterns of reasoning, detection of logical fallacies, and recognition of both proper and improper emotional appeals and uses of emotive language."

From Michael Osborn and Suzanne Osborn, *Alliance for a Better Public Voice* (Dayton, Ohio: National Issue Forums, 1991), p. 24.

a club's financial problems. You set the following criteria: members' dues must not be raised, and any fund-raising activity must generate money quickly without extensive planning. To match these criteria, you propose that the club stage a lottery and sell raffle tickets.

In applying **comparative advantage reasoning**, you begin by stating the possible solutions, including the status quo (the present mode of operation). You then demonstrate how the proposal you are presenting is the most workable (how it can solve the problem), the most desirable (why it does not cause any greater problems), and the most practical (how it can be put into operation). You also show that your proposal has fewer disadvantages than any other. To use comparative advantage reasoning to solve the fund-raising problem, you would explain why a lottery is a workable plan by indicating that other organizations have used it and by presenting statistics on the amounts of money they have raised. You then would indicate that the lottery is desirable because it will not cost club members a great deal of money, it is not illegal, it will probably not lose money, and it does not place a heavy responsibility on any one club member. Next, you would show that the proposal is practical because a local printer can have the tickets ready by the next week and the finance committee of the club has already worked out a plan for distributing the tickets and handling the money. Finally, you would explain why this solution is better than other options: raising dues, dissolving the organization, continuing the status quo, or having a bake sale.

☰12.3   Components of the Persuasive Message

The classical Greek philosopher and rhetorician Aristotle first described persuasive speech in Western culture as based on the use of three components.[2] In today's terms, these three components can be identified as speaker credibility (**ethos**), logical arguments (**iogos**), and psychological appeals (**pathos**). Though Aristotle wrote more than two thousand years ago, his theories still characterize the development of an effective persuasive message.

As we examine these three elements, consider how important each of them is in affecting your ability to persuade others or the ability of others to persuade you. Also consider how these three elements must interrelate for a persuasive message to be as effective as possible. Note, however, that listeners responding to a persuasive message do not necessarily separate (and may not be able to separate) the logical arguments from the psychological appeals. Research has illustrated that listeners rarely distinguish the rational from the emotional.[3] Indeed, because people may respond on an emotional level to a well-reasoned argument, each person will have different interpretations of and reactions to the persuasive techniques speakers use.

Speaker Credibility   The reputation, prestige, and authority of a speaker as perceived by the listeners all contribute to **speaker credibility**. In most persuasive speaking situations, listeners need to accept the speaker before they will accept the message. Thus, a speaker's credibility is related to the impact of the message and may in fact be the most potent of all means of persuasion.

If you as a listener dislike, mistrust, or question the speaker's honesty, you will have a difficult time accepting what the speaker tells you.

A speaker's prior reputation with an audience can help or hinder the persuasive task. For example, if Dr. Albert Bruce Sabin, developer of the polio vaccine, had addressed the American Medical Association about the need for a national immunization program for communicable diseases, he would have had initial credibility, and his ideas would probably have been accepted. But a speaker who has no reputation as an expert in immunization, or who has been accused of research fraud, would have had a much more difficult persuasive task.

If you are unknown in a public speaking setting, you can build your credibility by advance publicity or by adjusting the introduction to your speech. Try to determine what your listeners know about you before preparing your speech. You must be aware of whether your credibility is nonexistent, positive, or negative. In a beginning speech class, you may find you have little or no credibility early in the semester. One of the ways to compensate for this is to describe the research you have done to develop the speech or the personal connection you have to the material. Presenting your material confidently may also lead the audience to perceive you positively. The more you speak and the less you read, the more you use eye contact and the stronger the documentation that develops your ideas, the more confidence your listeners will have in you.

If you feel your credibility is positive, enhance that advantage by developing a well-documented and logical presentation. If your credibility is poor, compensate for it. Try to alter your listeners' perceptions by emphasizing qualities about yourself they may respond to positively. A former convict who was attending college as part of an educational release program started his presentation about the need for altering prison procedures by saying:

> I am a paroled convict. Knowing this, some of you may immediately say to yourself, "Why should I listen to anything that an ex-jailbird has to say?" Well, it is because I was in prison, and because I know what prison can do to a person, and because I know what negative influences jail can have on a person, that I want to speak to you tonight.[4]

If you know that your listeners have a negative perception of you, make a special effort to develop a well-documented speech, one that admits areas of disagreement and asks the audience to give you a fair chance to be heard. A Democratic candidate, speaking before a predominantly Republican audience, might state:

> I realize that I am a Democrat and you are Republicans. I also realize that we are both after the same thing—a city in which we can live without fear for

our lives, a city in which the services such as trash and snow removal are efficient, and a city in which taxes are held in check. You, the Republicans, and I, the Democrat, do have common goals. I'd appreciate your considering how I propose to help all of us achieve our joint objectives.

Factors of Credibility   Several factors contribute to a speaker's credibility: occupation, education, clothes, personal looks, personality, respect for others, sensitivity to trends, knowledge of the problem being discussed, ability to verbalize, vitality, trustworthiness, and general expertise.[5] Some of the factors in this list, such as clothing and personal appearance, may surprise you, but dress, voice, and manners truly do affect an audience's attitude toward a speaker. Because persuasion is cumulative—because many factors combine to urge listeners to reach conclusions—each factor in the process is important to consider.

Politicians recognize that physical appearance, clothing, and hair style contribute to their public image, and they pay close attention to these factors. The Kennedy-Nixon television debate during the 1960 presidential campaign illustrated how extensively such physical factors can influence speaker credibility. The rhetorical analysis following the debate centered on Nixon's waxen, perspiring appearance and Kennedy's vigorous, healthy, and suntanned look. Since then, political critics have claimed that proper make-up and attire could have improved Nixon's image significantly.[6] This important historical event has guided political consultants ever since in carefully tailoring a candidate's image to appeal to voters, especially if the candidate will appear on television, which has become a major means of political persuasion.

Perceived trustworthiness also affects credibility. Listeners appear to be more willing to consider new ideas when they perceive the speaker to be a trustworthy source. The professional position speakers hold, for example, may make it easier or more difficult for them to gain the respect of an audience. In a poll taken by the Gallup organization, interviewers asked a sample of Americans how they would rate the honesty and ethical standards of people in different fields. The results of this poll (Table 12.1) reflect the perceived credibility of the various occupations studied. As a listener, you may be deciding whether or not to accept a speaker's views based on his or her occupational status, or other similar factors.

Establishing Credibility   An unknown speaker has little initial credibility. If you are a beginning speaker, it is wise to consider some techniques for gaining personal acceptance from the audience. Above all, you should demonstrate that you are trustworthy, competent, and dynamic. These three factors operate as dimensions of a speaker's credibility during a speech.

Table 12.1

*Credibility Ratings of
Various Occupations*

	Very High, High	(% change, 1991 vs. 1990)	Very High	High	Average	Low	Very Low	No Opinion
Druggists/pharmacists	60%	(−2)	13%	47%	32%	4%	1%	3%
Clergy	57	(+2)	16	41	31	6	2	4
Medical doctors	54	(+2)	9	45	37	6	2	1
Dentists	50	(−2)	8	42	41	5	1	3
College teachers	45	(−6)	7	38	35	6	1	13
Engineers	45	(−5)	7	38	39	3	1	12
Police officers	43	(−6)	7	36	42	10	3	2
Funeral directors	35	0	6	29	43	9	2	11
Bankers	30	(−2)	3	27	52	11	3	4
TV reporters/commentators	29	(−3)	5	24	49	15	4	3
Journalists	26	(−4)	3	23	52	13	3	6
Newspaper reporters	24	0	2	22	54	14	3	5
Lawyers	22	0	4	18	43	20	10	5
Business executives	21	(−4)	3	18	55	14	2	8
Building contractors	20	0	3	17	49	19	3	9
U.S. senators	19	(−5)	2	17	48	24	6	3
Local officeholders	19	(−3)	2	17	54	19	4	4
Congressional representatives	19	(−1)	2	17	44	24	8	5
Real estate agents	17	(+1)	1	16	54	18	4	7
State officeholders	14	(−3)	1	13	53	21	7	5
Stockbrokers	14	0	2	12	46	17	4	19
Insurance salespeople	14	(+1)	2	12	47	26	7	6
Labor union leaders	13	(−2)	2	11	41	25	9	12
Ad practitioners	12	0	2	10	46	26	6	10
Car salespeople	8	(+2)	2	6	37	36	13	6

Source: "Pharmacists and Clergy Rate Highest for Honesty and Ethics; Senators and Police Decline," The Gallup Poll News Service, 56, no. 4 (May 2, 1991), p. 1.

Trustworthiness follows from a person's integrity. You want to convince your audience that you are honest, reliable, and sincere. For example, if you are attempting to persuade your listeners to sign pledge cards to donate their eyes to an eye bank upon their deaths, show them a card that certifies you yourself as a potential donor. If your personal experiences show that you follow your own recommendations, your audience is more likely to accept your advice as reliable. As a listener, you

A speaker establishes credibility with the audience by demonstrating that he is trustworthy, competent, and dynamic.

should be aware that you tend to perceive speakers as persuasive if you feel they are trustworthy.

Competence, another component of credibility, refers to the wisdom, authority, and knowledge a speaker demonstrates. Prepare yourself to be an expert on your topic so that listeners will have confidence in what you are saying. You can demonstrate competence by including up-to-date research findings, documenting sources of information, and connecting yourself to the topic.

You can also strengthen your position by quoting recognized experts in the field. In this way, listeners will draw the conclusion that if experts agree with your stand, then your stand must have merit. Quotations from experts let your audience know that you have taken the time to probe the attitudes and findings of others in the field before reaching conclusions.

For this reason, when you use supporting material, be certain to document your sources. Tell the audience the source and date of your material as well as the identities of the people responsible for creating or developing the information. If the sources are unfamiliar to your listeners, establish their credentials. For example, if you are attempting to persuade your listeners that there are advantages to living in our age of change and uncertainty, you can quote an expert:

Dr. Rollo May, a practicing psychotherapist and professor at Harvard, in his book *Love and Will,* supports my contentions when he writes, "One of the values of living in a transitional age—an age of therapy—is that it forces upon us the opportunity, even as we try to resolve our individual problems, to uncover new meaning in perennial man and to see more deeply into those qualities which constitute the human being."[7]

If possible, associate yourself with the topic. For example, if you are proposing a plan of action concerning safety regulations at construction sites, refer to your experience on a construction crew. Your listeners will more readily accept your point that the construction industry needs more stringent safety regulations than if you did not have the personal experience.

Although you want to reinforce your qualifications while developing your presentation, your audience may lose interest if you begin with a lengthy review of your research, experiences, or general qualifications. The person who introduces you should highlight your expertise. Let your credibility emerge directly throughout your speech: "It has been my experience that . . ."; "I have observed that . . ."; "My research indicates that . . ." Remember that specifics documented by time, place, and description are usually perceived to be more valid than personal opinion, especially if the presenter is inexperienced in the field.

As you listen to persuasive speeches, evaluate what the speaker is saying. Does he or she appear to be competent? Does the presentation include up-to-date research findings and documented sources of information? If it is appropriate, does the speaker connect himself or herself to the topic?

Another characteristic of credibility is **dynamism**, the projection of a vigorous, concerned, powerful image. President Ronald Reagan, sometimes called the "great communicator," developed his reputation as a speaker not necessarily from what he said but from how he said it—his oral dynamics. Many years as an actor had taught him how to present words and ideas in a forceful and convincing manner. As a speaker, speak directly to the audience, be animated in your vocalizations, and try to appear relaxed and comfortable. As a listener, be aware that some audience members are fooled by speakers who are dynamic but actually say very little of substance. What is said should be more important than how it is said. Understand that an audience can be carried away by a well-presented speaker.

By demonstrating trustworthiness, competence, and dynamism throughout your speech, you can help listeners accept you as a person of credibility and possibly move them toward accepting your message. Calculate carefully—on the basis of your audience analysis—what will most enhance your trustworthiness, prestige, and authoritativeness, and use these factors to build your message. As a listener, try to be a discerning and critical listener of persuasive messages.

Logical Arguments

In Western cultures, as we saw in an earlier chapter, critical thinking is the foundation on which most persuasive messages are built. Thus, if you want to present a well-thought-out speech, you must determine what your audience believes about your central idea and build your arguments on that information. Remember that although listeners may be swayed by a highly credible, dynamic speaker, over the long run they may forget the impact of the presentation style and remember only the basic premises. Consequently, you must make certain that your arguments are well substantiated.

There is some evidence in communication research to suggest that listeners cannot distinguish sound arguments and evidence.[8] However, especially when confronted with information that is new or that they are skeptical about, most listeners probably look for logical connections in the messages they receive.[9] Communication analysts have suggested that a well-reasoned message can have a decided impact on the speaker's credibility. As one source noted, "When listeners want reasons spelled out, they mercilessly put down as stupid or too sloppy to be trusted communicators who do not reason or who do it badly. It is easy to show that general absence of clarity, consistency, completeness, and consecutiveness in discourse is, in the world's eye, the mark of the fool."[10]

Remember that all factors in the persuasive speaking situation ought to be centered on the audience and that an audience is influenced by clarity of ideas, vividness of language, examples, and specifics that illuminate the reasons for the chosen solution. Consequently, organize and package your materials in such a way that they lead to the conclusion that only one solution is possible—the solution you are proposing. As a listener, you should be concerned about whether a persuasive speaker's contentions lead to the proposed solution. As a critical listener, evaluate whether the conclusion proposed is logical and in your best interest.

Patterns of Logical Argument

Your audience analysis should help you determine whether to use the inductive or deductive pattern of argument development. As a listener, evaluate the impact of a sender's persuasive message by being aware of how inductive and deductive arguments work and whether the development of the speech is logical and sequential. Realize that you don't have to commit to changing your beliefs or buying an idea that doesn't make sense to you and is not in your best interests.

Inductive Argument.   An **inductive argument** is based on probability—what conclusion is most likely to be expected or believed from the available evidence. Thus, the more specific instances you can draw on as evidence in an inductive argument, the more probable and believable your conclusion will seem to the audience. Inductive argument can take one of two patterns: the generalization conclusion or the hypothesis conclusion.

In the **generalization conclusion**, the speaker examines a number of specific instances and attempts to predict some future occurrence or explain a whole category of instances. Underlying this is the assumption that what holds true for specific instances will hold true for all instances in a given category. For example, speaking in Atlanta to the National Conference on Corporate Community Involvement, the vice-president of the American Association of Retired Persons described the "graying" of America. He developed an inductive argument by a series of claims:

> Because of better medical care, nutrition and activity, more people are gliding into their 60s and beyond in good physical shape. . . . Mental ability does not diminish merely because of age, according to researchers. In fact, it may improve. . . . The economic health of today's older generation has improved to the point where advertisers are already targeting the "Maturity Market." [Using evidence to support each of the claims, he drew an inductive conclusion:] The upshot of all this change in better physical, psychological and economic well-being is that we are looking at a new breed of older person vastly different from former negative stereotypes.[11]

In the **hypothesis conclusion**, the speaker uses a hypothesis to explain all the available evidence. For such an argument to have substance, however, the hypothesis must provide the best explanation for that evidence. Reviewing a number of cases in which terrorists had been tried and convicted throughout the world, the U.S. Department of State Ambassador-at-Large for Counterterrorism offered the hypothesis that "the rule of law is working against terrorists and fewer terrorists are being released without trial." His aim was to convince his audience that "we, the people of the world's democracies, will ultimately prevail over those who would through terror take from us the fruits of two centuries of political progress."[12]

Deductive Argument. The **deductive argument** is based on logical necessity. In other words, if one accepts the premise of the deductive argument—the proposition that is the basis of the argument—then one must also accept its conclusion. One type of deductive argument is the **categorical syllogism**, an argument that contains two premises and a conclusion. For instance, you might argue:

> All "A" students study hard (*premise*).
> You are an "A" student (*premise*).
> Therefore you study hard (*conclusion*).

If your listeners accept the premises of this argument, then they must accept the conclusion because it is the only one that can be drawn.

In developing an argument using the categorical syllogism, make sure you present a clear set of premises and that these lead to the conclusion. For example, in a speech with the purpose of persuading the audience that specific symptoms lead doctors to diagnose chronic fatigue syndrome, a speaker might state:

(*Premise*)   A proven sign of chronic fatigue syndrome is an off-balance immune system, with a positive diagnosis of Epstein-Barr disease.

(*Premise*)   A proven sign of chronic fatigue syndrome is a positive diagnosis for human herpesvirus 6.

(*Premise*)   A proven sign of chronic fatigue syndrome is a positive diagnosis for human B-cell lymphotropic virus.

(*Conclusion*)   Therefore, a person diagnosed with Epstein-Barr disease, human herpesvirus 6, and human B-cell lymphotropic virus can be diagnosed as having chronic fatigue syndrome.

Public speakers typically use a special form of deductive syllogism, the **enthymeme**, in which one premise is not directly stated because the speaker and listener both accept the premise.[13] For example, while speaking to those attending a conference on writing assessment, a speaker concluded, "If we can teach our children, from all backgrounds, to write with joy, originality, clarity and control, then I don't think we have much else to worry about."[14] This conclusion is based on the premise accepted by both speaker and listeners that children should be taught effective writing skills. Make sure when using the enthymeme that your audience does, indeed, share common premises. As a listener, be wary of a persuasive speaker who leads you to a conclusion by assuming that you share acceptance of the premise. If you don't accept the premise, don't be led to the conclusion.

The **disjunctive argument** is an either/or argument in which true alternatives must be established. Talking about America and the collapse of the Soviet Empire to a university audience, then-Secretary of State James Baker pointed out that the United States faced an either/or choice:

> To follow our fears and turn inward, ignoring the opportunities presented by the collapse of the Soviet Empire, or to answer the summons of history and lead toward a better future for all.[15]

The **conditional argument** sets up an if/then proposition. In this pattern of argument, there are two conditions, one of which necessarily follows from the other. For example, the chief executive officer of a major accounting firm proposed that the federal government adopt a new accrual accounting system so that the public and Congress could monitor the federal budget. He argued that

> if citizens were to demand the financial information to which they are clearly entitled, incentives would be created for sound fiscal management—and, perhaps, for more enlightened political leadership. We could then expect to see better-informed decision making—less fiscal recklessness—and a reduction in the risks caused by the misallocation of capital.[16]

Persuasive Evidence   The persuasive speaker must not only structure the argument to meet the listeners' needs but must also support these contentions persuasively.

The most persuasive form of supporting material—**evidence**—includes testimony from experts, statistics, and specific instances. If you can offer solid data to support your contentions, they will serve both to strengthen your perceived credibility and to lend substance to the argument you present. For example, a speaker who attempts to persuade listeners that the U.S. Food and Drug Administration (FDA) needs more funds to hire inspectors might cite specific instances from the agency's files. Real cases are on record of potatoes that were contaminated with insecticide, turkey stuffing that contained glass particles, and ginger ale that contained mold—all of which were sold to consumers. For additional support, the speaker might cite statistics from congressional budget hearings indicating that only 500 FDA inspectors are available to monitor 60,000 food-processing plants in the United States.

Essentially, your evidence should support the central idea, connecting it, if possible, with the listeners' beliefs about the topic. Persuasive evidence should be carefully tied to the argument at hand and accurately reported from authoritative, reliable sources. For example, the speaker who argues for additional FDA inspectors would connect evidence from FDA files and the congressional budget hearings to the generally held belief that uncontaminated food is necessary for public health and welfare. It seems fairly safe to assume that most of the audience would agree with the need for uncontaminated food, but not all speaking situations are so clear-cut. Before trying to build a persuasive case, speakers must ascertain through audience analysis that their assumptions are consistent with those held by the audience.

Reasoning Fallacies   In addition to presenting carefully structured and supported arguments, you should ensure the validity of your arguments so that your listeners can reasonably draw the conclusions you wish them to reach. To accomplish a valid argument, you must avoid some common reasoning fallacies.

One reasoning fallacy that can trip up persuasive communicators is the **hasty generalization**. A speaker who makes a hasty generalization reaches unwarranted, general conclusions from an insufficient number of instances. For example, a speaker who argues that gun control legislation is necessary by citing a few freeway shootings in Los Angeles is probably making a hasty generalization. Such limited instances may not provide the listener with enough of a foundation on which to base an all-inclusive conclusion.

Another reasoning fallacy that limits the persuasiveness of a message is **faulty analogical reasoning**. No analogy is ever truly complete because no two cases, however comparable, are ever identical. Speakers use faulty analogies when they assume that the elements two items or events share are similar in every respect. The speaker who argues, for example, that the current AIDS crisis is completely analogous to the bubonic plague that ravaged medieval Europe overlooks the scientific advances that make the AIDS crisis a very different (although no less serious) medical problem.

Faulty causal reasoning occurs when a speaker makes an overstated claim that something caused something else. A speaker would probably be overstating the case by arguing, for example, that the bank scandal in the House of Representatives, in which many congresspeople wrote bad checks, directly resulted from a lack of moral accountability on the part of all federal public officials.

An entire set of reasoning fallacies can result if the speaker tries to ignore the issue. By **ignoring the issue**, the speaker uses irrelevant arguments to obscure the real issue. The **ad hominem argument**—an attack on the personal character of a source—is one example. For instance, the campaign of Bill Clinton, the 1992 Democratic presidential candidate, was damaged because of accusations of marital infidelity, draft evasion, marijuana use, and political influence on the part of his wife's law firm. Some political observers questioned whether these issues were at all related to Clinton's ability to be president.

The **ad populum argument**—an appeal to people in terms of their prejudices and passions rather than on the basis of the issue at hand—is another way of ignoring the issue. For example, despite the vast amount of negative publicity resulting from the financial scandal surrounding Jim and Tammy Bakker's PTL ministry in the late 1980s, devotees of PTL, stirred by passionate appeals from their leaders, continued to contribute millions of dollars to keep the religious organization going.

Yet another example of the fallacy of ignoring the issue is the **ad ignorantiam argument**—the claim that a statement is true because it cannot be disproved. For example, proponents of pit bull terriers argue that pit bulls are not dangerous pets because dog-bite statistics show that pit bulls rank ninth in number of bites—after poodles and cocker spaniels. Such a claim ignores the fact that pit bulls do cause harm. The issue is not whether poodles and cocker spaniels bite.

All reasoning fallacies can interfere with the persuasiveness of a message and can diminish the total impact of the speech. A discerning audience member can see through most such smoke screens. Therefore, as a speaker, analyze your arguments to make sure that the structure and supporting evidence lead to valid conclusions that your listeners can accept. As a public listener of persuasive messages, be aware that speakers sometimes use fallacious reasoning in developing arguments and be on guard so that you don't fall for misinformation.

Developing Persuasive Arguments

When developing a persuasive speech, you must consider the order in which to present the arguments. Two possibilities are available. Some studies support the idea that the strongest argument should come first so that it will have the greatest impact on listeners at the outset. Other studies, however, support the idea that the strongest argument should come last to ensure that listeners remember it.[17]

You also must decide whether to develop both sides of the argument (and thus refute opposing arguments) or to present only your own stand. One potential problem in developing both sides of the argument is that you may raise issues and present ideas your listeners had not previously considered. If you are unable to refute these issues effectively, you may give your listeners a solution other than the one you intended—one they might not have considered if you had never mentioned it!

Because the research mentioned above is not definitive, it is sometimes difficult to decide how to best develop the issues in a persuasive speech. It is safe to assume, however, that the order of your arguments must be based on careful audience analysis. If you feel that the audience is on your side, state your arguments first and bring your listeners along with you for the rest of your presentation (a deductive mode of reasoning). However, if you perceive your audience to be hostile to your position, build the background first, and then present your arguments when you feel your listeners are ready for them (a more inductive mode of reasoning). This strategy requires thorough prior analysis as well as process analysis during your presentation so that you can make any necessary adaptations based on listeners' responses.

Speakers should be aware of the **inoculation strategy**, which suggests that just as people can be protected from disease through immunization, so too can listeners be inhibited from accepting subsequent counterarguments if they are armed with the means to refute them.[18] Let's say you plan to attend hearings favoring rezoning a residential area in your neighborhood. If your local citizens association bombards you with arguments against changing the neighborhood, you will go to the hearings more prepared to recognize the weaknesses in the opposing arguments and, ideally, strengthened in the support of your own stand.[19]

Another factor to consider in developing your arguments is **cognitive dissonance**, the mental discomfort that occurs when we accept an action or an idea that does not coincide with our previously held attitudes.[20] For example, if you are trying to persuade a group of new investors to purchase stock in a mutual fund, you should give reasons that reinforce the benefits of mutual funds, allay any fears about such funds, and diminish the attractiveness of alternative investment procedures. Your persuasive task will be especially challenging if your listeners have seen a decline in the value of mutual funds. If you present strong arguments and reassure your listeners that mutual funds are a sound, long-term investment, they will have more commitment to purchase the mutual fund after they reassess what you have said.

Here again, prior analysis can help you determine what persuasive strategies will be most reinforcing. If the potential buyers have young children, then your argument can center on the long-term proven profit increase of mutual funds over savings accounts, increased profits that can be used for the children's college educations. You can appeal to persons of limited finances by emphasizing that a mutual fund broadens the opportunity for profit and lessens the possibility of financial loss because clients are spreading their investments over more than one company.

Structuring the Body of a Persuasive Speech

The structure of a persuasive speech should allow the listener to reach the behavioral or mental change the speaker desires. The most common method of developing a persuasive message is to use the problem-solution arrangement (see discussion of problem-solution arrangement in Chapter 7).[21] The speaker identifies what is wrong and then presents the cure or recommendation for its cure.

The structure of the body of a speech which develops inductively would be:

III. Body
   A. Identify the situation (what is wrong).
   B. Identify the problem (what has to be changed).
   C. List the possible solutions to the problem.
   D. Evaluate the solutions for workability, desirability, practicality.
      1. Workability—Can the solution solve the problem?
      2. Desirability—Can the solution cause bigger problems?
      3. Practicality—Can the solution be put into effect?
   E. Recommend the solution that is most workable, desirable, and practical.

An alternative to this, the see-blame-cure-cost method, develops the speech by stressing the evil or problem that exists, determining what has caused the problem, investigating possible solutions, and then presenting the most practical solution. The see-blame-cure-cost technique allows the audience to see the problem, know who or what is to blame, hear of the possible cures, and then realize the costs involved in making the change such as increased taxes, giving up personal rights, and the emotional confusion that often accompanies any alteration.

Psychological Appeals

Psychological appeals, which constitute the final component of the persuasive message, enlist listeners' emotions as motivation for accepting your arguments. Just as you must select your arguments and enhance your credibility on the basis of what you know about your listeners, so must you select psychological appeals on the basis of what you think will stir your listeners' emotions. The purpose of incorporating some emotional appeals in your speech is to keep your listeners involved with you as you spell out your persuasive plan, even though they may not discern the emotional from the rational in your presentation.[22] One way to develop psychological appeals is to use Maslow's hierarchy of individual needs.

Maslow's Hierarchy of Individual Needs

Abraham Maslow, the psychologist noted for developing the concept of self-actualization, proposed a hierarchy of human needs (Figure 12.1) that can help speakers analyze the emotional needs of an audience. To use this theory, a speaker must determine the level of need of a particular group of listeners and then select appeals aimed at that level.[23] Although Maslow's theory is hierarchical, in reality these levels of need can function simultaneously. Therefore a speaker need not appeal to listeners on only one level at a time.

Maslow suggested that all human beings have five types of need. At the first, most basic level are **physiological needs**—hunger, sleep, sex, and thirst. These needs must normally be satisfied before a person can be motivated by appeals to other levels of need. Recognizing this, the U.S. Agency for International Development appeals to the physiological needs of people in developing nations as a means of persuading them to adopt a democratic form of government. A speaker might address a group of potential organ donors by pointing out the physiological needs of transplant patients, or persuade a group of homeless people to go to a shelter or an assistance center by appealing to their physiological needs.

The second level, **safety needs**, encompasses security, stability, protection, and strength. In presenting speeches to laid-off workers, employers may soften the blow by sharing information on job-search seminars,

Figure 12.1

Maslow's Hierarchy of Needs

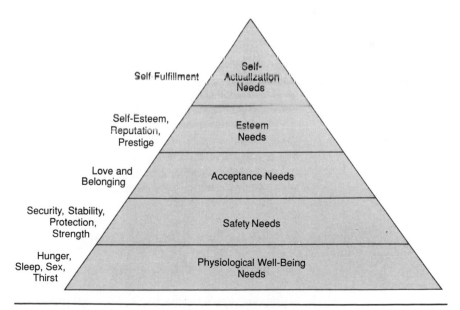

résumé preparation, and other career skills. Successful political candidates often key in on this second level of human needs when tailoring persuasive campaign speeches. An incumbent who can claim responsibility for a high level of police protection, for efficient trash disposal and snow removal, and for a vibrant economy is very likely to get re-elected. However, if an opponent can prove that the present officeholder is not satisfying these types of needs, the incumbent may well be voted out.

The third level consists of **acceptance needs**, for love and a sense of belonging. Americans are highly motivated by the need to belong, as evidenced by their affiliations with many different types of social and work-related groups. Persuasive speakers may appeal to a listener's desire to be "a good American" in order to motivate audiences. **Esteem needs**, at the fourth level, involve both self-esteem (desire for achievement and mastery) and esteem from others (desire for reputation and prestige). A coach giving a half-time speech is appealing to the esteem needs of team members.

Self-actualization needs, the desire for self-fulfillment or the achievement of one's greatest potential, is the fifth level in Maslow's hierarchy. This is a lofty level that few people ever reach but many strive for. A persuasive speaker can appeal to listeners' needs for self-actualization by setting high goals to reach. For example, entertainer Bill Cosby challenged 1992 University of Maryland graduates to make a difference in the world and in their own lives.

Group Needs   The needs of audience members may be strongly influenced by the needs of the groups to which they belong. Many Americans who have gone through the 1970s "me" decade of self-indulgence and the 1980s "no" decade in the wake of smoking, drunken driving, and AIDS are now into the 1990s "back to basics" decade of a simpler lifestyle.[24] Adapting to trends in group needs thus becomes a challenge for the persuasive speaker.

The desire to motivate a group also may be a legitimate objective of the speech itself. Organizations are booking motivational speakers for meetings and conventions in record numbers. The main goal of these speakers is to inspire self-improvement or financial improvement in salespeople, marketing personnel, and other staff groups. An official of the Washington Speakers Bureau observed that "the thousands of motivational speakers currently in the circuit make up the largest segment of the speaking industry."[25]

Appeals to   Once you have determined your audience's needs (perhaps using Mas-
Motivate Listeners   low's hierarchy), you can then build into your speech the psychological appeals that will help you persuade listeners to accept your point of view. A considerable variety of motivational appeals are available. Many speakers experience success by making an appeal to:[26]

1. *Adventure.* Here the speaker stresses the listener's desire to explore new worlds, see exciting places, take part in unusual experiences, or participate in different events. A speaker representing the travel industry might motivate potential travelers by describing what it would be like to go on a tour.

2. *Companionship.* Speakers often tap our desire to be with others. A speaker might make this appeal in an attempt to recruit volunteers for a local youth center.

3. *Deference.* Showing respect for a wiser, more experienced authority can be a successful speaking strategy. A speaker on international issues might defer to an officer in the Foreign Service for an assessment of a thorny international situation. Such deference can assure an audience that the speaker is in touch with key people who do make a difference. Speakers often use this appeal when they refer to a knowledgeable researcher who supports their point of view.

4. *Fear.* This appeal is used to raise apprehension in an audience. Identifying fears that threaten listeners or their values can motivate an audience to take action to overcome a potential danger. For example, speakers for the American Cancer Society's antismoking campaign stress the negative effects of smoking not only on the smoker but also on those in the same household and on a developing fetus. Though the fear appeal can be powerful, research shows that a speaker must be careful not to overdo it. A listener can become too frightened to accept the proposed action because the situation is perceived as hopeless, or the listener may become desensitized because of oversell. This is the case of some overeaters who decide that they have already jeopardized their physical health.[27]

5. *Gender.* This can be a powerful persuasive tool. Appealing to women's rights, stressing the need for more women leaders in upper levels of management, and criticizing sexual harassment have all been useful approaches for speakers who attempt to rally support for women's causes.

6. *Guilt.* Religious speakers often use this approach to persuade people to change their ways, or to feel badly about actions they have committed or might wish to commit.

7. *Humor.* Speakers who appeal to a listener's sense of humor demonstrate that they do not take themselves or their subject overseriously, so everyone can relax a bit. However, some speakers hesitate to use humor in a persuasive speech, especially one on a serious topic, since they feel the audience may be offended and more difficult to persuade. Note the number of humorous advertisements you see daily on television. These ads are attempts to persuade you. Advertising agencies realize that if humor is appropriate and helps make the point, it can be an effective motivating tool.

Profile: Patricia Fripp, *professional motivational speaker*

"Come out punching!" Counsel from an enthusiastic boxing trainer? No, this is sound public speaking advice from Patricia Fripp, a popular motivational speaker. Although her informational brochures quietly promote her as "A Speaker for All Reasons," she has been hailed as "electrifying," "highly energetic," and "a forceful presence."

In 1966, at age twenty, Fripp left her native England and set foot in the United States armed only with a positive attitude, $500, and her skill as a hair stylist. She had no job, nowhere to live, and no contacts. But, she says wryly, she "knew everyone in America was rich, and movie stars flocked through the streets!" Fripp worked as a hair stylist in San Francisco and eventually began traveling as a demonstrator of various beauty products and techniques. Because her stories and chats about her business experience added noticeable flair to her demonstrations, audience members soon began inviting her to speak at their Rotary Clubs, Kiwanis Clubs, and other civic organizations.

In 1977 Fripp attended her first National Speakers Association Convention. Seven years later, she became the National Speakers Association's first woman president. She is a Certified Speaking Professional (CSP) and has received the Council of Peers Award of Excellence (CPAE), the highest recognition for professionalism in speaking. In general, her work ranges from 25-minute keynote speeches to all-day seminars. She has spoken to government agencies, at independent rallies, and at meetings for such corporate giants as IBM, AT&T, and General Electric. Her presentations have titles such as "Creative Thinking for Better Business" and "Adapting to Change." Fripp states that her job is to present a message that is "in harmony with, and reflects the philosophy of" the company or organization that hires her.

Fripp's list of "Basics on Speaking for Your First or Fiftieth Talk" includes twenty-one noteworthy recommendations, such as

◆ Come out punching! Because people tend to remember a speech's beginning and end, make them worth remembering. Use startling statements or other attention grabbers rather than saying "Good evening ladies and gentlemen. It's a pleasure to be here."

◆ Recognize that because television has helped shape today's audiences, they demand more powerful speakers and have shorter attention spans. Be unique and interesting.

◆ People do not remember what you say as much as what they "see." Tell stories to illustrate your points and make them come alive. A story or vignette should be able to stand alone as a short talk.

Public speaking skill is important for almost all of us. "Your value in the marketplace depends very much upon how easy or difficult it is to replace you," Fripp says. "If you can learn to stand up and speak eloquently with confidence, you will be head and shoulders above your competition." The self-motivated young woman who arrived from England took her own advice and has forged a successful career for herself in the business of motivating others.

8. *Loyalty.* Our feelings of loyalty—to nation, to friends and family, and to organizations—are important to us. During Operation Desert Storm in 1991, appeals to national loyalty made by President Bush and others constituted probably the greatest persuasive motivator in getting near unanimous approval for the military action. The same is true of the "Buy American" speech campaign conducted by representatives of the U.S. clothing and automobile industry. We demonstrate loyalty to and defend those things and people of whom we are proud and with whom we identify.[28]

9. *Power and authority.* People often want to hold positions of power over others, to be the leader, to be in charge. The speaker who emphasizes American military initiatives may well appeal to the power and authority many Americans want to maintain as a world-leading nation.[29]

10. *Reverence.* Audiences are sometimes motivated by hero worship of sports figures, performers, astronauts, and other prominent figures. Referring to heros or important people who back your cause can convince others to accept your ideas. For example, in attempting to get a large turnout for a national "Freedom of Choice" rally held in Washington, D.C., in 1992, the president of the National Organization for Women stressed that marchers would include Hollywood stars Jane Fonda, Joanne Woodward, Cybill Shepherd, Molly Ringwald, Morgan Fairchild, and Mary Steenburgen.[30]

11. *Revulsion.* If used with care, the appeal to disgust can be effective. A speaker might illustrate the effects of water pollution by showing the listeners some samples from Chesapeake Bay, and then ask them to support legislation to clean up the bay. Astute speakers do not, however, arouse such a strong sense of revulsion that listeners tune out the message. Anti-abortionists and anti-vivisectionists sometimes overwhelm their listeners with revolting photographs of aborted fetuses and maimed laboratory animals.

12. *Worship.* Concern for the religious beliefs of people is a powerful persuasive tool. Forty percent of American adults attend church or synagogue in a typical week.[31] Using this information, persuasive speakers can appeal to a listener's religious convictions as a way to gain support for their side. The founder of a major anti-abortion organization, in a speech intending to persuade an audience, said, "We want to define for you the nature of the battle. And the nature of the battle is this: Whose God and whose God's laws will dominate the culture? It's good versus evil, good guys against bad guys."[32]

13. *Sympathy.* By showing photographs or films of starving children, impoverished elderly, or the homeless poor, a speaker can compel listeners to give time, money, or other resources. A sympathetic

bond, often coupled with guilt, is thus created with those less fortunate.

As this list shows, speakers have a wide variety of options from which to choose in developing persuasive appeals. Speakers must analyze the audience to determine need levels, select appeals that will meet these needs, and place the appeals in the speech at points where they will have the greatest persuasive impact. For example, if you determine that your listeners are operating at the level of acceptance needs, you would select appeals that motivate them at this level. Let's say you wish to persuade the employees of a particular organization to form an employees' association. You might explain how the association will satisfy their needs for meeting and interacting with other people and for participating in group decision making.

≡12.4   The Persuasive Process in Action

Psychological appeals, coupled with speaker credibility and well-reasoned and supported arguments, provide a sound approach to influencing others to change their beliefs or actions. The sample persuasive speech in Figure 12.2 illustrates the interaction of these components.

Figure 12.2

Outline for a Sample Persuasive Speech

Purpose statement: To persuade audience members to do their part to save the environment by listing the environmental problems this nation faces and how problems of the environment can be addressed through a combination of concern and control.

Attention material to gain audience interest	I. Introduction A. Attention material: Humans have the power to destroy all life on the earth. As environmental specialists have observed, "That power may be released at any time, for it is harnessed only by fallible humans, and, increasingly, by fallible machines."
Orienting material to get listeners involved in the topic	B. Orienting material: The future of our environment should be of concern to all of us.
Central point of the speech	II. Central Idea: Do your part to save the environment.

First main point Discussion and development of the first point with statistics, factual information, explanation, persuasive appeals	III. Body
	    A. Here are the environmental problems facing us:
	        1. Nuclear winter—the detonation of even a small number of nuclear weapons could send enough nuclear fallout into the atmosphere to trigger major climatic disruptions and create a global nuclear winter.

Figure 12.2 Cont.

2. Energy—78 quadrillion BTUs of energy were consumed in 1992 in the United States alone.
3. Water—more than 50 percent of the nation's wetlands have already been destroyed.
4. Air—more than half of the U.S. population lives in areas where air pollutants still exceed health standards at least part of the time.
5. Wildlife—the world faces a major threat of the loss of wild species, destroying the balance of nature.
6. Land—natural areas today are lost to development, further upsetting the balance of nature.
7. The destruction of the natural environment is the result of many factors—population expansion, industrial demands, and unplanned and uncontrolled urbanization and development.

Transition

(The problems of our environment are staggering. However, there is much that we can do to begin to address these problems.)

Second main point

B. The problems of the environment can be addressed through a combination of concern and control.

Discussion and development of the second point with suggested strategies

1. All of us, decision makers and taxpayers alike, need to recognize the impact of governmental decisions and actions on the environment.
2. Sound resource management and careful protection of the environment are critical.
3. The nation needs a new agenda that takes a global approach to dealing with population growth that is exceeding world capacity; toxic chemicals; burning of fossil fuels; and nuclear destruction.
4. What you can do as an individual—conservation consciousness and strategies, recycling, consumer and taxpayer pressure.

IV. Conclusion

A. Summary

Restates major points of the body of the speech

1. The environmental problems facing us include nuclear winter, the overuse of energy, the destruction of the nation's wetlands, unclear air, the destruction of the balance of nature, and the destruction of the natural environment.
2. These problems can be addressed by citizen demand for government environmental decisions, sound resource management, a global agenda to deal with the problems, and individuals becoming conservation conscious.

B. Clincher

Appeals for action on the part of the listener

1. Carrying out the environmental agenda will require the cooperation of individuals from all walks of life. The involvement and assistance of industry, labor, educators, scientists, lawyers, students, government workers, homemakers, etc., will be needed.
2. You can do your part by becoming involved. Write your political representatives, become an environmental doer rather than an environmental destroyer. Recycle rather than trash!

Summary

In this chapter on persuasive speaking, the key ideas presented were:

◆ Persuasion is "the process by means of which one party purposefully secures a voluntary change of behavior, mental and/or physical, on the part of another party by employing appeals to both feelings and intellect."

◆ The basic process of persuasion requires that the speaker make a claim and back it up in such a way that listeners accept the claim.

◆ Successful persuasive strategies center on the use of speaker credibility, logical arguments, and psychological appeals.

◆ A speaker's credibility incorporates trustworthiness, competence, and dynamism.

◆ Effective arguments can be structured inductively or deductively, depending on the listener's prior acceptance of the argument.

◆ A speaker should avoid such reasoning fallacies as hasty generalization, faulty analogical reasoning, faulty causal reasoning, and ignoring the issue.

◆ In arranging the issues in a persuasive speech, a speaker should take into account the positioning and development of arguments, inoculation strategy, and cognitive dissonance.

◆ Effective use of psychological appeals requires careful analysis of listeners' needs.

◆ Maslow's hierarchy of needs—physiological, safety, acceptance, esteem, and self-actualization—provides a framework for understanding listeners' needs.

◆ The speaker has a wide variety of psychological appeals from which to choose.

◆ The effective persuasive message combines ethos, logos, and pathos in an honest, straightforward presentation.

Key Terms

persuasion
coercion
theory of field-related standards
group standards
individual standards
critical reasoning
comparative advantage
  reasoning
ethos
logos
pathos
speaker credibility
trustworthiness

competence
dynamism
inductive argument
generalization conclusion
hypothesis conclusion
deductive argument
categorical syllogism
enthymeme
disjunctive argument
conditional argument
evidence
hasty generalization
faulty analogical reasoning

faulty causal reasoning
ignoring the issue
ad hominem argument
ad populum argument
ad ignorantiam argument
inoculation strategy
cognitive dissonance

psychological appeals
physiological needs
safety needs
acceptance needs
esteem needs
self-actualization needs

Learn by Doing

1. Prepare a speech on a topic about which you have strong feelings. Propose a change in present procedures, take a stand on a view concerning the subject, or propose a plan of action. The topic should be one to which your listeners can relate and react so that you can persuade them. A sample central idea for this speech might be "——— College (University) should not raise tuition."

2. Select a controversial topic and prepare a speech in which you advocate a particular solution to the problem. Your task is to persuade your listeners to accept your solution. A sample central idea for this speech might be "Euthanasia should be a legal option for terminally ill patients."

3. Prepare a speech analyzing the persuasive strategies used by some group in advocating a particular cause (for example, women's rights, gay rights, Native American rights). Select a number of persuasive messages by spokespersons for the group you choose, and use examples from these messages to illustrate your analysis of the persuasive strategies.

4. Find print, radio, or television ads illustrating the various psychological appeals described in this chapter. Prepare to describe and analyze the use of the appeals in the ads you select.

5. Consider the components of a persuasive message—credibility, logical arguments, and psychological appeals—and determine what you perceive to be the most influential persuasive strategies with American listeners today. Why do you think so?

6. What do you think is the difference between preparing persuasive speeches and preparing informative speeches? Do you think these differences are valid?

7. Analyze the "credibility crisis" of any of the recent American presidents or presidential candidates. What do you think an official could or should do to maintain credibility in the eyes of the American public?

8. Attend a persuasive speech by someone in a public forum, or analyze a persuasive manuscript in *Vital Speeches of the Day*. Prepare a descriptive analysis of the use of persuasive strategies by this speaker.

Notes

1. Robert Goyer, based on class notes, Purdue University, West Lafayette, Ind., 1965.

2. Aristotle, *The Rhetoric of Aristotle,* trans. Lane Cooper (New York: Appleton-Century-Crofts, 1932).

3. Stanley F. Paulson, "Social Values and Experimental Research in Speech," *Western Speech Communication,* 26 (Summer 1962), 133–139.

4. From a speech by an inmate from the Grafton Prison Farm, Grafton, Ohio, May 1976. Name withheld by request.

5. For a classical discussion of the dimensions of credibility, see James C. McCroskey, *An Introduction to Rhetorical Communication* (Englewood Cliffs, N.J.: Prentice-Hall, 1972), Chapter 4. Also see James C. McCroskey and Thomas J. Young, "Ethos and Credibility: The Construct and Its Measurement After Three Decades," *Central States Speech Journal,* 32 (Spring 1981), 24–34.

6. See, for example, Joe McGinniss, *The Selling of the President, 1968* (New York: Pocket Books, 1970), pp. 27–29.

7. Rollo May, *Love and Will* (New York: Norton, 1969), p. 20.

8. Wayne Thompson, *Quantitative Research in Public Address and Communication* (New York: Random House, 1967), pp. 50–53.

9. Carroll Arnold, "What's Reasonable?" *Today's Speech,* 19 (Summer 1971), 19–23.

10. Ibid., p. 22.

11. Robert B. Maxwell, "The 'Graying' of America," *Vital Speeches of the Day,* September 15, 1987, p. 710.

12. Jim Courter, "Step By Step," *Vital Speeches of the Day,* July 15, 1987, p. 581.

13. The role of the enthymeme as a rhetorical syllogism has been reassessed by Thomas M. Conley, "The Enthymeme in Perspective," *Quarterly Journal of Speech,* 70 (May 1984), 168–187.

14. Donald M. Stewart, "Good Writing," *Vital Speeches of the Day,* August 1, 1987, p. 633.

15. James A. Baker III, "America and the Collapse of the Soviet Empire," speech presented at Princeton University, December 12, 1991, and published in *Vital Speeches of the Day,* January 1, 1992, p. 167.

16. Duane A. Kullberg, "Accounting and Accountability," *Vital Speeches of the Day,* July 15, 1987, p. 608.

17. For a discussion of some of these research studies, see Raymond S. Ross, *Persuasion: Communication and Interpersonal Relations* (Englewood Cliffs, N.J.: Prentice-Hall, 1974), pp. 187–193.

18. William J. McGuire, "Inducing Resistance to Persuasion," in Leonard Berkowitz, ed., *Advances in Experimental Social Psychology* (New York: Academic Press, 1964), pp. 196–203. Also see W. Richard Ullman and Edward M. Bodaken, "Inducing Resistance to Persuasive Attack: A Test of Two Strategies of Communication," *Western Speech Communication,* 39 (Fall 1975), 240–248.

19. Thomas B. Harte, "The Effects of Evidence in Persuasive Communication," *Central States Speech Journal,* 27 (Spring 1976), 42–46.

20. Leon Festinger, *A Theory of Cognitive Dissonance* (Stanford, Calif.: Stanford University Press, 1963).

21. For a discussion of problem-solution arrangement, see Chapter 8 of this text.

22. Paulson, "Social Values and Experimental Research in Speech."

23. Abraham Maslow, *Motivation and Personality* (New York: Harper & Row, 1970), pp. 35–58. How Maslow's hierarchy reflects today's societal needs is demonstrated in M. Joseph Sirgy, "A Quality-of-Life Theory Derived from Maslow's Developmental Perspective," *American Journal of Economics and Sociology*, 45 (July 1986), 329–342.

24. Bob Spichen, "New Attitude: AIDS, Crusades Promote Change of Habits," *Norfolk Virginian Pilot*, August 12, 1987, pp. 1, 3; and David M. Gross and Sophfronia Scott, "Proceeding with Caution," *Time*, July 16, 1990, pp. 56–62.

25. Michael Adams, "Motivational Speaking: Is It Just a Quick Fix?" *Successful Meetings* (June 1987), p. 27.

26. This discussion is adapted from Douglas Ehninger et al., *Principles and Types of Speech Communication*, 9th ed. (Glenview, Ill.: Scott, Foresman, 1982), Chapter 6, and subsequent editions.

27. A comprehensive summary of research on fear appeals is provided by C. William Colburn, "Fear Arousing Appeals," in Howard Martin and Kenneth Anderson, eds., *Speech Communication: Analysis and Readings* (Boston: Allyn and Bacon, 1968), pp. 214–226. Also see Ronald W. Rogers, "Attitude Change and Information Integration in Fear Appeals," *Psychological Reports*, 56 (February 1985), 179–182.

28. For a discussion of the problem with loyalty in work, see Wayne Sage, "The Discontented Worker," *Human Behavior*, 2 (June 1973), 64–65.

29. For a discussion of power as a motivator, see David C. McClelland, "Love and Power: The Psychological Signals of War," *Psychology Today*, 9 (January 1975), 44–48.

30. "Major Rallies Return Focus on Abortion," *Baltimore Sun*, April 4, 1992, p. 3A.

31. George Gallup, Jr., "4 in 10 Adults Attended Church in Typical Week of 1986" (Princeton, N.J.: Gallup Poll, December 28, 1986).

32. "U.S. In Life-death Struggle, Terry Says," *Baltimore Sun*, April 4, 1992, p. 4B, quoting from a speech by Randall Terry given in Columbia, Md.

Ceremonial Speeches

13

Chapter Outline

**Learning
Outcomes**

After reading this chapter, you should be able to:

Understand the role of ceremonial speeches (epideictic discourse) in public communication.

Recognize what constitutes an effective ceremonial speech, including introductions, welcomes, farewells, award presentations, acceptances, thank-yous, after-dinner speeches, sermons, prayers, and commemorative presentations.

Know how to prepare and present an effective ceremonial speech.

Speakers are frequently called on to present **ceremonial speeches**, special types of short speeches on various social or ceremonial occasions. Traditionally, these presentations have had three functions: (1) *to explain a social world to listeners* as in commencement addresses; (2) *to display the speaker's eloquence* as in entertaining speeches; and (3) *to shape and share community ideals* as in inaugurals and keynotes.[1] White House speechwriters tend to dismiss ceremonial remarks that U.S. presidents usually present in the White House Rose Garden as "Rose Garden Rubbish," but such presentations serve important functions.

Public speakers should be able to develop and present ceremonial speeches, for they can be part of both career and social responsibilities. When preparing a speech for a special occasion, it is essential to analyze the audience carefully and to adapt the speech specifically to those particular listeners. Remember that listeners will have expectations as to what the occasion requires; it is important for the speaker to know what these expectations are. Common types of ceremonial speeches include: introductions, welcomes, farewells, award presentations, acceptances, thank-yous, toasts, after-dinner speeches, sermons, prayers, and ceremonial speeches such as tributes, keynotes, inaugurals, and commencement speeches.

≡13.1 Introductions

A **speech of introduction** precedes a public presentation. Its purpose is to give the audience the information they need to have about the speech. In addition, it fills in any details that the audience must be aware of,

On Listening

A speaker who uses eloquent language may very well create a compelling speech that can be enjoyed for the sake of the language itself. The Reverend Martin Luther King, Jr., certainly had that ability as a speaker. The rhythm, tone, and color of the words he selected created a sense of beauty of language that had a poetic effect on his listeners.

> So let freedom ring from the prodigious hilltops of New Hampshire.
> Let freedom ring from the mighty mountains of New York.
> Let freedom ring from the heightening Alleghenies of Pennsylvania!
> Let freedom ring from the snowcapped Rockies of Colorado!
> Let freedom ring from the curvaceous peaks of California!
> But not only that; let freedom ring from Stone Mountain of Georgia!
> Let freedom ring from every hill and mole hill of Mississippi.
> From every mountainside, let freedom ring.[1]

[1] Martin Luther King, Jr., "I Have a Dream," Washington, D.C., August 28, 1963, audio recording.

such as whether a question-and-answer session will follow the speech and the format of that session.

Too often, these introductions are poor because the speaker has not carefully prepared the remarks to be appropriate to the listeners' needs. In introducing a speaker, be sure to include such material as who the speaker is, where the speaker is from, what the speaker's accomplishments are, and when these accomplishments took place. Try to establish the credibility of the speaker, highlighting significant aspects of his or her background that relate to the speech topic. It is just as important, however, to portray the speaker as a person in whom the listeners will be interested. You might want to offer comments on how important the topic is and how significant the speaker is. Do not overstate your own connection to the speaker. (If you've just met the person, it seems inappropriate to introduce her as "my old friend.") Above all, a speech of introduction should be short and to the point. Remember, the listeners have come to hear the speaker, not the person making the introduction.

One note of caution is important with this type of speech. Be careful to prepare the listeners to be interested in the speaker, but avoid overpraising the speaker so much that he or she cannot possibly live up to the expectations you have raised. Probably we have all looked forward to hearing a speech by someone praised as "the best speaker you'll ever hear"—who then fell far short of that label!

If possible, get the necessary information from your speaker in advance of the presentation. If you can't interview the guest in advance, telephone or write. Request specific information, including how to pronounce the speaker's name and what background material to highlight.

If there are special circumstances concerning the speech or the speaker, it is the responsibility of the introducer to ease the speaker's way. For example, when Wellesley College invited First Lady Barbara Bush to present the June 1990 commencement address, the announcement sparked considerable controversy. Writer Alice Walker had been the first choice for speaker, and some Wellesley students felt that Mrs. Bush was not an appropriate speaker, for she is most known as "wife of . . ." rather than as a professional woman in her own right. While Mrs. Bush's speech itself was a masterful example of rhetorical strategy in deflecting the criticism, the president of Wellesley, Nannerl Keohane, established the proper rhetorical tone for the address in her splendid introduction:

> In a sermon delivered at the opening of Wellesley in 1875, Henry Fowle Durant directed that Wellesley should prepare women for great conflicts, for vast reforms in social life, for "noblest usefulness." And to instill that message, the chosen motto of the College, still constantly familiar to all of us today, was "Non ministrari, sed ministrare"—not to be the passive recipient of good works, but to do them. And thus service to other human beings, to family and community and the world became (and has remained) an integral part of the Wellesley tradition. Barbara Bush clearly exemplifies that tradition of "noblest usefulness." The most popular First Lady in our time, Mrs. Bush has used the visibility and clout of her position to work untiringly to heal wounds and combat evils—AIDS, drugs, homelessness, and the breakup of families. Her work is best known in the field of literacy. . . . She has worked in public, and she has worked behind the scenes, caring more about what she accomplishes than what she is given credit for. . . . Barbara Bush exemplifies what she believes: "to live a complete life, you need to help other people. . . . You have a choice: you can love your life, or not, and I have chosen to love my life."[2]

13.2 Welcomes

A **speech of welcome** is in order if you are called on to provide greetings to a visitor to your organization, to new members, or to make your own remarks on joining a group. Essentially, you will want to extend your greetings, pointing out that it is important or appropriate for the persons being welcomed to be with the group at this particular time. Remember that a good speech of welcome is sincere and personal.

If you are asked to present brief remarks upon joining a group, you may want to take the opportunity to extend your own personal greetings to the members of the organization. A newly confirmed secretary of state addressed U.S. Department of State employees with these words:

> As I looked into your faces, and heard your greetings, and felt your touch, you've made me feel very much at home already. . . . I don't know how much of a future together we have. But I would like that future to be active, creative, innovative, positive. I hope and expect to be learning a great deal from you about what is going on in this building—but more importantly what is going on around this planet that affects us, our interests, and our people.[3]

≡13.3 Farewells

A **farewell speech** can take two forms. You may be saying farewell as you move on to another position or retire; or, you may be extending your group's farewell to a departing member. Regardless of the approach taken, the farewell speech should be characterized by sincerity, warmth, and brevity and should give a memorable message. Good speakers will express true feelings, sentimentality that will not embarrass themselves or someone else, and offer an uplifting, optimistic speech. Using humor or a dramatic statement, recounting common experiences with those assembled, recalling events or people you'll remember— all these options are very appropriate.

Early in 1992, Magic Johnson, one of the most popular players in the history of the National Basketball Association, showed composure in the face of a terrible personal tragedy when he announced that he was retiring from basketball because he had tested positive for HIV, the virus that causes AIDS (see Figure 13.1 at the end of this chapter). Later that day, his former Los Angeles Lakers coach, Pat Riley, fought back tears in leading an arenawide prayer. Riley grabbed the microphone at midcourt. He asked for everyone, "in your own voice, in your own beliefs, in your way, to pray for Earvin and for the one million people who are afflicted with an insidious disease who need our understanding."[4]

≡13.4 Award Presentations

When an individual or a group achieves some distinction, officials are usually called upon to give an **award presentation**—a commendation to the recipient. The presentation of an award should include some discussion of the award itself, including the basis for selection, its history, and its significance. The speech should also detail the achievements of the person or group receiving the award so that it is clear to the listeners that the recipient is qualified. As the award is actually presented to the person, it is a nice touch to read the inscription so that everyone can share in this honor.

President George Bush joined Walter Massey, director of the National Science Foundation, in presenting the National Medal of Science and Technology to a number of recipients in the White House Rose Garden on September 16, 1991:

> Today, your Nation recognizes your monumental accomplishments, honors the differences you have made: Advancing human understanding, improving the human condition, helping mankind conquer ignorance and illness, helping this Nation compete and prosper. . . . In honoring each of you, this Nation honors the boundless horizons of the human mind, the soaring spirit of inquiry, the special genius of the architects who fashion today's fantastic idea into tomorrow's usable tool. Your work stands as its own reward; so let me simply add your Nation's thanks.[5]

13.5   Acceptances

A **speech of acceptance** normally follows an award presentation, an election victory, or a success. A good acceptance speech should include a sincere thank-you to those responsible for your recognition. It is also appropriate to discuss the significance of the award or victory. An acceptance should also be brief.

Hollywood producer and director Steven Spielberg received the Irving G. Thalberg Memorial Award at the 59th Academy Awards in 1987. While many Academy Award acceptance speeches are ineffective rambles, Spielberg's remarks showed thought and preparation:

> The Thalberg Award was first given 50 years ago in 1937. . . . I'm told Irving Thalberg worshiped writers. And that's where it all begins. That we are first and foremost storytellers. And without, as he called it, "the photoplay," everybody is simply improvising. He also knew that a script is more than just a blueprint. That the whole idea of movie magic is that interweave of powerful image, and dialogue, and performance, and music that can never be separated. And when it's working right, can never be duplicated or ever forgotten. I've grown up—most of my life has been spent in the dark watching movies. Movies have been the literature of my life. . . . [The] audience, who we all work for, deserves everything we have to give them. They deserve that fifth

draft, that tenth take, that one extra cut, and those several dollars over budget. And Irving Thalberg knew that. . . . I am proud to have my name on this award in his honor. Because it reminds me of really how much growth as an artist I have ahead of me, in order to be worthy of standing in the company of those who have received this before me. So my deepest thanks to the board of governors of the Academy, and the audience out there in the dark . . .[6]

≡13.6 Thank-Yous

The **speech of thank-you** is your acknowledgement of services or aid given to you by others. Like the acceptance speech, a heartfelt thank-you will be appreciated by your listeners, especially if they have been instrumental in supporting you, doing a good job, and so on. In such a presentation it is customary to include a tribute to those you are recognizing. General Norman Schwarzkopf, who led the U.S. military in Operation Desert Storm in the Persian Gulf, thanked America for its support in a speech before a Joint Session of Congress at the close of the operation:

> I am awed and honored to be standing at the podium where so many notable men and women have stood before me. Unlike them, I do not stand here today for any great deed that I have done. Instead, I stand here because I was granted by our national leadership the great privilege of commanding the magnificent American service men and women who constituted the Armed Forces of Operation Desert Shield and Desert Storm. . . . I must . . . tell each and every one of those extraordinary patriots that . . . I will never, ever in my entire life receive a greater reward than the inspiration that I received every single day as I watched your dedicated performance, your dedicated sacrifice, your dedicated service to your country.[7]

≡13.7 Toasts

The **toast** is a recognition of or tribute to a person or a group, in which a short speech is given and a celebratory liquid is sipped. It is an important form of communication at certain occasions, such as governmental functions. Diplomats, for instance, find that an effective toast is sometimes integral to their work with foreign dignitaries. Toasts are also common at celebrations such as weddings and anniversaries, as well as at dedications. An effective toast, like many special forms of speeches, should be short and to the point. The U.S. Department of State Office

An effective toast should be short and to the point.

of Protocol suggests that toasts at White House state dinners not exceed three minutes in length.[8]

As the speaker presenting the toast, you will want to highlight the reason that the guests are gathered together and establish some bond in the speech you make. Some toasts are humorous, others dramatic. If the gathering is in honor of some person or event, this should certainly be mentioned. For example, in marking Columbus Day at a luncheon at the Italian Embassy in Washington, President Ronald Reagan responded to a toast by the Italian ambassador with a toast honoring Italian-American ties:

> It's particularly fitting that we gather here on a day honoring Christopher Columbus, a remarkable Italian who altered the course of history by exhibiting great moral character and individual courage. . . . Our precious liberty, so important to Italians and Americans, depends on the quality of character that we honor on Columbus Day. Italy has long been a particularly close and important ally of the United States. In our commitment to genuine arms reductions and to the maintenance of a stable balance of power so necessary for peace, Americans and Italians are of one mind.[9]

≡13.8 After-Dinner Speeches

Another speech frequently used at luncheons, dinners, and banquets is the **after-dinner speech**, whose purpose is usually to provide an entertaining or compelling message on a theme. Common settings are athletic banquets, personality roasts, retirement dinners, and fund-raisers. The speaker should decide on a theme and then structure a speech around that theme. The case method of organization is appropriate for this type of presentation (see Chapter 8). In this way, a speaker can set out a unifying thesis and then put together a series of examples, anecdotes, or jokes. After-dinner speeches are often humorous. As an expert on humor observed, "Humor has often been the key that unlocks an audience's receptivity."[10]

It is important to recognize that not everyone can be an effective humorous speaker. It takes a good sense of timing. There is nothing more embarrassing than trying to be funny but failing; it will make both you and your listeners uncomfortable. As a result, not all after-dinner presentations ought to be humorous. It should be possible to develop other types of speeches—speeches that use mystery, suspense, or adventure, for example—as effective ways of entertaining an audience.

For a sample of an after-dinner speech, read the presentation made by Art Buchwald, the columnist, humorist, and television and movie commentator, at the end of this chapter (Figure 13.2).

≡13.9 Sermons

Religious services typically include some form of **homiletics**, or **sermonizing**, presented by a member of the clergy or of the congregation. An effective sermon has several characteristics: (1) unity, a sense of coherence around a theme; (2) memory, recalling the traditional beliefs of the religious community; (3) recognition, to enable members of the congregation to affirm their own faith; (4) identification, a sense of familiarity and relevance for the listeners; (5) anticipation, to sustain listener attention; and (6) intimacy, to create a personal relationship between the speaker and the listener.[11]

A sermon is usually placed in the context of some scriptural reference and developed to extend a religious thesis for the listeners in the congregation. Sermons usually center on a passage from a sacred text or on a moral or ethical issue and follow the basic structure of any informative or persuasive speech, with emphasis on statements that are backed up with supporting material. One of the most common negative perceptions

Profile: Lucky Childress, *Presbyterian minister*

W. K. "Lucky" Childress, pastor at Geneva Presbyterian Church in Potomac, Maryland, specializes in interesting, timely, well-structured, and dynamic speeches. A Princeton-trained minister, Lucky presents forty-five or more sermons a year and provides corporate workshops on conflict resolution, human dynamics, and team building. One of those rare public speakers who has carefully thought through his craft and artistry, Childress believes that a good sermon should be engaging, enlightening, and entertaining.

Engaging: "For communication to be effective, it must engage the receiver. I think of three areas of engagement whenever I preach. First, I engage physically. By that, I mean that I strive to be dynamic (using frequent gestures and a range of voice inflections), walk around the sanctuary, make direct eye contact, and place my hands on the receiver's pew (I do not touch the person directly). Secondly, I engage the mind. I want people to think. Therefore, I ask provocative questions. . . . Thirdly, I engage the emotions. I purposely use stories that will evoke laughter or tears, create feelings of peace or tension, or recall times of delight or distress. While some may consider this manipulative, I think it is effective in that it offers a total experience, not simply a one-dimensional (i.e., intellectual) one."

Enlightening: "I think a good sermon should offer some innovative ideas or some new approach to old ideas. I always review what I am going to say by asking the question, What is new about this? What do I want to offer that my listeners haven't heard or thought of before?"

Entertaining: "People want to have fun and enjoy themselves. People access communication activities for entertainment, including movies, television, music, books. Yet I often hear the same people talk about how boring worship services or sermons are. I want my congregation to enjoy worship. I frequently use humor, human interest stories, poetry, lyrics, visual images . . . to provide something that is enticing and interesting."

Childress has solid advice to offer to others who want to become effective speakers: (1) Watch a variety of speakers, noting what is effective and ineffective about them; (2) select several of your favorite speakers and attend their speeches or review audio- or videotapes of them; (3) experiment and eventually develop your own style; (4) practice with a live audience by volunteering to speak at various functions; and (5) have fun—"enjoy speaking and let it excite you so that you will excite others."

about sermons is that they are too long, but sermons need not be long to be effective. Both ordained and lay ministers are increasingly developing a conversational style in the preparation and presentation of sermons.

On the occasion of her niece's bat mitzvah (a ceremony in which a girl, on her thirteenth birthday, dedicates herself to being an adult member of the Jewish faith), a speaker connected the message of the Torah to the congregation at both the personal and the group level. She stated:

The message of Haazinu is a communal and national one. It serves as a paradigm for Jewish history, and roots a sense of Jewishness in a recognition that Jews are not just a community of faith, but a people with a past. But, can we make some personal connections to Haazinu as well? . . . Perhaps like the children of Israel on the edge of the Jordan, a rite of passage like this [the bat mitzvah] closes the pages of one chapter of a life and inexorably leads to the next. . . . Each stage has its own pitfalls and responsibilities. In order to come to terms with oneself, one should listen to and understand the voices from the past which root you in the present and guide you to the future. Those voices can perhaps help in keeping you from becoming involved with the "new" gods, but instead anchor you to that which has endured for generations.[12]

13.10 Prayers

In addition to presenting sermons, members of a congregation may be called upon to present **prayers**—statements of faith and concern addressed to the congregation's God. A prayer should be worshipful, setting the proper tone and mood and also expressing the joy or the concern that may be at the center of the religious occasion. Though some presenters use prayers written by others, some people prefer to develop their own. The typical prayer opens with an address to God and concludes with a meditation that expresses thoughts that the listeners share. A well-presented prayer can be a true work of art, requiring all the speaker's resources to fashion an eloquent call to worship.

Mother Teresa affords an example of a simple but meaningful prayer:

Dearest Lord, may I see you today and every day in the person of your sick, and whilst nursing them minister unto you. Though you hide yourself behind the unattractive disguise of the irritable, the exacting, the unreasonable, may I still recognize you. . . . Lord, give me this seeing faith, then my work will never be monotonous. I will ever find joy in humoring the fancies and gratifying the wishes of all poor sufferers. . . . Sweetest Lord, make me appreciative of the dignity of my high vocation, and its many responsibilities. Never permit me to disgrace it by giving way to coldness, unkindness, or impatience. . . . Lord, increase my faith, bless my efforts and work, now and for evermore.[13]

13.11 Commemorative Speeches

Commemorative speeches are presented to recognize a person or an event. These types of speeches offer brief, memorable remarks about the focus of the commemoration and draw some type of point for the individual listeners.

A **tribute** should stress the reasons the recipient is being honored and point out the recipient's accomplishments. Its function is "to deepen the appreciation and respect of the listeners for the person, persons, event, institution, or monument" and to "impress them with the worth of the ones to whom you pay tribute."[14] It is tempting in a tribute to become overly sentimental and to exaggerate the praise. Keep in mind that the listeners are in attendance because they understand the need to honor the recipient, so the focus of the speech should be on offering honor and drawing some point from it.

A **eulogy** is a tribute presented in recognition of an individual who has died. One of the most moving eulogies in contemporary history was President Ronald Reagan's televised speech commemorating the crew of the space shuttle *Challenger,* which exploded on January 28, 1986, killing all aboard. Televised news reports of the explosion had captured the world's attention throughout the day, but Reagan's speechwriter used her rhetorical skill to develop an eloquent tribute to the crew and their pioneering efforts:

> I know it's hard to understand, but sometimes painful things like this happen. It's all part of the process of exploration and discovery. It's all part of taking a chance and expanding man's horizons. The future doesn't belong to the fainthearted. It belongs to the brave. The *Challenger* crew was pulling us into the future, and we'll continue to follow them. . . . The crew of the space shuttle *Challenger* honored us by the manner in which they lived their lives. We will never forget them nor the last time we saw them—this morning—as they prepared for their journey and waved goodbye, and slipped the surly bonds of Earth to touch the face of God.[15]

Tributes may also commemorate a beginning. The keynote speech, inaugural address, and commencement address are all types of tributes and are intended to motivate listeners in some way. The key to effective speeches of this type is to identify the appropriate appeals for the intended listeners so that they are sufficiently involved in and responsive to your ideas.

A **keynote speech** usually serves as the focus of a conference or convention and typically is presented early in the proceedings to function as the "rallying cry" for those involved. The keynote speaker sets the tone for the entire conference, so it is important to target the appeals and present the speech effectively. Political conventions, for example, normally start with a keynote speech that informs the delegates and the television audience of the party's philosophy.

John F. Kennedy's inaugural is well remembered.

As the keynote speaker for the American Institutes of Chemical Engineers meeting in Houston, the chief executive officer of Occidental Petroleum Corporation spoke about the need for U.S. industry to create not only environmental awareness but also environmental literacy through increased cooperation:

> As we look for environmental solutions in the 1990's we're going to be challenged as never before to have better dialogue among industries. Industry cooperation, both horizontally and vertically, will be necessary to undertake the technological remedies needed to overcome formidable environmental problems. Look at the synergy that is taking place between the automotive, petroleum and chemical industries in the search for cleaner burning fuels. This is an excellent example of the type of cooperation I'm talking about.[16]

An **inaugural speech**, given when a new officeholder assumes responsibilities, is also designed to set the tone for new beginnings. A good inaugural speech must establish the transition from the old to the new and highlight expectations that accompany that transition.

The mayor of Washington, D.C., Sharon Pratt Kelly, presented a stirring inaugural when she assumed office, stressing that her motto—

"Yes We Will!"—should be considered more than a theme for a day: "It is an attitude and an ethic we must embrace to move our city beyond the troubles of drugs and crime, racial polarization and mounting financial problems."[17] Mayor Kelly characterized her transition to office in the sense of "a time and a season for everything and everyone":

> So it is with our great city. In their time and in their season, Commissioner John Duncan, Mayor Walter Washington and Marion Barry, each in his own way, made a telling contribution to the progress and growth of our community. Now, we begin a new time; a new season of coming together. A season where the international city, the federal city, the many neighborhoods, the many constituents, move to become one. For in this togetherness we have the power to meet the staggering challenges we face and do more to allow this city to become all of what she was meant to be—a great cosmopolitan community—a beacon for a 21st century America.[18]

A **commencement address** commemorates old events and new beginnings for members of a graduating class. The traditional commencement speech offers praise for members of the graduating class and encourages them to greet their future. The speech is difficult to present, for it must be targeted both to graduates and to families and friends who are attending the ceremony. A commencement speech, while usually the central point of the ceremony, is not really the focus; the awarding of the degrees is the main purpose for all in attendance.

Joel Conarroe, president of the Guggenheim Foundation, speaking at a commencement ceremony at the University of Maryland, used his own address to poke fun at the traditional format of a commencement speech:

> First, he (or she) should say something funny so as to win over the graduates and their by now penniless parents. Second, he is supposed to say something agreeable about the host institution, then, third, offer some advice, and in so doing work in an anecdote about his own college years. Fourth, he should say something challenging. And finally, he is required to quote from somebody who is smarter than he, thus ending the talk on an elevated note that leaves everyone not only pleased that it's over but also impressed by his reading habits.[19]

A sample commencement speech is presented at the end of this chapter (Figure 13.3).

Ceremonial speeches are an important part of the ritual of human life. A memorable speech can be exactly the right touch needed for any special event. As a result, speakers should take their ceremonial role seriously and spend time preparing the most effective presentation possible.

Figure 13.1

Sample Speech of Farewell
(Source: From Earvin "Magic" Johnson, press conference, November 7, 1991.)

Magic Johnson, considered by many to be one of the finest professional basketball players ever, gave this speech of farewell to announce that he was infected with the HIV virus and would retire from the Los Angeles Lakers team.

Because of the HIV virus I have obtained, I will have to retire from the Lakers today. I do not have the AIDS disease. My wife is fine. She's negative. I plan on going on living for a long time and going on with my life. I guess I get to enjoy the other sides of living.

I'm going to miss playing. I'm going to be a spokesman for the HIV virus, helping young people to realize they can practice safe sex. You can be naive. You think it will never happen to you. It has happened. I'll deal with it and my life will go on.

My life will change. I'll still be a part of the game, working with the Lakers and the league. Basketball will still be a part of my life. I want kids to understand that safe sex is the way to go. We think only gay people get it and that it's not going to happen to me.

I feel really good. My wife is healthy and I'm going to go on. I'm still going to pursue my dream of owning a team. I took the test due to a life insurance policy. They found nothing in terms of the flu, and they kept testing.

I think everybody will be more careful. That's what I want to preach. Most of all, what I'm going to miss is the camaraderie. I can do all the things a normal person can do.

I'm going to come out swinging. All I can do is have a bright side. That's why I am here right now.

Figure 13.2

Sample After-Dinner Speech (Source: Speech presented by Art Buchwald at a roast for David Wolper, May 2, 1990. Reprinted with permission of the author.)

Art Buchwald, the columnist, humorist, and television and movie commentator, presented this after-dinner speech:

My Fellow Americans,

My name is Art Buchwald and I am in the movie business. It is a great honor to be your speaker this evening. I got a call last week from one of the people involved with this program. He said, "Please don't speak more than twenty minutes."

I was ready to follow orders when I got a call from David [Wolper, the person to whom the tribute was being made] who said, "Look, if you're going to talk about me take as long as you want."

This is the one thousand two hundred and thirty-third dinner where we've paid tribute to David Wolper. As a matter of fact, you get 10,000 miles on your frequent flyer account if you attend a David Wolper Dinner.

I don't plan this evening to point out what a fine and revered family man David Wolper really is. That will be done next week at the dinner honoring David given by the National Conference of Christians and Jews.

Figure 13.2 Cont.

And I do not intend to tell you what David has done for race relations in the country. You will hear more about that next month when David is honored by the Malibu Anti-Defamation League.

And it is not my role this evening to tell you what a great and wonderful filmmaker David Wolper really is—David will tell you that later.

This evening I will tell you about USC where David and I both went to school. I first met David in front of the Student Union when he was selling tables for a dinner he was giving himself to celebrate his getting a "C" in freshman English. We hit it off immediately. David scalped tickets for the gridiron games—and I took the English tests for the football team. I did pretty good until a tackle complained that I had gotten him a "D" in Shakespeare and was hurting his chances of getting into medical school.

I was the editor of the humor magazine *The Wampus* and David became my business manager. David was in charge of the magazine's money and I should have learned a lesson from him which would have saved me a lot of trouble. David always insisted on taking the gross profits for himself and giving me the net. After we left school in 1948 David took all the gross from *The Wampus* and bought a movie company. I took my net and bought a map of the movie stars' homes.

I went to Paris to make my career and David chose to stay in Hollywood. I could tell you how David took the fledgling Flamingo Films and turned it into one of the great tax shelters of all time. But, if you attend the City of Hope Prayer Breakfast for David next Tuesday, you will get a much more detailed picture of that part of his life.

Also, I wish to announce there will be a David Wolper cookout on June 1st at the John the Baptist Savings and Loan in San Marino with the money going for victims who had money invested in Drexel Burnham.

Who is David Wolper and why do we keep honoring him with dinners? He is an artist who has made pictures about presidents, spacemen, and just ordinary people like Ronald Reagan and Gerry Ford.

Needless to say, David's great triumph was *Roots.* The story of how Wolper acquired that property is part of this nation's history. I was going to tell it at the Night of a Thousand Stars honoring David Wolper in Ventura, but I'll tell it to you tonight instead.

Some years ago Wolper was at the National Archives in Washington hoping to find a hot property in the public domain, so he wouldn't have to pay for it, when he heard a man in the next cubicle mumbling, "And the first one from our family to come to this country was the African. His name was Kunte Kinte and he called the river Kamby Bolongo. He was captured when he went into the woods to make a drum—and he later married Bell—and their child was a girl named Kizzy."

Wolper said, "What on earth are you doing?"

The man replied, "I am looking for my roots. I can only trace them back as far as a slave ship in Annapolis. If I could find out where the Kamby Bolongo River is I could sell my book to the Literary Guild."

"No sweat," David said, "The Kamby Bolongo River is in Gambia."

"How do you know that?"

"That's the first thing we learned at USC."

Figure 13.2 Cont.

"If you're right," the man said, excitedly, "I'll sell you the TV rights to my story."

"I know I'm right," David replied. "My uncle comes from there."

The rest is history. Alex Haley's chance meeting with David Wolper, a USC alumnus, was serendipity because the University of Southern California is the only school in the nation that has made the study of the Kamby Bolongo River a required course.

After *Roots*, David decided to try something different. He was asked by Peter Ueberroth to put on the show for the Olympics in Los Angeles. Although you saw a great show, Wolper's original ending fell through. As a finale he wanted to have Rafer Johnson take the Olympic torch and set Michael Jackson's hair on fire. Jackson was willing to do it, but he wanted to be paid for it, and David said, "I've never paid for anything in my life."

After the Olympics, David went on to launch the Statue of Liberty festival. How could David Wolper afford to devote so much time to public service? How could he give so much to charity? It's quite simple. Throughout his entire career, David has always taken the gross and given everyone else the net. That's why the Hollywood accountants are honoring him at a dinner tomorrow night.

Figure 13.3

Sample Commencement Speech (Source: Speech as presented at Commencement Exercises of Elyria (Ohio) High School by Eric H. Berko, June 1984. Excerpt from "Bridge Over Troubled Water," by Paul Simon. Copyright 1969 by Paul Simon. Poem by Laurie Reinker. Used by permission of the authors.)

Eric Berko, a student at Elyria (Ohio) High School, presented this commencement speech, which stressed his perceptions of the past, present, and future of his classmates:

LOOKING IN, LOOKING OUT: THE LEGACY OF US ALL

I stood looking in through the window. It was the afternoon after our senior prom and a group of us had gone to Put-in-Bay for some fun in the sun. Unfortunately, it rained most of that day. Everyone else was really tired, but for some reason I wasn't. I wandered outside into the gentle mist, walked around, came back to the cottage, and looked in through the window. Sleeping bodies littered the floor. They seemed content to remember the great prom night we had all experienced. I came back inside and looked out the same window. My breath fogged up the pane and this, added to the rain gently running down the window, made the scene outside rather blurry and hard to see.

That after-prom experience forms the basis for what I'd like to share with you today.

Looking inside the house, seeing the people, and remembering the experiences we've had, was not difficult. It is symbolic of our past. The four years of high school that we've shared seem so clear. This is especially true today when the experiences all come together. High school has brought us many things, including many memories. Some of these will be remembered with joy, and others we will wish to forget. High school has also provided us with knowledge. But we have gained more than just book knowledge—we have gained more than facts and figures, names of famous people, and dates of

Figure 13.3 Cont.   important events. We have gained values, life skills, and maybe most significantly, meaningful relationships.

The values that we've gained will help us throughout our lives. You may remember a bit of sage advice given to us by one of our English teachers: "Hard work guarantees nothing, but the lack of it does." It's a motto that, in reality, teaches us all that we are responsible for our own destiny, and if we fail to succeed, it will probably be from a lack of desire to succeed, and a lack of effort on our part. And then there's a science teacher's chemically inspired battle cry, "You can't mix apples and oranges together, because all you get is fruit salad." We are responsible to make sure that what we do, and the way in which we do it, has a clear purpose. If not, the result will be a lack of unity.

During the past four years, through participating in extracurricular activities, in school functions, and the requirement of going to classes, we have gained lifelong skills. Our class has had a series of successes that have been the direct result of our working together and striving for excellence. Whether it was winning the spirit week competitions, the excellence of the senior-led athletic teams, the participation in the activities of the music department, the Academic Challenge team's success, or the effort that resulted in selection to such organizations as The National Honor Society and Thespians, we have gained the knowledge of working together. Without this spirit of cooperation, we could not and would not have been able to succeed. There's a song in the movie *Fame* that says, "We're always proving who we are, always reaching for that rising star to guide me far and shine me home, out here on my own." Often, this could have been considered the motto of our class.

From the responsibilities we've assumed as leaders of the various school clubs and organizations, we have learned the importance of setting goals and following through on our responsibilities. These patterns will hopefully continue with us throughout our lives. Even those who assumed the responsibility for playing practical jokes, thus making entrance into school each morning a challenging and often frustrating experience, have added to our understanding of who and what we are. How many of you have heard your name called by the phantom voices, or looked for the turtle tracks on the ceilings, or leaned down to tie your socks? Ridiculous? . . . maybe. A learning experience? Of course. The practical jokers pulled it off each and every day with dedication and creativity—qualities that people who succeed in life carry with them and exercise.

And then there were classes. How often did each of us feel that these were the less important part of school? As Mark Twain put it, "I have never let schooling interfere with my education." The last-minute cramming for exams, getting balled out by the teachers for doing our homework for the next class in the class right before, and the headaches and sore throats that magically appeared the day term papers were due all seem like normal parts of everyday life. Through these experiences we *have* learned. We *have* learned the facts and figures; we *have* learned the names of famous people; we *have* learned the important dates in our history; and, most important, we've hopefully learned to be responsible human beings. We've learned that

Figure 13.3 Cont.   "the world steps aside to let any person pass if that person knows where he or she is going."

Look around you. You are surrounded with some of the most important people in your life. When you think back years from now, the most significant thing you will remember about your high school years won't be an event or a class, it will probably be the people with whom you shared these experiences. It could be the friend you turned to when things weren't going right, or the person who helped you when you had troubles with your parents, or the person who sat next to you in class and comforted you when a teacher unfairly picked on you. Most likely it will be the people who acted as your bridge over troubled waters. Who gave you the feeling that,

I'm on your side, when times get rough
And friends just can't be found,
Like a bridge over troubled water
I will lay me down.
I will comfort you.
I'll take your part.
When darkness comes
And pain is all around
Like a bridge over troubled water
I will ease your mind.

Thinking back now about that day at the cottage, I realize that trying to look out through the steam-covered window was a lot more difficult than looking in. It's the future, the uncertain, the unknown. It's blurred. It's scary. For the first time in many of our lives, our paths are not clearly marked for us. The decisions we make will affect our lives forever. Our class poet, Lauri Reinker expressed this beautifully when she wrote,

Now we've reached the Crossroads,
Many ways from which to choose.
It is a time to make decisions
Which will help us win or lose.
The time has come to take the chance,
We've earned through work and care,
To reach our goals, to meet our needs,
To climb the final stair.

When we reach that final stair, then you and I, the members of the Elyria High School class of 1984, will truly be able to find a way to use the values, skills, relationships, and knowledge that we've gained in high school to make the window clear, so that our future will be as bright as our past.

I got faith in our generation
Let's stick together and futurize our attitudes
I ain't looking to fight but I know with determination we can challenge
    the schemers who cheat all the rules
If we take pride
A fair shot here for me and for you
Knowing that we can't lose.
If we succeed, then we will leave a legacy of us all.

Summary

This chapter investigated the types and formats of ceremonial speeches. The major ideas presented were:

◆ There are many types of ceremonial speeches: introductions, welcomes, farewells, award presentations, acceptances, thank-yous, toasts, after-dinner speeches, sermons, prayers, and commemorative speeches such as tributes, eulogies, keynotes, inaugurals, and commencement speeches.

◆ Ceremonial presentations have three functions: to explain a social world to listeners, to display the speaker's eloquence, and to shape and share community ideals.

◆ Public speakers should be able to develop and present such speeches, for they can be part of both career and social responsibilities.

◆ When preparing a speech for a special occasion, analyze the expected audience carefully and adapt the speech specifically to those particular listeners.

◆ A speech of introduction precedes a public presentation.

◆ A speech of welcome is in order if you are called on to provide greetings to a visitor to your organization, to new members, or to make your own remarks on joining a group.

◆ An award presentation is a commendation to a recipient of a citation or recognition.

◆ In a farewell speech you may say good-bye as you move on to another position or retire, or extend your group's farewell to a departing member.

◆ A speech of acceptance normally follows an award presentation, an election victory, or a success of some kind.

◆ The speech of thank-you is your acknowledgement of services or aid given to you by others. It should include a tribute to those being recognized.

◆ The toast is a recognition or tribute to a person or a group, in which a short speech is given and some liquid sipped as a means of acknowledging the recipient.

◆ The after-dinner speech is frequently used at luncheons, dinners, and banquets. Its purpose is to provide an entertaining or compelling message on a theme.

◆ The characteristics of an effective sermon are unity, memory, recognition, identification, anticipation, and intimacy.

◆ Prayers are statements of faith and concern addressed to the congregation's God.

◆ The purpose of a tribute is to deepen the appreciation and respect of the listeners for the person, persons, event, institution, or monument.

◆ A eulogy is a tribute presented in recognition of an individual who has died.

◆ A keynote speech usually serves as the central point of a conference or convention and typically is presented early in the proceedings to function as the "rallying cry" for those involved.

◆ An inaugural speech, given when a new officeholder assumes responsibilities, is designed to set the tone for new beginnings.

◆ A commencement address commemorates old experiences and new beginnings for members of a graduating class.

Key Terms

ceremonial speeches	homiletics
speech of introduction	sermonizing
speech of welcome	prayers
farewell speech	commemorative speeches
award presentation	tribute
speech of acceptance	eulogy
speech of thank-you	keynote speech
toast	inaugural speech
after-dinner speech	commencement address

Learn by Doing

1. Secure the text of or a video- or audiotape of a ceremonial event. Analyze the style of the speech. Ceremonial presentations may be obtained by researching in professional journals or newspapers, or asking sources such as religious leaders and politicians for copies of presentations they have made.

2. Select a type of ceremonial speech and prepare it for presentation in class.

3. Find a copy of a famous presidential inaugural speech. Analyze the speech to determine what characteristics made this such a memorable speech.

4. During a regular round of speeches in your class, your instructor will assign each of you a classmate to introduce.

4. Your instructor will assign you the name of a person in your class whom you will later be introducing as a speaker. Interview that person and collect all the information you will need to prepare a speech of introduction (topic of the speech, some background information on the speaker, why the speaker chose the topic, the qualifications of the speaker to present a speech and so on). On the appointed day, introduce your partner.

Notes

1. Celeste Michelle Condit, "The Functions of Spideictic: The Boston Massacre Orations as Exemplar," *Communication Quarterly,* 33, no. 4 (Fall 1985), pp. 284–300.

2. From text of speech by Nannerl Keohane, President of Wellesley College given at Commencement Ceremonies of Wellesley College, Wellesley, MA, June 1, 1990. Reprinted by permission of the author.

3. Edmund S. Muskie, speech to U.S. Department of State employees, Washington, D.C., May 9, 1980. Department of State Press Copy of Remarks.

4. Mark Asher and Dave Sheinin, "NBA Offers Its Prayers to a Friend," *Washington Post,* November 8, 1991.

5. George Bush, Presentation Ceremony for the National Medals of Sciences and Technology, Washington, D.C., September 16, 1991. Reprinted in *Weekly Compilation of Presidential Documents,* 27 (September 23, 1991), Washington, D.C.: Office of the Federal Register, National Archives and Records Administration, pp. 1277–1288.

6. © Copyright Academy of Motion Picture Arts and Sciences, 1987. Reprinted with permission.

7. H. Norman Schwarzkopf, "Operation Desert Storm," *Vital Speeches of the Day* 57, June 1, 1991, p. 482.

8. Rudy Maxa, "Here's to the Toast," *The Washingtonian* (September 1986), p. 159.

9. Ronald Reagan, luncheon toast at the Italian Embassy, Washington, D.C., October 12, 1983. Reprinted in *Weekly Compilation of Presidential Documents,* 19 (October 17, 1983), Washington, D.C.: Office of the Federal Register, National Archives and Records Administration, p. 1421.

10. Bob Orben, "How to Spice Up Those Dull Speeches," *Current Comedy Newsletter,* 440 (February 19, 1981), p. 4.

11. Fred B. Craddock, *Preaching* (Nashville: Abingdon Press, 1985), Chapter 8.

12. From sermon presented by Dr. Hasia Diner at the Bat Mitzvah of Rebecca Fink. Used by permission of the author.

13. Daily Prayer of Mother Teresa, from *Morning, Noon and Night,* edited by Rev'd. John Carden. London: The Church Missionary Society. Reprinted with permission.

14. Robert G. King, *Forms of Public Address* (Indianapolis: Bobbs-Merrill, 1969), pp. 64–65.

15. Ronald Reagan, text of speech, January 28, 1986. Reprinted in *Weekly Compilation of Presidential Documents,* 22 (February 3, 1986), Washington, D.C.: Office of the Federal Register, National Archives and Records Administration, pp. 104–105. For insight into the background and development of this

speech, see Peggy Noonan, *What I Saw at the Revolution* (New York: Random House, 1990), Chapter 13.

16. Ray R. Irani, "Environmental Literacy," *Vital Speeches of the Day* 57, June 15, 1991, p. 543.

17. Sharon Pratt Kelly, "Inaugural Address," Washington, D.C., January 2, 1991. Text of speech, p. 2.

18. Kelly, p. 1.

19. From "Books and the Good Life," by Joel Conarroe, presented at the Commencement Exercises of the University of Maryland, May 25, 1989. Used by permission.

Professional Public Communication

14

Chapter Outline

Learning Outcomes

After reading this chapter you should be able to:

Understand the role of public speaking as a profession.

Understand the role of a speakers bureau, press conference, internal corporate communication, motivational speaking, speechwriting, speech coaches, image management, international public communication, promoters, rhetorical criticism, training and public speaking organizations.

Recognize some of the professional issues related to public communication.

Identify potential careers in the field of public communication.

ublic communication has become big business. Trained speakers make careers presenting speeches to various audiences. As a result, public communication has taken on a professionalism unparalleled in the history of the field.

14.1 Speakers Bureaus

Whereas many organizations rely on their chief executive officer to be the corporate spokesperson, others have found it useful to develop a **speakers bureau**, which enables them to respond efficiently to requests for speakers and messages pertinent to the organization's mission. Many speakers bureaus pay company representatives, and others release speakers from part or all of their previous work responsibilities. The speakers bureau is typically organized by a coordinator who recruits speakers from throughout the organization, handles the bookings to match speakers with audiences, and even assists in training speakers and developing speeches and related audiovisual support.

The Washington, D.C. Gas Light Company has a highly developed speakers bureau designed to provide speakers for requesting groups. Each year, speakers from throughout the company are solicited and trained. The bureau also helps them develop their individual speeches, which address energy and conservation issues. The efforts of a speakers bureau should be consistent with and supportive of an organization's philosophy. Consequently, the statements by participants in a speakers bureau can be perceived as a well-orchestrated public relations campaign designed to most positively present the organization and its goods, services, and mission.

On Listening

Most professional listeners work on an interpersonal level—customer service representatives, counselors and therapists, ministers, bartenders, and interviewers. Other listeners function on a more public level. The court reporter, for example, must listen to arguments and testimony presented in the courtroom and record a verbatim transcript of what is actually said in court proceedings. Likewise, an interpreter must listen to someone's speech and provide a simultaneous translation of it to an audience. Journalists also function as professional public listeners. They are required to listen to presentations by public officials and then report those remarks to newspaper readers, radio listeners, or television viewers.

Such professional listening requires disciplined concentration and the ability to mobilize considerable empathy in order to understand the speaker's full message. Public listeners often report that the key to their professional success is that they *care* about listening.

14.2 Press Conferences

Press conferences are an important part of the public communication agenda. Increasingly, organizations are finding it useful to announce significant decisions, communicate new initiatives, clarify issues, or respond to crises through formalized meetings with members of the media. Typically, a press conference begins when the CEO or the company spokesperson, often hired specifically for this function, presents an opening statement and then responds to questions from the invited journalists. As opposed to a printed press release that may well get lost on a newspaper editor's desk, a press conference offers the advantage of radio and television coverage and actual interaction with journalists.

A variation of the traditional press conference is the radio or television talk-show interview. Radio talk shows are popular and often feature a guest who fields call-in questions from listeners. Likewise, television talk shows offer opportunities for speakers to present their messages in the context of interviews and conversations with talk-show hosts and even viewers who call in with questions. Many talk-show guests are paid for their appearances.

≡14.3 Internal Corporate Communication

In addition to making an effort to communicate to the public, companies today are increasingly attending to better communication within, or **internal corporate communication**. Organizations have found that disseminating information within and between departments increases job satisfaction by giving credit to outstanding employees and highlighting the contributions of staff members. By knowing what is happening within the organization, workers feel that they are part of the team rather than outsiders. Keeping employees abreast of changes and plans also eliminates rumors and unnecessary confusion.

One approach to internal corporate communication is the use of company forums where officers or managers appear before employees to address issues, provide information, and respond to questions. The job descriptions of these speakers specify that a portion of their time will be spent in making public presentations. Company forums can be useful in opening up channels of communication and giving people in the organization the information they need to understand management decisions and employee responsibilities. Some companies have even taken to scheduling regular "employee press conferences." These internal forums are structured just like press conferences except that employees are the ones asking questions of corporate officials or their representatives.

Corporations also find it effective to hold regular annual or even semi-annual meetings of their sales and management staffs.

≡14.4 Motivational Speaking

Motivational speaking, which encourages listeners to fulfill their potentials and reinforces the need for a high level of job performance and organizational commitment, is more popular than ever. According to the Washington Speakers Bureau, "the thousands of motivational speakers currently on the circuit make up the largest segment of the speaking industry." Media figures, authors, entrepreneurs, journalists, and other professionals whose sole job is to present this type of speech make considerable money as speakers at national staff meetings and conventions. The National Speakers Bureau stresses that the most popular motivational speakers are those "who can articulate their own past successes, who speak *from* success, not *about* success.[1]

A good example of a popular speaker is Debbi Fields, founder of the Mrs. Fields Cookies chain. She generally presents a motivational speech describing her experience starting out with a cookie recipe in her own kitchen and then developing a multibillion-dollar empire. Her experience and credibility as a business success serve as an inspiration to those in her audience.

A key to effective motivational speaking is to target the presentation to the specific audience rather than give a "generic" speech. One professional speaker notes that he always requests job descriptions of those who will be attending, a demographic profile, the product or service of the group, the firm's position in the market, the company goals, and the potential barriers to meeting those objectives.[2]

Because motivational speakers are so popular and so in demand, many of them have agents who take care of bookings and billings. One speech agency is the National Speakers Forum, headquartered in Washington, D.C., which handles such speakers as Ed Bradley of CBS, psychologist Joyce Brothers, columnist Ellen Goodman, former diplomat and Iranian hostage Bruce Laingen, management expert Tom Peters, fitness specialist Richard Simmons, and sports figure Joe Theismann. The agency offers an extensive array of client services including audience surveys, topic suggestions, press kits on speakers, tailored presentations, and a video library of preview tapes for selection of speakers.[3]

The extent to which motivational speaking has become big business is reflected in the fees that noted speakers can command. Here is a representative list of approximate fees for single speeches: entertainer Bill Cosby, $100,000–$200,000; former president Ronald Reagan, $50,000; author Alvin Toffler, $30,000; former secretary of state Henry Kissinger, $25,000; futurist John Naisbitt, $25,000; and basketball coach Pat Riley, $20,000.[4]

≡14.5 Speechwriting

Speechwriters are professional writers who put a speaker's ideas into manuscript form or into "talking points" to be presented. Speechwriting is a major industry, a profession as old as the history of the speech discipline itself. Historians can demonstrate that even George Washington had speechwriting help, but the first "official" White House speechwriter was Judson Welliver, who wrote for President Calvin Coolidge. Today, the White House speechwriting staff consists of a number of writers, typically with journalism backgrounds, who create individual and group drafts of speeches for the president. One of the most famous is Peggy Noonan, who wrote speeches for President Ronald Reagan.

Speechwriting extends beyond the political arena, however. Corporate executives and even university presidents today are likely to use speechwriters, individuals who are part of the corporate communication staff or the executive staff. As CEOs, like American presidents, become increasingly occupied with their responsibilities, professional writers must supply the speeches that these individuals are called upon to present in many different public settings.

As a profession, speechwriting can be highly rewarding. Experienced writers can command top corporate salaries, and the intellectual and creative process of researching and assembling a manuscript appropriate to the thoughts and style of another person can be quite challenging.[5] Robert Friedman, the editor of *Speechwriters Newsletter,* observes that effective speechwriting "takes the ability to get into someone else's head and understand what they want to say."[6] Effective speechwriters must be able to function under the pressure of deadlines and to write speeches that are appropriate both to the speaker's verbal and nonverbal style and to the listener's ear. They must adapt to the speaking style of their clients, not promote their own style. Since word choices, phrasing, and speaking patterns differ from person to person, the speechwriter must learn how to make adjustments so that the material sounds like the speaker who will be presenting it.[7]

☰14.6   Speech Coaches

Speakers in the public arena are supported further by **speech coaches**, individuals who provide training and feedback in presentation skills. As the need for effective public speakers has intensified, so too has the demand for coaches who work on speech development and delivery techniques. "At a time when firms are spending extravagantly to promote just the right corporate image," notes one observer, "perhaps it's only natural that executives are paying more attention to the image they themselves project."[8]

☰14.7   Image Management

Image management—developing and communicating to the general public a vision of a person or a corporation—has become so lucrative that entire companies have formed to offer training and consulting to speakers in organizations. The focus of much of this training centers on delivery skills and may very well include videotaping, replays, and critiques that help speakers see and hear what they do effectively and what they could improve.

One such firm that provides image management training is a company in Atlanta called Speakeasy. It offers speaker training in its own Atlanta studios or in an organization's facilities on site. Training seminars focus on such topics as "Planning for Results," "How to Face an Audience Without a Tranquilizer," and "How to Talk So People Listen."

The demand for speech coaches has grown with the need for more effective public speakers.

☰14.8   International Public Communication

A special dimension of public speaking is **international public communication**, speaking to people from differing cultures. As we find ourselves increasingly part of a global village in which business and industry are highly interconnected, it is important for public speakers to be able to communicate with audiences in many different cultures. It should be recognized that different countries have different speaking conventions. In some European countries, for instance, the question-and-answer session is usually not part of a formal speech presentation. Listeners in Asian cultures may expect a different speech structure and style than the typical Western deductive approach to argument. And American humor generally does not "play" to audiences in other countries.

The international speaker also faces the challenge of working with an interpreter. If your audience speaks a different language, it is necessary to have someone translate your message. Speakers who work with an interpreter must be careful that all terms can be translated to convey meaning within the context of the message and that the presentation is paced to the translator.

One experienced speaker in the international arena offers seven suggestions for speakers who are asked to address foreign audiences:

1. Keep in mind that different cultures react to humor in different ways.
2. Avoid telling a joke that is based on a pun or word play.

3. Be careful, for a joke might be taken seriously.

4. Know the most sensitive issues in the country where you are going to speak.

5. Listen carefully to your contact person so that you know the expectations of the audience.

6. Arrive early for the event to be sure you are in the right place at the right time.

7. Use the question-and-answer session to measure your success.[9]

☰14.9 Promoters

Whether the public speaker is communicating in an international or domestic arena, it is likely that he or she will command considerable attention. Media organizations today are quite interested in covering significant public communications as newsworthy events, so it is useful to portray communication efforts as news. This requires public speakers to extend their role to that of **promoter**—a seller of media images. Promoters specialize in getting audience attention, which may well extend beyond the immediate group of listeners to a broader population or through the media to local, regional, national, or even international coverage. Promotion activities involve cultivating interpersonal relationships with newspeople and others whose assistance you need to reach your intended public. Promoters create their own audience by determining who should receive their message and how best to get that message to them. Professional public relations people sell not only their own images but cultivate media images for clients.

☰14.10 Rhetorical Criticism

Public speaking and media events today draw the attention of **rhetorical critics**, people who evaluate and analyze speeches in both academic and media settings. The study of rhetorical strategies is of interest to people, especially during heated political campaigns, so attention is paid to how effectively communicators are presenting their messages. These critics can be network newspeople or specialists in speech communication who are hired specifically to analyze speeches and debates.

During the 1988 presidential campaign as television networks covered the debates between George Bush and Michael Dukakis, much postspeech analysis focused on the speakers' communication styles and techniques rather than on their approach to the issues. Commenting on George Bush, for instance, one reviewer observed that "many of his remarks emerge less elegantly than he would like."[10] From this and other critical comments evolved Bush's reputation as a less than dynamic speaker.

A critical review of one of the 1988 debates between then–Vice-President George Bush, the Republican nominee, and Massachusetts governor Michael Dukakis, the Democratic nominee, in part stated:

> Thursday night's debate was the most interesting confrontation in this year's election, as a broader variety of subjects and issues were probed.
>
> Dukakis attempted to make a major issue of the concept that military and economic security go hand in hand and that the Bush administration would favor the military. He continued to repeat his themes, his record, the differences between Bentsen [the Democratic vice-presidential nominee] and Quayle [Bush's running mate]. In the end, however, these issues don't appear to be enough to get the voters off center track. He didn't quite sell himself and his policies because he seemed unable to find the open wounds that would make the electorate believe that what we have now isn't the basis for optimism.
>
> The format for the debate doesn't allow for the head-to-head confrontation that would afford the electorate glimpses of what happens when the candidates really are challenged to defend their views. Maybe, if that happened, voters would be judging on the real issues, the substance of a debate, and less on style.[11]

The 1992 presidential nomination trail was filled with rhetorical criticism. Presidential hopeful Paul Tsongas was continually referred to as a lackluster speaker, and candidate Bill Clinton picked up the name "Slick Willie" because of his ability to verbally counter attacks on his personal life. One rhetorical critic called contender Edmund "Jerry" Brown a political terrorist because of his ability to verbally attack and damage the other candidates' stances and reputations.[12] Rhetorical critics, appearing in print and on the air, have great power to sway the attitudes of voters.

≡14.11 Training

Proficient public communicators often find successful careers in training. **Training** is the process through which companies and other organizations help employees improve performance and increase job satisfaction.[13] Speech professionals train others how to perform effectively as communicators. Effective trainers must be skilled public speakers, and most have backgrounds with a major emphasis in public communication and educational methodology. Many specialize in such speech fields as group work, interpersonal communication, listening, conflict resolution, interviewing, problem solving, evaluation, and persuasion. Since many

Profile: M. Jean Berns, *president, MJ Solutions, Inc.*

"As a consultant, trainer and speaker, I am continually using speaking and debate skills."

So says M. Jean Berns, a former college speech professor who is president of an international communication consulting firm specializing in witness preparation, advocacy, public speaking, and small-group communication. A former intercollegiate champion debater, Jean became a Top Merit Professor before leaving the academic profession. Within three years she was the first female operating vice-president of a major northeastern consulting firm. She is listed in *Who's Who of American Women* and the *World's Who's Who of Women*.

Berns has built an international reputation for incisive analysis of highly technical data. She has worked with more than 3,500 executives, managers, and technical experts in over 100 companies. Her advice to people interested in becoming effective public speakers is

◆ Practice—Practice—Practice. It's an old adage but still true. Speaking is a skill you can study *about* for only so long. To develop the skill, you must use it. And the basis for the practice should be a well-developed message. If you have something worthwhile to say, people will listen—there is no substitute for substance!

◆ To develop your own personal style, watch others and experiment to learn what works for you. For instance, you can be entertaining without being humorous. You can be dynamic without being a dynamo. Or—you can be humorous—or a dynamo. The point is, there is no one way to be effective. Be ready to allow your own personality to come through.

◆ Read good speeches. Just as reading good articles helps one become a better writer, reading good speeches helps one become a better speaker. You begin to "feel" the power of the speaker coming through the written words. You begin to identify the transitions and the logic being used to persuade or inform. We don't read speeches nearly as much as we ought to as vehicles for self-improvement.

◆ Get some good instruction or coaching somewhere along the way. The diagnosis of an expert will save you time and move you forward.

placements in training are in the corporate world, business experience or knowledge is advisable.

Trainers understand that there is a need for strong interpersonal communication, negotiation, and advocacy skills in organizations. They possess the research skills needed to evaluate communication networks within organizations, to determine critical communication issues, and to clarify the values and attitudes held by people in organizations. They understand how to develop communication capabilities in employees. Trainers function differently than teachers or collegiate instructors, as they deal mainly with adult learners. If you are interested in becoming a trainer, you should become familiar with the differences between academic teaching and adult training.

Speech trainers often handle media training as well. Preparing speakers to effectively function in press conferences or especially in television talk-show interviews is an important part of training. The approach that many trainers take is to provide the opportunity for role-play in simulated press conferences or interviews that are videotaped, reviewed, and critiqued. Many trainers also attempt to provide some hard-hitting questions so that, in a "real" situation, the speaker will be prepared to respond with skill and poise.

The field of training is ever increasing. More and more businesses and social service agencies recognize the possible financial loss due to poor communication skills among employees. Organizations may hire in-house trainers or external consultants. In-house trainers work exclusively with the organization's employees. External consultants are freelance trainers who market themselves to various companies on a contractual basis. These individuals are in the field either full-time or part-time. Full-time trainers usually have consulting firms that market themselves as specialists in one type of training, such as teaching employees to be more efficient. College communication professors are among the largest core of part-time trainers. They make themselves available to organizations as trainers during nonteaching hours or vacation periods.

Individuals interested in entering the speech training field can enroll in specifically designed university programs usually offered in the department of human resource development or speech communication. Another way to become a trainer is to work for an organization that has a training department and to attend its programs. Many college students do an internship in a training department in order to learn the skills necessary to enter the field.

≡14.12 Professional Speech Organizations

Professional speech organizations have been established to hone the skills of the professional communicator. The National Association for Corporate Speaker Activities, for instance, is an organization "for people who write speeches, train speakers and manage speakers bureaus."[14] Professional speakers belong to the Professional Speakers Association or the International Platform Association, and speechwriters may join a Speechwriters Forum. Toastmasters International, which has thousands of chapters around the world, offers a forum in which speakers can pratice their skills. Chapters hold frequent meetings at which members present speeches and receive feedback from other professionals. The purpose of the Speech Communication Association, a national organization of high school, college, university, and individual members involved in corporate and public speaking occupations, is to disseminate new materials dealing with the profession and to hold regional and state meetings to educate people in the field.

Public communicators are in great demand today. As the field develops further, it will become more and more professional. There are broad career opportunities available to people who are well-trained and proficient public speakers, and professional organizations to help speakers gain experience and practice and to refine their public communication skills—skills that require a lifetime of attention and development.

Summary

♦ Trained speakers make careers of presenting speeches to various audiences.

♦ Many corporations and associations have developed speakers bureaus to enable them to respond to requests for speakers and messages pertinent to the organization's mission.

♦ Organizations often announce significant decisions, communicate new initiatives, clarify issues, or respond to crises through formalized press conferences.

♦ Companies are increasingly attending to better communication within the organization, or internal corporate communication.

♦ Motivational speaking often reinforces job performance and organizational commitment on the part of listeners.

♦ Speechwriters are professional writers who put a speaker's ideas into manuscript form or into "talking points" to be presented.

♦ Speech coaches provide training and feedback in presentation skills.

♦ Image management is developing and communicating to the general public a vision of a person or corporation.

♦ International public communication is speaking to people from differing cultures.

♦ A promoter is a seller of media images.

♦ Rhetorical critics evaluate and analyze speeches in both academic and media settings.

♦ Training is the process through which companies and other organizations help employees improve performance and increase job satisfaction.

♦ Professional speech organizations have been established to hone the skills of the professional communicator.

Key Terms

speakers bureau
press conferences
internal corporate
  communication
motivational speaking
speechwriters
speech coaches

image management
international public
  communication
promoter
rhetorical critics
training
professional speech organizations

Learn by Doing

1. Locate and interview a professional speaker or the manager of an organization's speakers bureau. How does this individual view the field of public communication?

2. Observe a speaker's televised presentation and note some of the strategies the individual utilizes. Does the speaker appear to be trained and coached? Why or why not?

3. Listen to a speech by the president of the United States and observe how the style of the speech is or is not appropriate to the listening ear. If possible, locate a printed text of the speech (reproduced in your local newspaper, in the monthly *Presidential Documents* in your library, or in *Vital Speeches of the Day*) and note which segments are especially listenable or not listenable.

4. Locate a local organization that provides speech and media training and coaching for individuals. Interview one of the trainers to determine what training techniques are used.

Notes

1. Michael Adams, "Booking Speakers: Get 'em While They're Hot," *Successful Meetings* (May 1987), p. 33.
2. Adams (June 1987), p. 42.
3. Enumerated in the National Speakers Forum brochure (Washington, D.C., National Speakers Forum, n.d.)
4. Nichole Bernier, "Money Talks," *Meeting News* (February 1991), pp. 32–33.
5. Carol Kleiman, "Speechwriters Join the Corporate Team," *Chicago Tribune*, February 12, 1989, p. 8–10.
6. Ibid.
7. See Judson Smith, "Writing for the Eye and Ear," *Training HRD* (March 1981), p. 65.
8. Brian Hickey, "People Packaging," *America West Airlines Magazine*, 5 (September 1990), pp. 61–62.
9. Based on Roland Leuschel, "Some Advice on Addressing Foreign Audiences," *Wall Street Journal*, March 3, 1986, p. 18. Used with permission.
10. Charles Paul Freund, "Bush's Remarkable Randomness," *Washington Post*, May 16, 1989, p. A19.

11. Roy Berko, "C-T Analyst: Bush Wins on Warmth," *(Elyria, Ohio) Chronicle-Telegram,* October 14, 1988, p. A-1, A-6.

12. For details of these comments, see "It's Now Clinton's Race to Lose," *Baltimore Sun,* March 20, 1992, p. 1; "Front-Runner Took Charge, Got Noticed," *USA Today,* March 18, 1992, p. 1.

13. For an extensive discussion of training and development and its relationship to communication, see William Arnold and Lynne McClure, *Communication Training and Development* (New York: Harper and Row, 1989).

14. Letter from Victor Pesqueira, Executive Director, National Association for Corporate Speaker Activities, August 23, 1988.

Index